DATA STRUCTURES FOR COMPUTER INFORMATION SYSTEMS

DATA STRUCTURES

FOR COMPUTER INFORMATION SYSTEMS

ROY S. ELLZEY
Corpus Christi State University

 ®

SCIENCE RESEARCH ASSOCIATES, INC.
Chicago, Henley-on-Thames, Sydney, Toronto
A Subsidiary of IBM

Acquisition Editor	Alan W. Lowe
Project Editor	Judith Fillmore
Production Coordinator	Greg Hubit
Compositor	Marin Typesetters
Illustrator	Carl Brown
Copy Editor	Ruth Cottrell
Cover Designer	Henry Breuer
Text Designer	Paul Quin

Library of Congress Cataloging in Publication Data

Ellzey, Roy S.
  Data structures for computer information systems.

  Includes bibliographical references and index.
  1. Data structures (Computer science) I. Title.
QA76.9.D35E44   001.64'2   82-5640
ISBN 0-574-21400-3   AACR2

Printed in the United States of America

10 9 8 7 6 5 4

To my students, because they asked for it,
and to a few good friends who gave me
the support to see it through

PREFACE

This book was developed for a one-semester course in a curriculum intended to prepare individuals for careers as applications programmer/ analysts. It is assumed that the student has a background that includes a minimum of an introductory course to computers and programming and competency in at least one of the languages: COBOL, PL/1, BASIC, or FORTRAN. A one-semester course in computer organization and assembly-language programming is helpful in understanding the rationale in the use of certain structures and the accompanying examples, but it is not essential.

Emphasis is placed on the understanding and manipulation of standard data structures and the accompanying algorithms that perform the creation and manipulation of these structures. Examples of the use and application of the structures are provided throughout the text, along with guides for conditions under which one structure or technique should be chosen over another.

It is important to understand that a decision was made to provide the student with the tools necessary to make a good choice with respect to structures and techniques, but not necessarily a best choice. This was done so that the level of mathematics used and the amount of mathematical analysis needed could be kept to a minimum.

Algorithms are presented as *structured flowcharts* (and in most cases paralleled with pseudocode) as opposed to any specific programming language, so that they can be readily understood by a wide audience despite programming-language preference. The structured flowcharts are designed so that all algorithms are constructed using only the PROCESS, IF-THEN-ELSE, and WHILE DO constructs of structured programming; they should not be confused with the unstructured flowcharts that abound in earlier literature. I have simply taken a modern approach to an old and familiar format to provide a precise and graphic description of specific logical processes. The algorithms should be a bit simpler to implement in COBOL or PL/1 than in BASIC or FORTRAN, partly because COBOL and PL/1 possess greater flexibility in defining complex data structures and both facilitate the writing of structured programs, and partly because the algorithms were constructed under the guidelines of: "Can the competent COBOL programmer understand and implement this?"

The reason for the slight philosophical preferential treatment of COBOL is twofold. First, COBOL is currently the dominant programming language in the world of applications programming in this country, and it is likely to remain so for the next few years. Second, given the great flexibility in defining and grouping data elements and its powerful file-handling capability, COBOL becomes a very reasonable language choice in its own right.

It is intended that the student will study the accompanying algorithms and will incorporate the majority of these, or ones that are functionally equivalent, in programming assignments such as those suggested in the exercises. Students in our own university have benefitted from this approach in the following ways:

1. Reinforcement of concepts involved

2. Additional practice in writing modular programs

3. Appreciation of the relative effort and resources required to utilize the various structures and techniques

The exercises were implemented in the language that was preferred by the student on an individual basis. These included the four languages already mentioned and IBM 360/370 assembly language. The most commonly chosen language was COBOL, which was to be expected since the majority of our students are preparing for commercial applications and because of the slight bias of the text.

As for traditional computer-science curricula, this book would seem appropriate for a C-5 type course as described in the ACM "Curricula '78" or as a supplementary text for a C-7 course; in the latter case, however, it may lack the depth of formal analytical development that is usually desired.

The precise role of data structures in curricula that are being developed for computer information systems is not as clear-cut as it is for computer science proper; however, course IS2 of the ACM Curriculum for Information Systems seems very close to that contained in this book. The bulk of the material offered in this book and the philosophy under which it is presented has served as a key course in the curricula of professionally oriented programs offered at two Texas universities (American Technological University and Corpus Christi State University) over the past eight years. Regular monitoring of the graduates of these programs and the agencies they serve seems to indicate that both are well satisfied with the preparation received.

In addition to the results from the two academic programs just cited, I have received strong favorable response from professionals working in business, government, and industry who have taken the course at either of the two universities, and this response was reinforced by seminars taught using portions of this material in state agencies and business over the past few years.

Therefore, it has seemed to me that there is a need for a book that presents data structures without the use of formal disciplines such as graph theory, and in a manner that is familiar to the countless numbers of applications programmers. This I have tried to do in the pages that follow.

ACKNOWLEDGMENTS

I am indebted to a number of individuals for their contributions to this book. First, there are the people at SRA, namely: Charles McCormick, who said the right thing on the right day to get me started; Alan Lowe, who believed in the project enough to guide me through the conversion of a stack of class notes into an acceptable manuscript; and Judith Fillmore, who saw to the polish and other particulars in the final stages.

Second, I thank the following reviewers, who assessed the manuscript as it evolved into its final form:

J. W. Baker, Kent State University

Della Bonnette, University of Southwestern Louisiana

William F. Denny, McNeese State University

Fred Harold, Florida Atlantic University

J. B. Harvill, North Texas State University

M. H. McKinney, Corpus Christi State University

James E. Miller, University of Western Florida

James A. Schaefer, Rhode Island College

James D. Schoeffler, Cleveland State University

Oberta Slotterbeck, Hiram College

I am particularly indebted to J. B. Harvill, who participated in each round of the review and supplied valuable suggestions and encouragement.

Next, I am grateful to Jill Strauss and Yvonne Herrera for their careful and patient typing and artwork for the various versions of the manuscript.

Finally, I thank the students at CCSU who provided me with the opportunity of testing the manuscript in the classroom. It was they who ferreted out most of the bugs and evaluated the clarity of the material.

Roy S. Ellzey

CONTENTS

DATA STRUCTURES FOR COMPUTER INFORMATION SYSTEMS

I. INTRODUCTORY CONCEPTS

If we accept the premise that a computer is primarily a machine that facilitates the processing of data, then the manner in which data is stored and accessed for processing should be a major concern for those who wish to program computers. The proper choice of a structure, or set of structures, for the data in a particular computer application can simplify the programmer's job, whereas a poor choice can result in wasted effort for the programmer or the computer or both. Therefore, the principal goal of this book is to study a variety of structures in which data can be arranged for storing and accessing. We concentrate on how these structures are created and manipulated, and we investigate the conditions under which a particular structure would be a good or poor choice with respect to efficiency. Understanding these structures and their uses is important not only to the programmer who employs them directly in an implementation, but also to the individual who must evaluate a program or software package that uses these structures.

Chapter 1 prepares the readers for the overall goal of the book. Readers will have different academic preparation and programming experience. Most of this material can be treated lightly; however, we suggest that the readers give at least cursory attention to these topics since most will be encountered later in the book or prove useful in implementing the programming exercises.

We assume that the readers have at least the equivalent of an introductory programming course and are reasonably proficient in a higher-level programming language, such as COBOL, BASIC, FORTRAN, or PL/1, with preference given to COBOL and PL/1 because of their extensive data description facilities and their appropriateness for writing structured programs. COBOL is given a slight preferential treatment in the book, primarily in Chapter 1, because of its prominence in the marketplace of applications programming; however, all data structures topics are presented independent of any particular programming language, and all algorithms are presented as structured flowcharts and/or pseudocode so that they are appropriate for study for all programmers, no matter what their programming language preference is.

BASIC TERMINOLOGY

To study any subject, we need a few basic terms and concepts from which we can develop other concepts and define new terms. Some of these are presented here; we assume the rest have been learned in a beginning programming course or through experience.

DATA AND INFORMATION

Data are values or sets of values that have no implied meaning until they are associated with a particular attribute. For instance, the values 78.2, 81.6, 85.1, and 82.4 are data. But what data? If we are told that these values are for the average noon temperatures for the weeks in last April for Corpus Christi, Texas, then our data have meaning or information. (We may also have an ad for the Corpus Christi Chamber of Commerce.) *Information*, then, is defined as data that have been given attributes and organization so as to have meaning.

An *entity* is something we have information about. The entity has *attributes* or properties, and we assign values to these attributes (that is, information is a collection of attribute, value pairs). Examples:

Attribute	Value
NAME	JOHN SMITH
ID	426720412
WEIGHT	165
EYES	BROWN

Attribute values have a *range*, which is the set of all values a particular attribute can have. This range may be discrete, such as the set {BROWN, BLUE, BLACK, GRAY} or continuous, such as $\{X: 0 \leq X \leq 1\}$.

ENTITY, ENTITY SET, INFORMATION UNIVERSE

An *entity* is described by attributes and defined by a set of attribute, value pairs. An *entity set* is a collection of entities that possess the same attributes or at least a common set of attributes. An *information universe* is a collection of entity sets that contain the information we need to perform a particular application or set of related applications (see Figures 1-1 and 1-2).

DATA BASE, FILE, RECORD, FIELD

In computer applications, an information universe is represented by a *data base* or library, whereas an entity set is represented by a *file*. An entity is represented by a *record*, and an attribute is represented by a *field*, which is a subdivision of a record that has meaning. Field contents correspond to attribute values.

A field by which a record is identified is called a *key field* or simply a *key*.

ORDER

Order is a property that can be ascribed to sets of real numbers. We say a set of numbers is ordered if, for any two numbers a and b belonging to the set, one of the following relationships is true: $a < b$, $a = b$, or $a > b$. And $a < b$ and $b < c$ implies $a < c$, where c is also a member of the set.

In computer applications, we can view the locations of records as a set of real numbers, and we can view the contents of their key fields as a set of real numbers. Each fits the definition of an ordered set; however, we are usually more interested in whether or not the order relationship between successive keys is constant (that is, whether exactly one of the following is always true between any two successive keys: $<, \leq, =, \geq, >$). For the remainder of this book, therefore—unless noted otherwise—*ordered will mean ordered with a constant relationship.*

We define a file as *physically ordered* if both the keys of the records of the file and the corresponding locations of the file are ordered.

Given a file consisting of records $R_1, R_2, R_3, \ldots, R_n$ with corresponding keys $K_1, K_2, K_3, \ldots, K_n$, the file is in *ascending order* if R_i precedes R_{i+1} implies that $K_i \leq K_{i+1}$ for $1 \leq i \leq n$. The file is in *descending order* if R_i precedes R_{i+1} implies that $K_i \geq K_{i+1}$ for $1 \leq i \leq n$ (see Figure 1-3).

FIGURE 1-1 ENTITY SET OF EMPLOYEES FOR ACME COMPANY

	Attribute			
Entity	Name	ID Number	Weight	Eye Color
Employee 1	JOHN SMITH	426720412	165	BROWN
Employee 2	MARY BROWN	475249021	115	BLUE
Employee 3	SUE LARKINS	531261429	120	BLACK
Employee 4	TOM LEWIS	465075802	180	BROWN

FIGURE 1-2 DIAGRAM OF INFORMATION UNIVERSE FOR ACME COMPANY

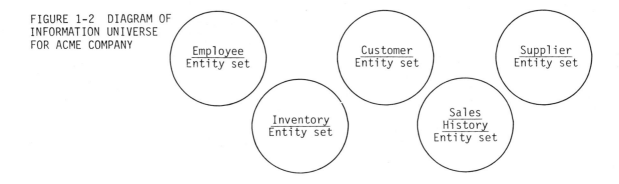

MATHEMATICAL SYMBOLS AND CONCEPTS

This book, by design, minimizes the use of mathematics and limits that used to the level of finite mathematics or college algebra. However, certain symbols and concepts appear frequently enough so that a brief presentation is given here in case the readers have not encountered some of them before or, perhaps, have forgotten them.

1. $\lfloor x \rfloor$: This notation means the greatest integer that does not exceed x. It is called the *floor* of x. Examples:

$$\lfloor 2.6 \rfloor = 2$$

$$\lfloor 3.1416 \rfloor = 3$$

$$\lfloor 5 \rfloor = 5$$

$$\lfloor 0.99 \rfloor = 0$$

$$\lfloor -1.5 \rfloor = -2$$

2. $\lceil x \rceil$: This notation means the least integer that is not less than x. It is called the *ceiling* of x. Examples:

$$\lceil 1.4 \rceil = 2$$

$$\lceil 0.99 \rceil = 1$$

$$\lceil 5 \rceil = 5$$

$$\lceil 0.0001 \rceil = 1$$

$$\lceil -1.5 \rceil = -1$$

3. $n!$: This notation is called *n factorial* and is the product of all integers from 1 to n, inclusive. Therefore

$$n! = 1 \times 2 \times 3 \times 4 \times \cdots \times n \qquad 0! = 1 \text{ by definition}$$

FIGURE 1-3

	Ascending Order			Descending Order	
Rec. No.	Key	Data	Rec. No.	Key	Data
1	ADAM		1	95	
2	AMY		2	90	
3	DAVID		3	85	
4	JAMES		4	85	
5	KAREN		5	80	
6	SUSAN		6	70	

Examples:

$$5! = 5 \times 4 \times 3 \times 2 \times 1 = 120$$

$$6! = 6 \times 5! = 6 \times 120 = 720$$

$$\frac{10!}{6!} = \frac{10 \times 9 \times 8 \times 7 \times 6!}{6!}$$

$$= 10 \times 9 \times 8 \times 7 = 90 \times 56 = 5040$$

4. $n(\text{mod } k)$: In its purest sense $n(\text{mod } k)$ has a slightly different meaning in mathematics than it does here, but, for our purposes, this is the remainder function such that $n(\text{mod } k)$ is the integer remainder of n divided by k where both n and k are integers. Examples:

$$18(\text{mod } 7) = 4$$

$$20(\text{mod } 5) = 0$$

$$5001(\text{mod } 2) = 1$$

$$8(\text{mod } 32) = 8$$

5. $\log_b a$, $\log_2 n$: $\log_b a$ is the logarithm of a to the base b. The logarithm is a number that represents the power to which we raise b to equal a—that is, if $x = \log_b a$, then $b^x = a$.

Likewise $\log_2 n$ is the power to which we raise 2 to equal n. Thus, if $n = 8$, then $\log_2 8 = 3$ or $2^3 = 8$. Examples:

$\log_2 1 = 0$ because $2^0 = 1$

$\log_2 2 = 1$ because $2^1 = 2$

$\log_2 32 = 5$ because $2^5 = 32$

$\log_2 18 = 4.17$ because $2^{4.17} = 18$

The last example cannot be readily calculated since 18 cannot be represented as an integral power of 2, and even when n is an integral power of 2, we must usually compute the value of 2^x instead of calculating $x = \log_2 n$ directly. However, it is common to find $\log_e n$ or $\ln N$ (which represents the natural log of N) on handheld calculators, in most books of mathematical tables, and even on that ancient instrument, the slide rule.

Therefore, we can create a conversion formula by the following reasoning:

If $\log_2 N = X$

then $2^x = N$

Thus $\ln 2^x = \ln N$

and $x \ln 2 = \ln N$

giving

$$x = \frac{1}{\ln 2} \ln N = \frac{1}{0.693147} \ln N$$

or

$$x = 1.442695 \ln N$$

Therefore

$$\log_2 N = 1.442695 \ln N$$

Example:

$$L = \log_2 5000$$

$$L = 1.442695 \ln 5000$$

$$L = 12.288$$

Hence

$$2^{12.288} = 5000$$

PROGRAMMING CONVENTIONS

Since this book is intended for programmers or individuals preparing to become programmers, we place a strong emphasis on the development of algorithms that create and manipulate the structures presented. The programming philosophy followed in the development of these algorithms can be summed up by three terms: modular, top-down, and structured. No serious attempt is made to teach these concepts since a number of excellent books are available for that purpose. Here we describe briefly how they are used in this book.

MODULAR PROGRAMMING

Each algorithm is presented so that it can be encapsulated as a stand-alone subroutine. It is presented this way for two reasons. First, once a process has been formalized as a subroutine, it can be called on whenever it is needed, thus reducing the programming effort required. Second, the algorithms tend to become more complex as we progress through the book. However, they often include processes that we have already developed. Therefore, if we simply present these processes as modules or subroutines that perform a function, then we can keep the logic of the new algorithm to a manageable size.

In this book, most modules are presented as if they are formalized subroutines with a list of parameters to be shared with the subroutine and the module that calls it. In practice, the programmer must decide which modules should be formalized and which should simply be grouped as a set of instructions to be accessed when needed. In COBOL, we speak of the difference between a PERFORM of a paragraph or group of paragraphs and a CALL to a formal subroutine.

A module is indicated in the book as a process symbol with double bars at each end. The name of the module is in capital letters with the list of shared parameters below it, as shown in Figure 1-4.

TOP-DOWN PROGRAMMING

The top-down programming philosophy is presented implicitly rather than explicitly in this book since we present only specific algorithms and not complete programs. It is intended that this approach be used in implementing the programming exercises not only because it is good practice in general, but also because most of the exercises are presented as modifications or enhancements of previous exercises, and this progression of the exercises is facilitated by the top-down approach.

In top-down programming, we have a hierarchy of modules. There is a top-level module or set of instructions that controls the overall flow of the program and initiates the next level of modules that may, in turn, call lower-level modules.

The diagram in Figure 1-5 is a schematic of a top-down conceived program that illustrates the hierarchical relationship of the modules. The schematic should not be confused with a flowchart since it shows only the control structure between modules and not the specific execution order of the program it represents.

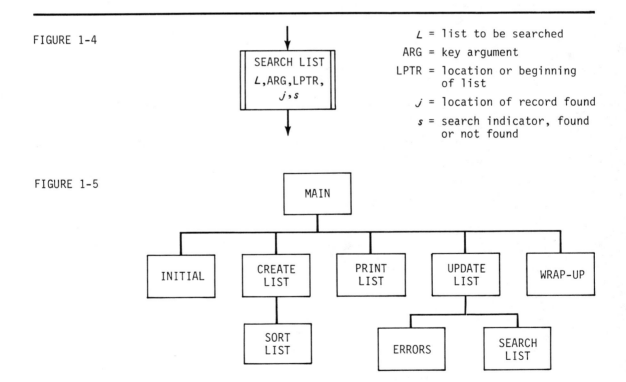

FIGURE 1-4

SEARCH LIST
L,ARG,LPTR,
j,s

L = list to be searched
ARG = key argument
LPTR = location or beginning of list
j = location of record found
s = search indicator, found or not found

FIGURE 1-5

MAIN

INITIAL · CREATE LIST · PRINT LIST · UPDATE LIST · WRAP-UP

SORT LIST

ERRORS · SEARCH LIST

In COBOL, the MAIN might appear as follows:

```
              .
              .
              .
         PROCEDURE DIVISION.
         MAIN.
              PERFORM INITIAL.
              PERFORM CREATE-LIST.
              PERFORM PRINT-LIST.
              PERFORM UPDATE-LIST.
              PERFORM PRINT-LIST.
              PERFORM WRAP-UP.
              STOP RUN.
              .
              .
              .
```

Within the CREATE-LIST paragraph, we might find a CALL to a sort subroutine such as:

```
         CREATE-LIST.
              .
              .
              .
              CALL 'SELSORT' USING LISTA, NUM-REC.
              .
              .
              .
```

In BASIC, the executable portion of the MAIN module might appear as follows:

```
                   .
                   .
                   .
         100    GOSUB   1000
         200    GOSUB   2000
         300    GOSUB   3000
         400    GOSUB   4000
         500    GOSUB   5000
         600    GOSUB   6000
         700    STOP
                   .
                   .
                   .
```

where each module coded ends in a RETURN statement that returns control to the next GOSUB statement in the MAIN module.

If the BASIC used supports a CHAIN statement, then formal subroutine calls can be issued as follows:

```
            .
            .
            .
2250     CHAIN    'SELSORT'  L,N
            .
            .
            .
```

STRUCTURED PROGRAMMING

All algorithms in this book are presented using only the three basic constructs of structured programming (that is, PROCESS, WHILE-DO, and IF-THEN-ELSE) in structured flowchart form and/or with pseudocode. In flowchart form, they appear as shown in Figure 1-6.

A process is any statement or subroutine whose execution will always result in the execution of the next sequential program statement. Examples of a process in COBOL are:

1. `ADD 1 TO RECORD-COUNT.`

2. `WRITE PRINT-LINE AFTER ADVANCING 1.`

3. `PERFORM SEARCH-LIST.`

4. `CALL 'SELSORT' USING LISTA, N.`

In BASIC, examples of processes are:

1. `200 LET N = N + 1`

2. `250 PRINT "X=" ; X; "Y=" ; Y`

3. `260 GOSUB 1000`

The IF-THEN-ELSE statement tests a condition. If the condition is true, the PROCESS specified by the THEN is done. If the condition is false, the condition specified by the ELSE is done. After either process is done, control returns to the next sequential statement.

Two examples are shown in structured flowchart form in Figure 1-7 and then as they might be coded in COBOL and BASIC. In COBOL, we have:

```
1.  IF SEARCH-CODE =1
        THEN PERFORM FOUND RTN
        ELSE PERFORM NOFIND-RTN.

2.  IF VOTE = 'YES'
        THEN ADD 1 TO YES-COUNT
        ELSE IF VOTE = 'NO'
                THEN ADD 1 TO NO-COUNT
                ELSE ADD 1 TO ABSTAIN-COUNT.
```

FIGURE 1-6

PROCESS

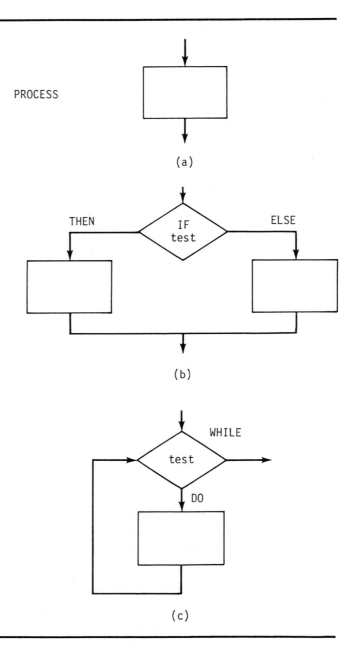

(a)

(b)

(c)

FIGURE 1-7

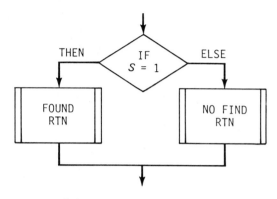

(a) Simple IF-THEN-ELSE

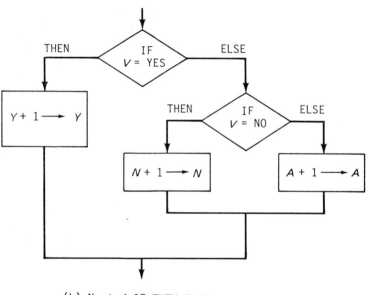

(b) Nested IF-THEN-ELSE

In BASIC, we have:

```
1. 100 IF  S = 1 THEN  130
   110 GOSUB  1000
   120 GOTO    140
   130 GOSUB  1500
   140

2. 100 IF V$ = "YES" THEN 160
   110 IF V$ = "NO"  THEN 140
   120 LET A = A + 1
   130 GOTO    170
   140 LET N = N + 1
   150 GOTO    170
   160 LET Y = Y + 1
   170
```

The preceding BASIC examples were coded assuming the BASIC used does not have the structured statements included in the language. If they are included, they can be used directly without GOTO statements.

The WHILE-DO construct tests a condition, and if the test is true, a process is executed. Control returns to the test and execution proceeds as before until the test fails. At this point, the next sequential statement that follows the WHILE-DO is executed as shown in Figure 1-8.

FIGURE 1-8

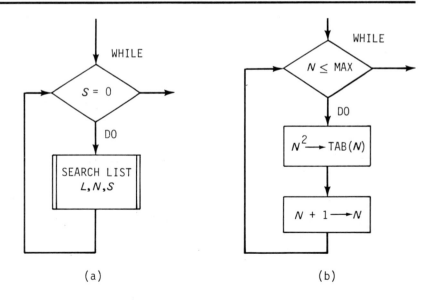

(a)   (b)

In COBOL , we have:

1.   PERFORM SEARCH-LIST UNTIL S NOT = 0.

2.   PERFORM LOAD-TABLE UNTIL N > MAX.

```
LOAD-TABLE.
    COMPUTE  TAB (N) = N * N
    ADD 1 TO N.
```

In BASIC, we have:

```
1.  100   IF  NOT S = 0 THEN 130
    100   IF  S < > 0 THEN 130   ◄──── in case the BASIC used has
    110   GOSUB 500                    no logical operators
    120   GOTO  100
    130       .
              .
              .

2.  100   IF  N  >  M THEN 140
    110   T(N) = N * N
    120   N = N + 1
    130   GOTO  100
    140       .
              .
              .

or  100   FOR N = N TO M
    110   T(N) = N * N
    120   NEXT N
    130       .
              .
              .
```

This example is simpler than the first; however, the FOR-NEXT loop in BASIC will not suffice for WHILE-DO constructs in general. For example, it is inappropriate in example 1 just given.

VECTORS AND ARRAYS

VECTORS

A *vector* is a one-dimensional structure containing a fixed number of contiguous elements all of the same type. In terms of our earlier definitions then, a vector is an entity set of fixed size such that each entity, or element, has exactly the same attributes and internal structure. Some authors restrict the elements of a vector to a single attribute inherent to programming languages such as BASIC and FORTRAN (but not COBOL or PL/1) but, for our purposes, the possibility of vectors composed of elements with multiple attributes is more useful. Opinion is divided on the fixed-size requirement for vectors. Authors like Knuth and Elson have elected to allow vectors to vary in size, which is a characteristic of languages like ALGOL. However, we have chosen the fixed-size requirement because it is consistent with equivalent structures found in COBOL, BASIC, and FORTRAN and because it is convenient to distinguish between this structure and a list that we define later. (Authors like Pratt, Tremblay and Sorenson, and Coleman have also chosen this requirement.)

Each element of a vector has associated with it an *index* that is a positive integer corresponding to the relative position of the element within the vector. It is through the index that we can access a specific element in the vector, as shown in Figure 1-9.

Examples of vectors are shown in Figures 1-10 and 1-11. Figure 1-10 shows the scores of six students on a GRE test. Figure 1-11 shows the same scores with the students' names.

In COBOL, Figure 1-10 might appear as:

```
            .
            .
            .

01   SCORE-TAB.
     02   SCORE PIC S9(4) USAGE COMP OCCURS 6 TIMES.
            .
            .
            .
```

FIGURE 1-9 DIAGRAM OF A VECTOR

Index	Elements
1	1st element
2	2nd element
3	3rd element
.	.
.	.
.	.
n	nth element

FIGURE 1-10 SCORES OF SIX STUDENTS ON A GRE TEST

Index	Elements
1	1120
2	950
3	1290
4	1080
5	840
6	1020

and a statement using this vector is:

```
MOVE  SCORE (N) TO SCORE-OUT.
```

(where N is the index and $1 \leq N \leq 6$).

In COBOL, Figure 1-11 might appear as:

```
01  SCORE-TAB.
    02 ELEMENT OCCURS 6 TIMES.
       03 SCORE PIC S9(4)  USAGE COMP.
       03 NAME  PIC  X(15).
```

which could be used as:

```
MOVE SCORE (N) TO SCORE-OUT.
MOVE NAME (N) TO NAME-OUT.
```

In BASIC, we could describe Figure 1-10 and an example of its use as:

```
050 DIM  S(6)
         .
         .
         .
200 LET  X=S(I)
```

(where I is the index and $1 \leq I \leq 6$).

Figure 1-11 is a bit more complex in BASIC since BASIC requires single values, all of the same type, for each element in an "array." Therefore, we can describe our vector in Figure 1-11 with two BASIC "arrays."

```
050 DIM  S(6),N$(6)
         .
         .
         .
200 LET  X=S(I)
210 LET  A$=N$(I)
```

It is important to keep in mind that a vector always has a fixed number of elements. Therefore, we can neither add nor delete elements from a vector. We can change the values of the attributes of an element of a vector, but we cannot change the set of elements that makes up the vector.

FIGURE 1-11 SCORES OF SIX STUDENTS
ON A GRE TEST INCLUDING NAMES

Index	Elements	
1	1120	ADAMS, MARY
2	950	BROWN, BILL
3	1290	GREEN, ROBERT
4	1080	HALL, JUDY
5	840	MEEK, KAREN
6	1020	TURNER, TOM

ARRAYS

A *one-dimensional array* is a vector. A two-dimensional array is a vector of vectors. An n-dimensional array is a vector of $(n - 1)$-dimensional arrays. A separate index is associated with each dimension of an array so that elements within an n-dimensional array are located by an appropriate set of n index values.

The size of an array is specified by the product of the length of the vectors in each dimension, which is also the number of elements in the array (a fixed number).

A two-dimensional array is usually depicted as a structure with its elements arranged in rows and columns as shown in Figure 1-12, where $E(r,c)$ represents the element located at row index r and column index c.

The arrangement in Figure 1-12 can be viewed as m vectors of length n, or n vectors of length m, as long as the elements of the rows and the columns are of the same type.

For example, consider the populations of the five largest cities in each of the 50 states in a two-dimensional array. All the elements are populations that we will arrange in 50 rows and 5 columns, or POP(50,5).

We could define this array in COBOL as:

```
01  POP-TAB.
    02 STATE OCCURS 50 TIMES.
        03  CITY OCCURS 5 TIMES.
            04  POPULATION PIC S9(8) USAGE COMP.
```

and we could obtain the population of the third largest city of the twenty-fifth state by writing:

```
MOVE  POPULATION (25,3) TO POP-OUT.
```

And in BASIC, we could have:

```
50  DIM  P(50,5)
200 LET  P1 = P(25,3)
```

FIGURE 1-12 A TWO-DIMENSIONAL
ARRAY

Col. Row	1	2	· · ·	m
1	$E(1,1)$	$E(1,2)$	· · ·	$E(1,m)$
2	$E(2,1)$	$E(2,2)$	· · ·	$E(2,m)$
3	·	·	· · · ·	·
·	·	·	· · · ·	·
·	·	·	· · · ·	·
n	$E(n,1)$	$E(n,2)$	· · ·	$E(n,m)$

Let us now examine another example of a two-dimensional array in which five students have each taken three tests so that a row defines all of the tests taken by a particular student and a column defines all of the grades made on a particular test, as shown in Figure 1-13. If the grades are denoted by G, then $G(2,3) = 95$, $G(1,2) = 69$, and $G(4,1) = 70$.

We stated earlier that all elements of a vector must be stored in contiguous locations, but since the array in Figure 1-13 can be viewed as a collection of row vectors or a collection of column vectors, we need to make a decision on how the elements will be stored. Actually, the elements will be stored in physically sequential locations; so the choice is as shown in Figure 1-14.

The choice is arbitrary and will be determined by the programming language used. Choice I is called *row major* and is the choice used by COBOL, PL/1, and at least some BASICs. Choice II is called *column major* and is the choice used by FORTRAN. The fact that some languages store their arrays in one order while others use another has brought surprise (and consternation) to unwary programmers trying to interface subroutines written in different

FIGURE 1-13 A TWO-DIMENSIONAL ARRAY

Student	Test		
	1	2	3
1	95	69	55
2	80	90	95
3	95	85	96
4	70	80	75
5	90	80	84

FIGURE 1-14

Relative Memory Location		I Element	Relative Memory Location		II Element
1		95	1		95
2	Row 1	69	2		80
3		55	3	Column 1	95
4		80	4		70
5	Row 2	90	5		90
6		95	6		69
7		95	7		90
8	Row 3	85	8	Column 2	85
9		96	9		80
10		70	10		80
11	Row 4	80	11		55
12		75	12		95
13		90	13	Column 3	96
14	Row 5	80	14		75
15		84	15		84

languages. Should you encounter this problem, you can remedy it quickly by reversing the roles of the row and column subscripts in one of the subroutines.

Just as a two-dimensional array can be viewed as a collection of one-dimensional arrays, a three-dimensional array can be viewed as a collection of two-dimensional arrays, and so on, such that an n-dimensional array can be viewed as a collection of $(n - 1)$-dimensional arrays. Since we will not need arrays beyond two dimensions for the remainder of the book, we will not carry the discussion of higher-dimensional arrays any further.

LISTS

A *list* is a one-dimensional structure consisting of a collection of elements. If the elements of the list are located in contiguous locations, the list is called a *linear list* or *dense list*. The only, although quite important, difference between a linear list and a vector is that a list may contain a variable number of elements (that is, we can add or delete elements from a list but not from a vector). Therefore, we can say that all vectors are linear lists, but not vice versa.

Since languages such as COBOL, BASIC, and FORTRAN do not give us the capability of directly defining a structure that varies in size within memory, we must implement a linear list with a vector that is equivalent to the maximum size of the list and let the list expand or contract within the confines of the vector that serves as the list area or host to the list.

There are many uses of linear lists; however, we see in Chapter 3 that the concept of elements residing in contiguous locations can be treated logically instead of physically without loss of usefullness. Therefore, we reserve much of our discussion of the applications of linear lists until then. One common application of a linear list is a sequential file of records stored on tape or disk; we explore these in the next section, "Files Considerations."

Because of their importance in a variety of computer applications, two special cases of linear lists, stacks and queues, are described here and then again as logical structures in Chapter 3.

STACKS

A *stack* is a linear list to which all additions and deletions are performed at one end. This list is also referred to as a last-in, first-out (LIFO) structure. As the name implies, the operation of a stack is analogous to a stack of trays in a cafeteria; a customer takes a tray from the top of the stack and fresh trays are placed on top of the remaining trays.

The simplest implementation of a stack is through the use of a vector with an integer variable called a *pointer* that contains the index value or location of the top or head of the stack. The stack "grows" from index position 1 downward. Figure 1-15 shows a host five-element vector containing a stack that initially contains three elements; then we delete one element and add two.

The process of adding an element to a stack is called *pushing* the stack. The process of deleting an element is called *popping* the stack.

Manipulation of the stack as described here is a relatively simple process. When we wish to add an element or push the stack, we add 1 to head pointer and move or assign the next element to this location. When pushing a stack, you should make sure that the stack area is not already full. If the stack is already full, you should invoke an error or overflow procedure.

A deletion from the stack, or a pop, is accomplished by performing whatever processing is needed to the element pointed to by the head pointer, and then subtracting 1 from the value of the head pointer. Once again, the current head pointer value should be checked prior to popping this stack since a head pointer value of 0 will indicate that the stack is empty.

Creation of a stack amounts to setting the stack pointer to 0 and then repeating the insertion procedure until all initial elements have been entered.

Stacks are useful when we want to process elements in reverse of the order that we encounter them, or when we want to backtrack through a series of processes; a nested set of subroutine calls is an example of this.

Suppose that routine A calls routine B, routine B calls routine C, and finally routine C calls routine D. If part of the calling process is to store the return address of the calling routine in a stack, then when routine D finishes, we can pop the stack and return to C; when C finishes we can pop the stack and return to B, and so on. If, after returning to routine C, routine C has called routine D before returning to routine B, then the new address of routine C is pushed into the stack ahead of the return address for B, which is exactly what is needed. Thus, when we pop the stack, we always return to the routine that called the current routine.

Stacks are also useful when we want to keep track of elements or tasks and when the order in which these are processed is of no concern. An example of this is seen when we study the quick sort in Chapter 2. Another example could be the case of I/O buffer management. An I/O buffer is a block of main

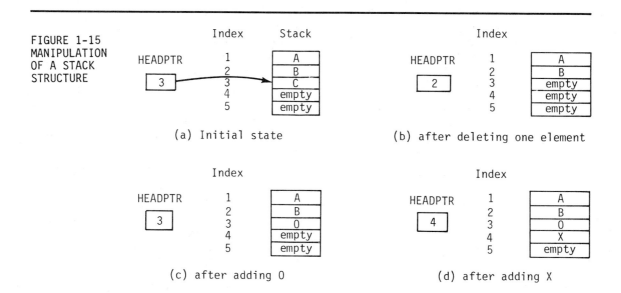

FIGURE 1-15
MANIPULATION
OF A STACK
STRUCTURE

(a) Initial state

(b) after deleting one element

(c) after adding 0

(d) after adding X

memory into which records are read from external devices for processing or from which records are written back to the device after processing. In multiuser environment, I/O processing can be facilitated without an undue waste of main memory if all users are assigned buffers from a common list of buffers called a *buffer pool.*

Initially, the locations of all available buffers are placed in a stack. As a buffer is needed by a process, the stack is popped and a buffer is assigned. When a buffer is no longer needed, its location is returned to the stack for reassignment. In this technique, it is very likely that some buffers will be used much more frequently than others, and it is possible that some may be assigned rarely if at all. For this reason, a stack is an appropriate mechanism for memory buffers since repeated use will not affect their longevity, but this process would hardly suffice in the assignment of rental cars! Figure 1-16 shows a buffer location stack.

As another example, compilers use stacks to evaluate expressions. Consider a simplified compiler in which expressions are limited to the operations =, +, −, *, /, () with the usual hierarchy of evaluation. We use two stacks for the process—one for operands and one for operations. Operations +, −, *, /, and = are always performed on the top two elements in the operand stack. Groupings are initiated by a "(" and ended by a ")". These groupings are treated as operations such that when a "(" is encountered, it is stacked without action and the stacking process continues until a matching ")" is encountered. At this point, the grouping is evaluated and left as a single temporary operand in the operand stack. The * and / operations are performed before a + or − is stacked. The evaluation of any operation followed by a (is delayed until the grouping marked by an) is first evaluated, and then it is performed. The + and − operations are performed only in the process of evaluating a grouping or in the process of emptying the stacks. When the end of the expression is reached the stacks are emptied until an = is encountered, at which time the final assignment is made and the process stops.

In Figure 1-17, evaluate the expression $TI = G − (1000 * D + R)$ from left to right. S1 is the operand stack and S2 is the operation stack. The sequence of the steps of the process is shown below the graphics of the stacks. In this illustration, we follow the "conceptual" notion of pushing elements in the top of the stack diagrams instead of representing the stacks in the upside-down method that we suggested in using vectors. (Actually, if one's aesthetic senses are offended, we can always fill the vectors from the bottom up and thus restore order.)

An algorithm is given in Figure 1-18 for the operation of a stack that is implemented as a simple linear list within a host vector. It is assumed that the first element in the vector is referenced by an index value of 1 and that the nth element would be referenced by an index value of n. The stack grows downward, as we described earlier, such that the top pointer p always contains the index value of the top element in the stack. When p contains a value of 0, the stack is empty.

The algorithm makes use of a status flag S to indicate two special conditions that must be taken into account. One of these conditions is an attempt to add (push) an element into a stack that is full. The other is an attempt to delete (pop) an element from a stack that is empty. In either case, no action is taken other than to set the flag S to the value that indicates the condition. The equivalent pseudocode accompanies Figure 1-18.

An error routine is included within the algorithm in case the procedure is invoked with an invalid request (that is, neither a push nor a pop). This practice is followed throughout the book as a recommended bit of preventative medicine for those who practice programming.

FIGURE 1-16
BUFFER ASSIGNMENT
USING A STACK

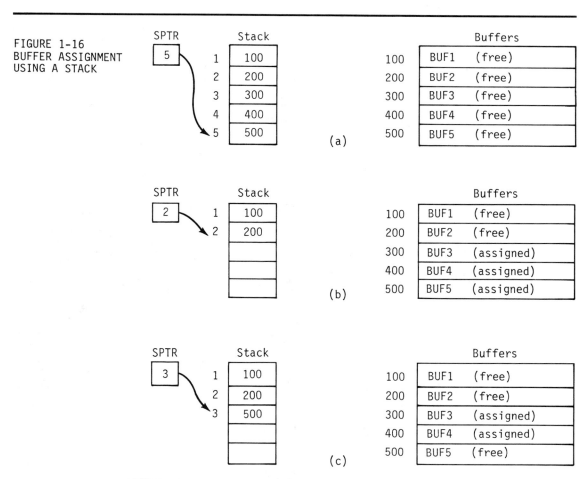

BUFFER LOCATION STACK: (a) initially, all buffers are free, and their locations are shown in the location stack for assignment; (b) after three buffers have been assigned; (c) after the buffer at location 500 has been freed and returned to the stack for reassignment.

FIGURE 1-17

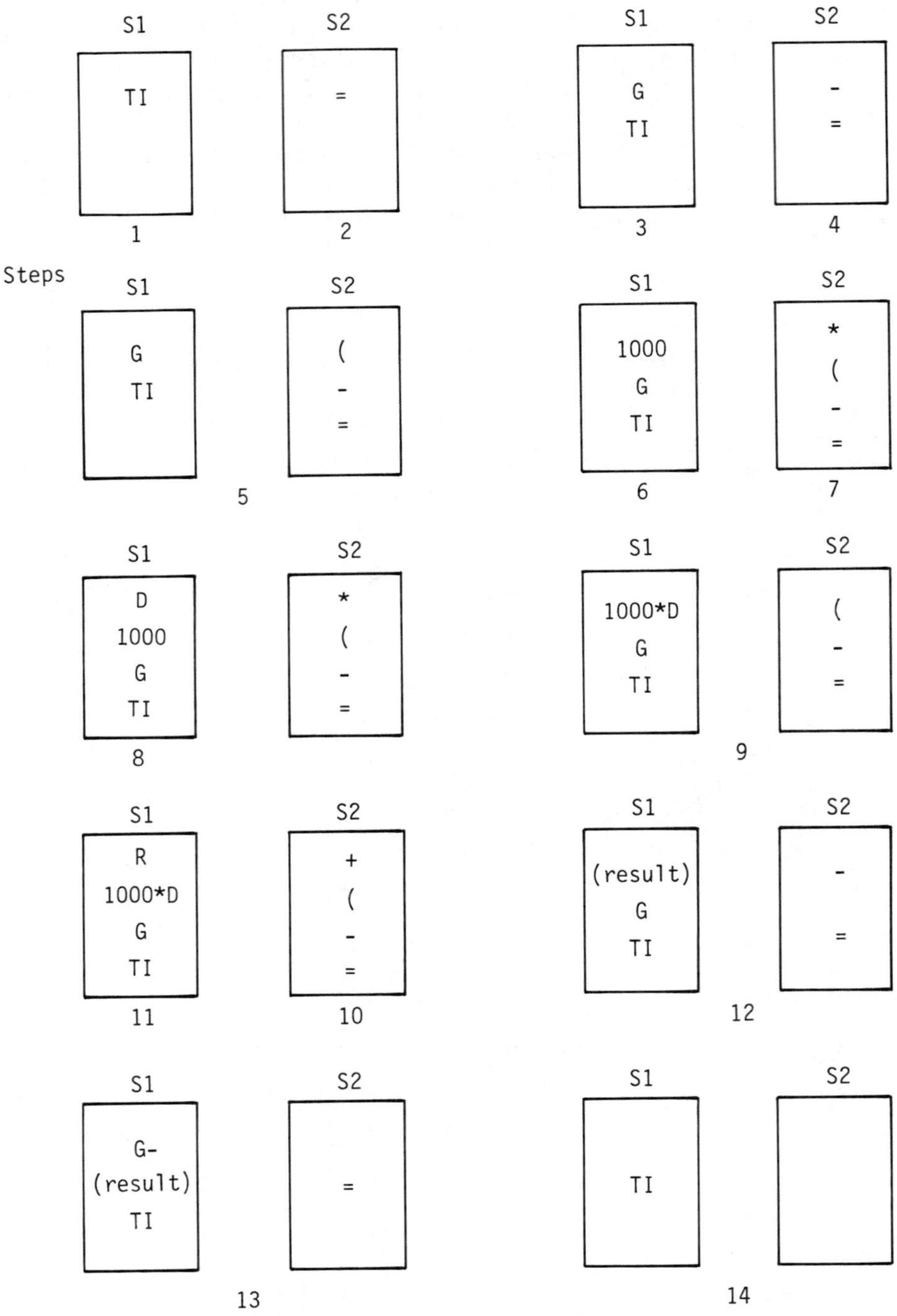

Steps

S1	S2		S1	S2
TI	=		G TI	- =
1	2		3	4

S1	S2		S1	S2
G TI	(- =		1000 G TI	* (- =
5			6	7

S1	S2		S1	S2
D 1000 G TI	* (- =		1000*D G TI	(- =
8				9

S1	S2		S1	S2
R 1000*D G TI	+ (- =		(result) G TI	- =
11	10			12

S1	S2		S1	S2
G- (result) TI	=		TI	
13			14	

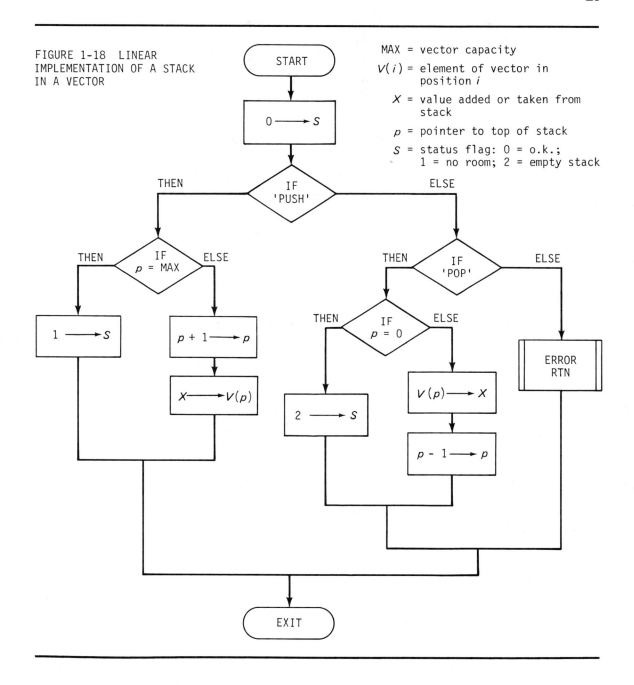

FIGURE 1-18 LINEAR
IMPLEMENTATION OF A STACK
IN A VECTOR

MAX = vector capacity

$V(i)$ = element of vector in
position i

X = value added or taken from
stack

p = pointer to top of stack

S = status flag: 0 = o.k.;
1 = no room; 2 = empty stack

START

$0 \longrightarrow S$

IF
'PUSH'

THEN

ELSE

IF
p = MAX

THEN

ELSE

$1 \longrightarrow S$

$p + 1 \longrightarrow p$

$X \longrightarrow V(p)$

IF
'POP'

THEN

ELSE

IF
p = 0

THEN

ELSE

ERROR
RTN

$2 \longrightarrow S$

$V(p) \longrightarrow X$

$p - 1 \longrightarrow p$

EXIT

LINEAR IMPLEMENTATION
OF A STACK IN A VECTOR

```
/*  MAX = vector capacity */
/*  V(I) = element of vector in position I */
/*  X = value added or taken from stack */
/*  P = points to top of stack */
/*  S = status flag: 0 = o.k.; 1 = no room; 2 = empty */
/*  A = action to be taken to stack; push or pop */


PROC  STACK
    S = 0
    IF  A = 'PUSH'
        THEN IF P = MAX
                THEN S = 1
                ELSE P = P + 1
                     V(P) = X
             ENDIF
        ELSE IF A = 'POP'
                THEN IF P = 0
                        THEN  S = 2
                        ELSE  X = V(P)
                              P = P - 1
                     ENDIF
                ELSE error routine
             ENDIF
    ENDIF
END PROC
```

QUEUES

A *queue* is a linear list to which additions are performed at one end and deletions are performed at the other, often referred to as a first-in, first-out structure (FIFO). Queues are abstractions of such natural occurrences as ticket lines at theaters or, from the recent past, cars in gasoline lines. A car enters the end of a line, progresses through the line one position at a time, and leaves from the head of the line with gas (hopefully).

We can implement a queue with a host vector and two pointers, one pointing to the head of the queue and the other to the tail. This type of arrangement is shown in Figure 1-19 where we delete from the head and add to the tail. We start with a queue containing two elements residing in a host vector of five elements. We then add one element, delete one, and add another.

As shown in Figure 1-19, using a physically sequential structure to represent a queue is not as satisfactory as it was for the stack because the deleted element's space is lost. As a result, we are much more apt to overflow our queue area than we were in the case of the stack. The problem can be eliminated if, after each deletion, we move each element forward one position, but this solution increases our processing time, which in turn creates another problem. Fortunately, both of these problems are eliminated by the circular implementation described here or by the use of linked lists, which we study in Chapter 3.

In any case, if we want to implement the basic arrangement shown in Figure 1-19, we can add or insert an element by adding 1 to the tail pointer and assigning the new element to this location in the vector. Deleting an element is accomplished by processing the element designated by the head pointer and adding 1 to the head pointer. As with stacks, we must take care not to overflow the queue. If, after a deletion, the head pointer exceeds the tail pointer, the queue is empty and both pointers should be set to indicate this.

A queue can be created by setting the head pointer to 1 and the tail pointer to 0 and then performing repeated insertions to the queue.

A solution to the storage management problem that occurs from the deletion of records from a queue that is implemented as a linear list residing in a host vector is to treat the vector as a circular arrangement of elements. This treatment is accomplished by using the MOD function described previously such that, if wraparound occurs after a deletion, the new head position is calculated as $(HEAD+1)MOD(n)$. Similarly, if wraparound occurs after an addition, the new tail position becomes $(TAIL+1)MOD(n)$, where n is the number of elements in the vector. We have, therefore solved the storage management problem by adding only the slight overhead of calculating the mod function to the first queue process described; it is this algorithm that we present in detail in Figure 1-20. (The equivalent pseudocode accompanies the figure.) The algorithm makes use of only a head position and a record count since a new tail position is always equal to (HEAD+COUNT)MOD(n), and the record count provides a more natural check for possible overflow or underflow conditions.

A common example of the use of queues in computer applications is a list of jobs waiting to be processed in a multiprogramming environment. Jobs waiting for execution are placed in a queue until an execution slot, or whatever is needed to accommodate the execution of another program, is available. In fact, operating systems make use of many queues: queues for jobs waiting for initiation, queues for active jobs needing service, and queues for jobs waiting for a resource. In other words, any time we want to process elements in order of their arrival, we use queues. More uses are discussed in Chapter 3 under the section on queues as linked lists.

FILES CONSIDERATIONS

In the section titled "Basic Terminology," we said that a file is an example of an entity set. More specifically, we define a *file* as an entity set whose entities or records have some common use. The data structures that we study

---

FIGURE 1-19
MANIPULATION
OF A QUEUE
STRUCTURE

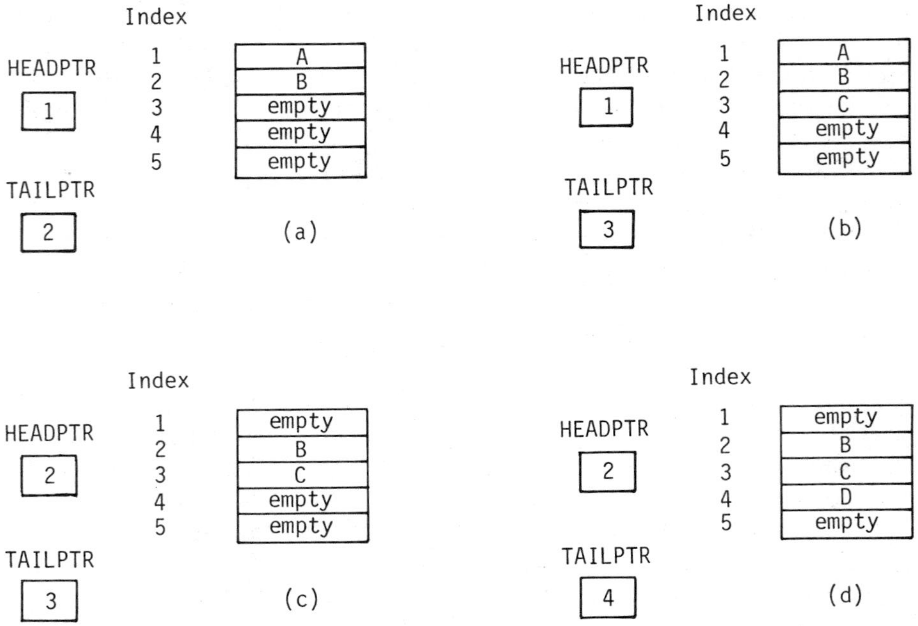

(a) Initial state; (b) after adding C; (c) after deleting one element; (d) after adding D can be thought of as file organizations, and we often refer to them inter-changeably. For this reason, we tend to use the terms *records* and *fields* instead of *entities* and *attributes* throughout the book.

It should be noted that the data structures and the associated algorithms studied in this book are presented from the viewpoint of being applied to files that reside totally in main memory; however, additional considerations in organizing and accessing files when they reside on external media, such as tape or disk, are discussed here and at other points in the book so that the reader can generally understand what must be done to extend the concepts involved to external files.

ACTIVITIES IN FILE PROCESSING

There are certain activities basic to file processing that we need to define to discuss file processing in general and various applications in particular. The most fundamental of these is searching. *Searching* is the process of locating a particular record within a file or data structure, or finding the position where the record should be or will be located. The search process can be as simple as moving to the next physical location in the file that contains a record, or it can involve a complex procedure (Chapter 4). If file processing is considered as an activity to be performed on the records of the file, then all file processing involves searching since nothing can be done to a record until it is first located.

Retrieval is the process of bringing a record into main memory for processing. If the file already resides in main memory, then retrieval amounts simply to searching the file to find the location of an existing record.

Updating is the process of changing the contents of a file, usually with the intent of making the contents more current. There are two types of updating: that which involves changing the structure of the file (that is, adding or deleting records), and that which involves simply changing the contents of fields within existing records.

The second type of updating involves nothing more than posting records in the file. *Posting* is defined as entering a value into a field of a record such that the value of the field does not affect the structure of the file. This may be an initial value for the field or the replacement of an existing value.

The reason that we restrict posting to fields whose contents do not affect the file structure is because file structure is often based on the values of the key fields, and changing a key field amounts to the deletion of the old record and the addition of a new one. For instance, suppose that we have an employee file containing records organized in ascending order according to employee names. If we change an employee's name, we are very likely to change the ordering of the file and require that the file be restructured. See Figure 1-21 as an example. If we change TAMES, R to JAMES, R, we have to rearrange our file to maintain the ascending order. The results of this change are shown in Figure 1-22.

28

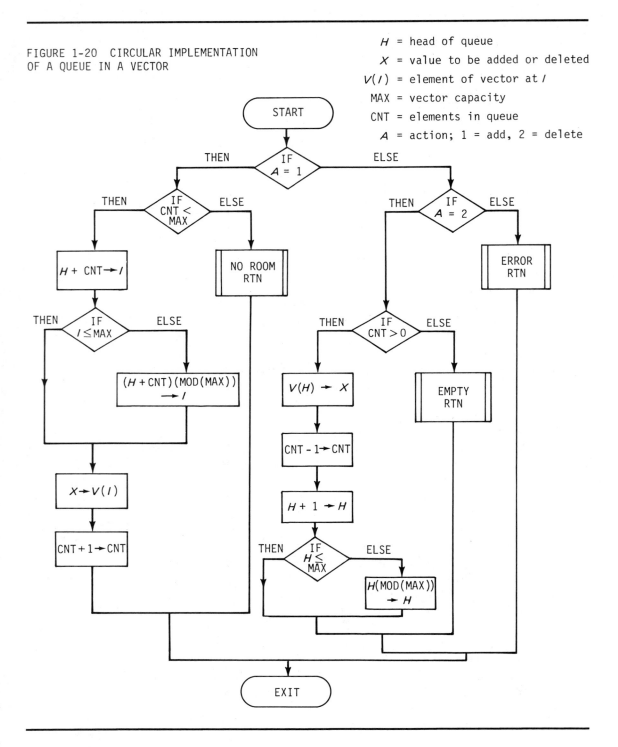

FIGURE 1-20 CIRCULAR IMPLEMENTATION
OF A QUEUE IN A VECTOR

H = head of queue
X = value to be added or deleted
$V(I)$ = element of vector at I
MAX = vector capacity
CNT = elements in queue
A = action; 1 = add, 2 = delete

CIRCULAR
IMPLEMENTATION
OF A QUEUE
IN A VECTOR

```
/*  V = the host vector; V(I) = element I of the vector */
/*  H = the head pointer of the queue */
/*  COUNT = the number of elements in the queue */
/*  MAX = capacity of the vector; X = value to be added or deleted */
/*  ACTION = action to be taken; add or delete */


PROC  CIRCULAR-QUEUE
    IF ACTION = 'ADD'
        THEN IF COUNT<MAX
                THEN I = (H+COUNT)
                    IF I≤MAX
                        THEN Continue
                        ELSE I=I(MOD(MAX))
                    V(I) = X
                    COUNT = COUNT+1
                ELSE  do no room routine
            ENDIF
        ELSE IF ACTION = 'DELETE'
                THEN IF COUNT>0
                        THEN X = V(H)
                            COUNT = COUNT-1
                            H = (H+1)
                            IF H≤MAX
                                THEN Continue
                                ELSE H=H(MOD(MAX))
                        ELSE  do empty routine
                    ENDIF
                ELSE  do invalid action routine
            ENDIF
    ENDIF
END PROC
```

Although posting is an important activity with respect to file processing, particularly if it involves something like one's bank balance, updating that is restricted to the posting activity is of little concern in a book on data or file structures since posting has no effect on these.

It is the first type of updating that concerns us: updating that involves addition or deletion of records. Therefore, for the remainder of this book, updating of this type is implied.

HARDWARE CHARACTERISTICS

Main Memory We stated that all algorithms presented in this book will be from the viewpoint that the associated data structures and files are totally contained within the main memory of the computer used to execute the algorithm. We assume that the readers have been exposed to the general characteristics of the main memory of a computer, but there are a few properties that need to be emphasized since they have a direct bearing on the physical organization of a file and on file processing efficiency.

1. Within that portion of memory allocated to a particular user, it is possible to access any location directly regardless of which location was accessed last.

2. Access to any location in main memory is equally fast, regardless of which location was accessed last, once the CPU has the

FIGURE 1-21
FILE PHYSICALLY ORDERED
ON A NAME FIELD

Location	Key	Other Fields
1	ADAMS, B	
2	BAKER, J	
3	DURAN, A	
4	MORRIS, W	
5	SMITH, F	
6	TAMES, R	

FIGURE 1-22
RESTRUCTURED FILE FROM
FIGURE 1-21 RESULTING
FROM AN ALTERATION OF
A KEY

Location	Key	Other Fields
1	ADAMS, B	
2	BAKER, J	
3	DURAN, A	
4	JAMES, R	
5	MORRIS, W	
6	SMITH, F	

address of this location. Virtual systems have additional conditions, such as address translation and paging, that can have considerable effect on how fast the CPU gets the next main memory address. The readers can pursue these in the appropriate vendor manuals.

3. Once the location has been determined, access to a record stored in main memory is many times faster than access to records stored on an external device. Access time to a particular location in main memory will generally range from the order of 100 nanoseconds to perhaps 2 microseconds, depending on the particular type of computer involved, whereas access time for even the fastest external devices is measured in milliseconds.

4. The amount of storage available for files in main memory tends to be quite limited. Once again, the specific amount will depend on the characteristics of the particular computer used and the total amount of memory that is allocated to a given user, but the amount of storage available for this purpose will normally be measured in terms of thousands of bytes instead of millions of bytes used for external devices.

Magnetic Tape A *magnetic tape* is a continuous strip of plastic that is coated with a substance that can easily be magnetized; it is wound on a reel. A typical length for a magnetic tape is 2400 feet, although it can be purchased in much shorter lengths.

Data are stored on the tape as serial strings of bits arranged in parallel tracks or channels. The purpose of the parallel channel arrangement is that one channel can be dedicated to error checking and the others can carry data. The number of data channels usually corresponds to the number of bits in the character code of the computer to be used so that when the tape is viewed as a whole, we have a serial string of characters. The type of error checking used is called *parity*, and this parity bit is such that the number of bits written for a vertical bit position in each of the channels is either even or odd, depending on vendor design. Parity is checked when the tape is read. A diagram of a nine-channel tape of this type is shown in Figure 1-23.

From Figure 1-23, we see that the bit positions within a byte for EBCDIC code do not follow the same order as the channels. The reason for this is that the bits set to 1 are the bits that are set during a write, and since write errors are more likely to occur toward the edges of the tape, the bit positions that tend to be set more frequently are arranged toward the center of the tape.

Based on the preceding discussion, we now assume a tape contains serial strings of characters.

The number of characters that we can store on a tape is dependent on three things: the length of the tape, the density of the tape, and the number of separate blocks of data on the tape.

Density is defined as the number of bits that can be stored in one channel in a length of 1 inch. It turns out that since a byte is represented vertically across the corresponding bit positions for the eight data channels, we may think of density as bits per inch or bytes per inch for a nine-channel tape. Typical densities are 800 bpi, 1600 bpi, and 6250 bpi. Thus, for a nine-channel tape 2400 feet long with a density of 1600 bpi, if we could store one solid string of data, it would contain $1600 \times 2400 \times 12 = 46,080,000$ bytes.

As it turns out, we don't store data in one continuous string. We don't store data this way because tape drives cannot start or stop on a bit, so to speak. They require some slack space on the tape to reach speed to read and also to stop. Therefore, data are arranged along the tape in a series of continuous blocks of data separated by gaps that contain no data and serve the purpose just described. These gaps are called *interblock gaps* (IBG) or *inter-record gaps* (IRG). Two common lengths for these gaps are 0.6 inch and 0.75 inch, but as technology improves, gaps become shorter, so that IBGs of 0.3 inch are not uncommon. The result is that a tape drive always reads or writes one complete block of data at a time. Another way of viewing this is that a tape drive processes from one IBG to the next.

Suppose that we write card image records (that is, 80 bytes) to a 1600 bpi tape such that each record is a block of data, and suppose that the IBG is 0.6 inch. In this case, a data block is $80/1600 = 0.05$ inch, which means that if we filled a tape to capacity with blocks of this size, we would use 7.7% of our tape for data and 92.3% for IRGs or empty space! (See Figure 1-24.)

FIGURE 1-23 DIAGRAM OF
A NINE-CHANNEL TAPE

Channel	Characters A	1	A	2	&	A	3	Corresponding bit positions for EBCDIC
0	0	0	0	0	0	0	0	4
1	0	0	0	1	0	0	1	6
2	1	1	1	1	0	1	1	0
3	1	1	1	1	1	1	1	1
4	0	1	0	1	0	0	1	2
5	0	0	0	0	1	0	1	parity
6	0	1	0	1	1	0	1	3
7	1	1	1	0	0	1	1	7
8	0	0	0	0	0	0	0	5

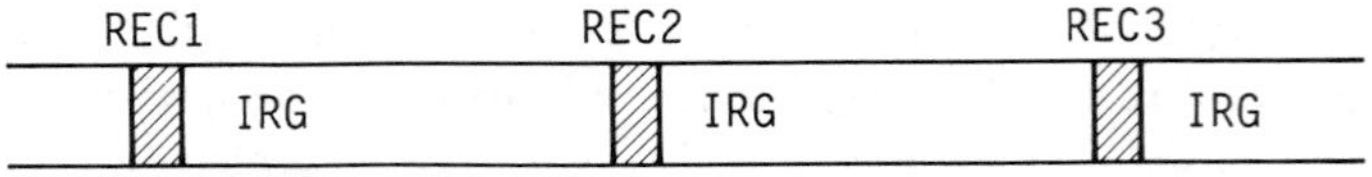

FIGURE 1-24 1600-BPI TAPE
WITH 80-BYTE DATA BLOCKS

REC1   REC2   REC3
IRG   IRG   IRG

In general, the percent of utilization of a given amount of tape can be calculated as:

$$U = \frac{BL}{BL + IBG} \cdot 100\%$$

where BL is the block length. Block length (BL) is calculated as:

$$BL = \frac{b}{d}$$

where b = bytes per block and d = density. Therefore, if our block length is given in bytes, we have:

$$U = \frac{b/d}{b/d + IRG} \cdot 100\%$$

Thus, continuing this example, if we have 400-byte blocks, we would use:

$$U = \frac{400/1600}{400/1600 + 0.6} \cdot 100\%$$

$$U = \frac{0.25}{0.85} \cdot 100\% = 29.4\%$$

This calculation leads us to Figure 1-25 for tape utilization of a 1600-bpi tape with various block sizes.

Figure 1-25 leads us to the conclusion that increased block size will lead to better tape utilization, but these gains will be less significant after block size has reached a few thousand bytes in length. Even though high tape utilization is desirable, other factors such as program size (discussed soon) are apt to limit this goal well before maximum utilization can be reached.

It would appear from the preceding discussion that tape utilization is directly related to record size. It will be if we create a tape file with only one record per data block, but if we group records together so that our data blocks contain several records, we can achieve an acceptable utilization of our tape regardless of the record size. The process of grouping records together to form one data block is called _blocking_, and the number of records per block is called the _blocking factor_ (see Figure 1-26).

FIGURE 1-25 TAPE UTILIZATION FOR
1600-BPI TAPE WITH 0.6-INCH IBGS

Block Size (in bytes)	Tape Utilization (in percent)
80	7.7
400	29.4
1000	51.0
2000	67.6
4000	80.6
8000	89.3
16000	94.3

Blocking of records not only improves tape utilization, it reduces the number of physical I/O operations required to sequentially process the records in a file by roughly the reciprocal of the blocking factor. For example, if we have a tape file consisting of 100 records with a blocking factor of 5, it would take only 20 physical reads to access all 100 records. This fact will limit the total amount of processing required of the operating system to retrieve all of the records, and will, in the end, reduce the execution time of the program. In a file of 100 records, this concern is a minor one, but in a file of 100,000 records, the savings can be substantial.

Since we always read a block of records with one physical read, the term *physical record* is frequently used to describe a block, while its component records are referred to as *logical records*. When we use unblocked records, the physical and logical records are equivalent.

A possible problem that can arise with blocking of records is program size overhead. The program that processes a file stored on an external medium, such as tape, must contain I/O buffers for passing data to and from the I/O device. These buffers are equal in size to the data blocks on the tape or other device. There must be a minimum of one buffer for the file, but normally there will be two or more for each sequential file to allow for overlap processing—the technique of allowing one buffer to be filled while another is being processed. Therefore, if the data blocks become too large, the increased size of the program may exceed the bounds of the available memory assigned to its execution. In view of this potential problem, one should choose a blocking factor that will provide a balance between tape utilization and program size.

One other characteristic of tape files that we must consider is a result of the limitation to only a sequential arrangement of records. This characteristic is a widely varying access time for a particular record. *Access time* is the time required to retrieve a given record. Average access time is the average of all the access times to a file. For a tape file from which each record in the file is processed in sequential order, the average access time is essentially constant, allowing for small variations due to blocking, and usually amounts to only a few milliseconds. If the same file is processed entirely in random order, then the average access time is approximately the time required to read half of the file in sequential order, which may take as much time as a few minutes for a file that covers an entire tape.

Magnetic Disk The most common of the direct-access devices is the *magnetic disk*. A direct-access device is one in which the record or an immediate neighborhood of the record can be accessed directly once the

FIGURE 1-26 BLOCKED RECORDS WITH
BLOCKING FACTOR OF *N*

physical address of a record is known. This greatly reduces the average access time for files processed in a random fashion. The magnetic disk can also be processed in sequential fashion similar to tape files, and access times are usually at least as fast as those possible with tape. Therefore, except for situations in which total cost is the deciding factor, or in cases where relatively large amounts of archival information must be stored, tape files are being replaced by disks. In smaller computer systems, flexible or floppy disks and single-platter hard disks—logically similar to the multiple-platter hard-disk packs described later—are in common use.

The physical properties of a magnetic disk are as follows. A *disk pack* is composed of a set of platters (resembling phonograph records) that are attached to a thick spindle that passes through their centers. The platters are separated from each other by enough space to allow arms containing read/write heads to be inserted between them. Data are stored on circular tracks, not on a spiral, as a serial string of bits, so that a byte appears as a linear series of bits instead of the parallel arrangement found on tape. Since all tracks can contain the same number of bits, the tracks near the center of a platter will necessarily carry a more dense arrangement than those near the outer edge. Within a disk pack, all tracks lying in the same respective position for each platter form a cylinder. This name comes from the concept of passing a hollow cylinder one track in thickness through the top of a pack and encountering exactly one track from each surface as it passes through. The importance of a cylinder is that all of the tracks in a given cylinder can be accessed with one positioning of the read/write arms (see Figure 1-27).

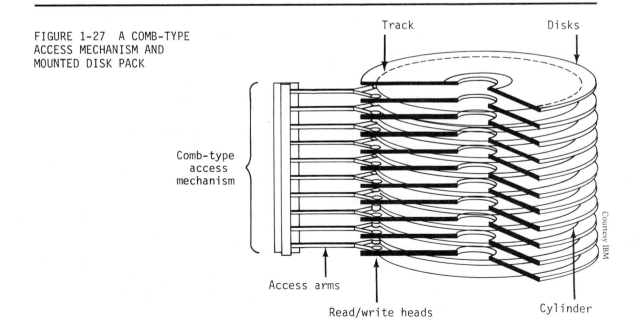

FIGURE 1-27 A COMB-TYPE
ACCESS MECHANISM AND
MOUNTED DISK PACK

Track   Disks

Comb-type
access
mechanism

Access arms

Read/write heads

Cylinder

Courtesy IBM

There are two types of disk devices with respect to the arrangement of the read/write heads: fixed and movable. The fixed type is the more expensive and is generally used only when the average access time of the movable type is unacceptable. A fixed-disk arrangement has one read/write head attached to a rigid arm for each track on the disk pack so that the disk pack is not removable.

The more common type of disk drive has a movable arm arrangement with one read/write head for each platter surface. The arms are attached to a comblike assembly that can move in and out between the platters to reach any cylinder in the pack. The time required to position the arms to the desired cylinder is called *seek time*. Seek time can vary from 0, when the arms are already in position, to somewhere around 100 milliseconds when the arms must cross the entire pack, but the maximum time will vary by a factor of 2 or 3 depending on the model and make of the drive used.

All disk drives require time to rotate the disk into position to access a given block of data, and this time is called *latency time*. Latency time will also vary depending on the position of the respective read/write head over the track in question, but maximum latency time is usually on the order of 20% of maximum seek time. To access a block of data from a track, the track must be rotated to a fixed starting position on the track called the *home address* (the physical address of the given track, along with certain status information), and then rotated to the desired block.

Data are stored on disks in blocks or sectors that can be viewed as fixed-sized blocks. The block arrangement is more efficient with respect to the use of available space on a track, but the sector arrangement is slightly simpler to access.

IBM normally uses the block arrangement for data. Figure 1-28 shows two formats used.

In both cases, the count block contains the physical address of the following data block along with the length of the data block and error checking information. The data block is similar to a block of data on tape

FIGURE 1-28

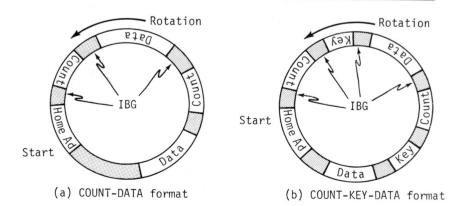

(a) COUNT-DATA format   (b) COUNT-KEY-DATA format

except that the data are one string of serial bits instead of parallel strings, and there are no parity bits since error checking is done by performing a calculation on the number of bits either read from or written to a block and by comparing this calculation to a cyclic check field at the end of each block.

The count-key-data format carries an extra block that contains the highest key value for the records contained in the following data block.

All blocks of any kind are separated by IBGs similar to those for tape; however, these gaps are not one fixed length as with tape. Therefore, the number of records that will fit on a track for a given format and a given blocking factor is normally supplied in vendor manuals.

Tracks can be searched by the physical address supplied in the count block or by the key value in the key block. A key value is usually more simple to obtain than a physical block address, but adding the key blocks to a track will reduce the capacity.

One very important aspect of searching a track on a disk is that even though a track must be searched serially to find an appropriate data block, only the appropriate data block will be read into memory because of hardware design.

Total capacity for data stored on a disk depends on the number of platter surfaces that can be used, the number of tracks per surface, the maximum capacity of a track, and the size of the data blocks to be stored. For example, the IBM 3350 contains 30 surfaces with 555 tracks, each having up to 19,000 bytes per track, for a maximum capacity of slightly more than 317,000,000 bytes per disk. The device has an average seek time of 25 milliseconds and an average latency time of 8.4 milliseconds, yielding an average access time of 33.4 milliseconds.

Recent advances tend toward increased capacities and slightly faster access times. Improvements have been aided by such techniques as disk modules (sealing the disk and access arms into an unremovable plastic shell) and using two sets of read/write heads per drive, but for our purposes, the basic characteristics of the multiple-platter hard-disk drive are essentially the same.

Floppy disks, which are commonplace with minicomputer systems, have the same concentric track arrangement and random access properties of the more sophisticated disk devices just described, but there are also notable differences.

The floppy disk consists of a single flexible oxide-coated disk, similar in size and appearance to a 45-rpm phonograph record; it is contained in a permanent, flexible square envelope. The envelope has a center cut out for mounting and a slit across the radius of the disk for access to the tracks. In comparison to the hard disks described earlier, the floppy disk has much less capacity and a considerably slower access time.

With respect to capacity, floppy disks are commonly found in 8-inch and 5-inch diameter sizes. A typical example of the 8-inch variety is the DEC RX211. This model has 77 tracks, with each track containing 26 sectors of 128 or 256 bytes each, for a maximum capacity of slightly more than half a million bytes per disk. Floppy disk drive units commonly contain two disks per unit. Only one side of the DEC disk is used for data, but other vendors provide models that record on both sides of the disk and thus double the capacity (for example, the IBM Model 4964).

The average access time of the DEC RX211 is 262 milliseconds, which is similar to the IBM 4964 and typical for the device in general. This access time is roughly an order of magnitude slower than access times for hard disks.

SEQUENTIAL FILES

A *sequential file* is a linear list to which all access is restricted to the natural order of the list. This means that, given a sequential file with 100 records, if we are positioned at record 5 and want to process record 57, we must pass through or read all records between records 5 and 57 before we can process record 57.

Card files and tape files are by default sequential files because of their physical characteristics. A main memory or disk file may or may not be treated as sequential.

Sequential files have several advantages:

1. They are *simple to create*. They are moved into position one after the other as they are received and either sorted or left in original order.

2. They are *simple to search*. Searching involves no more than moving to the next position in the list.

3. They are *space efficient*. No file organization is more space efficient since no additional information, other than the records themselves, is needed. That is, there is no requirement for directories and so on.

The disadvantages of sequential files are related to processing speeds:

1. *Searching time*: As long as a sequential file is to be processed along its natural order, and as long as most of the records encountered during the search are processed, its search time is very efficient. But if a sequential file containing n records is to be processed randomly, then, on the average, we have to examine $(n + 1)/2$ records for each record that we want to process! If the record that we want is missing, then it will again take $(n + 1)/2$ examinations for a file in ascending or descending order, and n examinations for a file ordered otherwise, to determine that the record is missing.

2. *Adding records*: If the file is not in ascending or descending order, adding is no problem since records can be added at the beginning or end of the list. If the file must be in a specific order,

then the file has to be sorted after each addition before it can be searched according to the specified order.

3. _Deleting records:_ Basically, deleting records presents the same problem as adding if the file is to remain a dense list. However, if we can tolerate the presence of null records in our files, we can simply set a field in the record—usually the key—to some value that indicates that this record has been deleted and the deletion process is improved. But the possible presence of null records means that our search must now examine each key twice during a search, once to see if the record is valid and then once again as before, which makes our search time even longer.

Given the advantages and disadvantages of a sequential file, there are applications for which a sequential file is not only appropriate but desirable. One such application is a payroll file for a company in which employee turnover is minimal (that is, it requires few additions or deletions) and each employee is paid every pay period. Another application for a sequential file would be a mailing list for subscribers to a magazine or catalog.

An inappropriate application for a sequential file is a bank's checking accounts file that is to be posted dynamically each time a customer makes a deposit or withdrawal. In this case, we would incur heavy search time overhead because of the random order in which customers make transactions.

Thus, we conclude that sequential files are appropriate when (1) there is a requirement to process all or at least a large portion of the records examined each time the file is processed, (2) the records are processed in the natural order of the file, and (3) addition or deletion of records is either minimal or can be batched and handled periodically.

ADDITIONAL TECHNIQUES

The following techniques are not particular to any data structure or file organization, but they are generally useful in file processing of all kinds. Consequently, they are offered here as a separate grouping.

Coding of Data   _Coding of data_ is the substitution of a code for a specific data value. For example, if we have a file in which every record is to carry the full name of a state, we can substitute a code for each state instead of the name, such as 01 for Alabama or 50 for Wyoming, and replace the code with the state name after a record is retrieved if it is needed. This technique can result in a considerable space saving for a file containing a large number of records.

In general, coding of data is desirable when the count of the possible data values for a particular field requires less storage than would be required to store the actual data values themselves. The preceding example in which we substitute integers from 01 to 50 for the names of states illustrates this.

Nonnumeric codes can also be used. A common example is the use of M and F for MALE and FEMALE. A nonnumeric mnemonic code such as M and F offers the advantage of possibly serving as an abbreviation for the actual data value and also makes visual checking of a record easier.

No matter what type of code we use, at some point we intend to replace a code with its corresponding data values. Therefore, we must devise a technique for doing this. A common method of substitution is through the use of data value tables, which allows us to match codes with corresponding data values. In this technique, numeric codes greatly enhance the use of the tables since the codes can serve as subscripts, or displacements, into the table, and once the code is obtained, its matching data value can be obtained directly. Consider the following example.

The job title of each employee must be stored in his or her record in an employee file. Job titles may contain as many as 30 characters; however, there are only 42 different job titles in the company.

By assigning code values of successive integers 01 through 42, the storage requirement for each person's record is reduced from 30 characters to one or two characters, depending on the numeric form of the code (for example, character, binary, decimal).

In COBOL, under working storage we have:

```
01   JOB TITLES.
     02   FILLER PIC X(30) VALUE IS 'PRESIDENT'.
     02   FILLER PIC X(30) VALUE IS 'VICE-PRESIDENT'.
                    .
                    .
                    .
     02   FILLER PIC X(30) VALUE IS 'ASSISTANT MANAGER'.
01   JOB-TABLE REDEFINES JOB-TITLES.
     02   TITLE OCCURS 42 TIMES PIC X(30).
```

If the coded field in the employee record is called JOB-CODE, in the procedure division we have:

```
                    .
                    .
                    .
     MOVE  TITLE (JOB-CODE) TO JOB-TITLE-OUT.
                    .
                    .
                    .
```

In BASIC, the job titles can be stored in a table of characters strings defined as:

```
50   DIM  J$(42)
```

Records can carry a number code defined as J1 and a job title could be assigned with 200 T$ = J$(J1).

In addition to saving space, coding of data can be useful in situations where the data values themselves change but the use and count of these values does not change. An example is the use of a price code for items carried in a retail store. When prices change, all that is necessary is a modification to a price table and not a modification to every record affected by this price change.

Variable-length Records and Fields

Records: In most applications, all of the records in a particular file will be of the same length. Fixed-length records may still be appropriate, even when one uses different record types with different formats, as long as one field in each of the record types is identical with respect to position, length, and data type and can be used to identify the type. Should a small amount of padding be required to maintain the fixed-length file, convenience normally outweighs the slight overhead.

A situation in which record types within the same file vary considerably will occasionally arise, and since every record must be as long as the length of the longest record type for a file containing fixed-length records, the overhead for using fixed-length records is unacceptable. Therefore, variable-length records should be used.

An example of fixed-length records being unacceptable is the student transcript records at a college or university. Each record requires a fixed portion consisting of descriptive information about the student, but it also requires variable information concerning each course taken by the student, such as course identification and grade. The variable information has a considerable effect on the size of a record. After all, some students take only one course, others take several, and most take less than 50. However, if only one student takes as many as 100 courses, all records would need to carry space to accommodate this many courses if we use fixed-length records, and this is hardly an efficient use of storage.

When we use variable-length records, we must have some way of determining where one record begins and ends. The simplest and most common way is to append a standardized record length field to the beginning of each record. This not only provides the boundaries for the current record but also provides the location at which the record length for the next record can be located (see Figure 1-29). In this case the record length includes the length of the record length field itself. By adding the record length to the address of the current record, we obtain the address of the next record.

Another method used with variable-length records is to precede each record with a special character or character string. A character string is usually less efficient since it requires examining every character in the record to determine the end (see Figure 1-30).

FIGURE 1-29

RL		RL		RL	
104	data	24	data	96	data

Length   4   100   4   20   4   92

FIGURE 1-30

**	data	**	data	**

Fields: Variable-length fields are fairly rare with respect to separate treatment within records. However, the techniques used for variable-length records—namely, a length at the beginning of the field or a special character—can also be used.

In addition, if the field has a relatively small set of values, then a fixed-length pointer field can be used to point to a specific value within a data pool (see Figure 1-31).

REVIEW EXERCISES

1. Define and give an example of:

   (a) information
   (b) attribute, value pair
   (c) range
   (d) ascending order
   (e) vector

   (f) array
   (g) linear list
   (h) stack
   (i) queue
   (j) sequential file

2. Evaluate:

   (a) $\lfloor 5.9 \rfloor$
   (b) $\lceil 0.12 \rceil$
   (c) $\lfloor 8 \rfloor$
   (d) $\lfloor -3.6 \rfloor$
   (e) $\lceil N + 0.5 \rceil$ where N is an integer

   (f) $\log_2 16$
   (g) $\log_2 50$
   (h) $7!$
   (i) $22 (\bmod 4)$
   (j) $5 (\bmod 7)$

3. Draw a structured flowchart for an algorithm that finds the maximum value for a set of values stored in a linear list.

4. Implement the algorithm from Exercise 3 as a structured program.

FIGURE 1-31

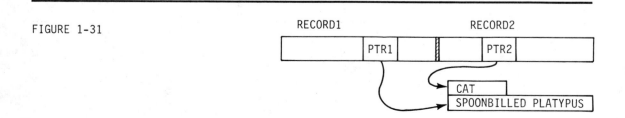

5. Show how the following 3×4 array will appear if it is stored in memory in (a) row major format and (b) in column major format.

5	7	2	8
1	6	3	4
8	4	9	0

6. Explain the relationship among file, record, and field.

7. Explain briefly:

   (a) search   (f) latency time
   (b) retrieve   (g) parity bit on magnetic tape
   (c) update   (h) IBG
   (d) access time   (i) blocking
   (e) seek time   (j) overlap processing

8. Give an example of an appropriate application for a sequential file.

9. Give an example of an inappropriate application for a sequential file.

10. If we write a sequential file containing 48-byte records to a 9-channel tape with a density of 1600 bpi and 0.6-inch IBGs using a blocking factor of 10: (a) what percent of the tape allocated to the file is used for data and (b) what blocking factor should be used to achieve a 60% utilization?

11. A file is built. It contains a record defining the status of each project in progress for a particular company. Each record has a field identifying the project leader for each project, and there are 10 project leaders. Show how coding of data can be used in this case.

12. Discuss the conditions under which variable-length records are desirable.

2. PHYSICALLY ORDERED LISTS

SORTING

Sorting is the process of ordering a file or a list; a *sort* is a routine that performs this function. *Internal sorts* are sorts that are performed totally in main memory; *external sorts* are sorts that use work areas external to main memory.

The study of sorting is important because first, it is one of the primary functions in the processing of information, and second, it is a preliminary step in the creation of many logically ordered data structures that are studied later. A complete study of sorting is not attempted for two reasons: the amount of material required exceeds a one-semester course, and many of the procedures needed to perform a theoretical analysis of the sorts involved require a level of mathematics beyond that assumed for the readers of this book. Should readers want more extensive presentation on sorting, two such works are: D. Knuth's *Sorting and Searching*, which is volume 3 of his *The Art of Computer Programming* (1973), and H. Lorin's *Sorting and Sort Systems* (1975). Of the two volumes, Knuth's tends to stress thorough mathematical analysis of the algorithms presented, while Lorin's work is a more descriptive approach with more attention given to empirical tests. Both books are listed in the References at the end of this book.

With respect to sorting then, our goals are the following:

1. To provide readers with a set of sorting algorithms so that, in any given situation requiring internal sorting, they will have a good sort available.

2. To give readers enough background in analyzing the sorts presented to make an appropriate choice of which sort to use.

3. To present a general introduction to external sorts with the assumption that if readers intend to write an external sort, they will study the topic elsewhere before attempting to do so.

INTERNAL SORTS

Sorting is an activity common to programming, but since there are many ways to sort a list or file, we need to develop the ability to make a good choice of sorting technique whenever the need arises. First of all, with respect to internal and external sorts, external sorts should be used only if the list will not fit conveniently into available main memory. This statement does not mean that every internal sort is faster than every external sort, but it does mean that for any list that does fit into available main memory, there is an internal sort that is faster than any external sort.

Most major computer vendors supply a good external sort-merge package. Therefore, it is highly unlikely that an application programmer will need to write an external sort. However, the need for writing internal sorts is commonplace. With this in mind, we present the following internal sorting techniques and algorithms.

The Basic Sorts   The three basic sorting types are selection, exchange, and insertion. We develop algorithms illustrating each of these basic types. Although each of these algorithms is preferable to the others in one situation or another, each is appropriate under general conditions for a short list, and each is simple to implement. A comparative analysis of the three basic sorting techniques is presented at the end of this section.

Selection Sorts: These sorts scan a list repeatedly, and they select one record on each pass according to a desired order. The basic example of this type of sort uses two identical list areas, one filled with the unsorted records and the other one empty.

The sort algorithm is just an extension of finding the maximum or minimum value in a list. If the list is to be sorted in ascending order, a search is made of the unordered list to find the lowest key value; then the corresponding record is moved to the top of the second list. Once a record has been chosen, its key field is set to a null or highest possible value, and the process is repeated to find the next lowest key, and so on, until all the records have been moved to the second list (see Figure 2-1). If there are n records, it will take n passes to sort the file with each pass scanning the complete list. A pass will require comparing $n - 1$ pairs. Therefore, the total number of comparisons or looks is $L = (n)(n - 1) = n^2 - n$ and the number of records moved is n. Figure 2-2 gives the algorithm for the selection sort in flowchart form; the equivalent pseudocode accompanies it.

A refinement of the preceding selection sort is a selection with exchange. This sort will require $n - 1$ selection passes for n records, but instead of moving a record to a duplicate list area, it exchanges the selected record, if necessary, with the record in its true position. This refinement saves the extra list area and, as it moves down the list, each successive pass requires the examination of one less pair of records than the previous pass since all records above the current position are in position. This reduces the average number of comparisons for each pass to $n/2$ and the total number to $(n - 1)(n/2) = (n^2 - n)/2$, which is half the previous number. The first version required

FIGURE 2-1 (a) Start;
(b) after first pass;
(c) after second pass

Key   Data

Key	Data
08	
02	
05	
03	
01	
04	
07	
06	
09	

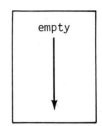

empty

(a)

Key   Data

Key	Data
08	
02	
05	
03	
99	
04	
07	
06	
09	

01	

empty

(b)

Key   Data

Key	Data
08	
99	
05	
03	
99	
04	
07	
06	
09	

01	
02	

empty

(c)

48

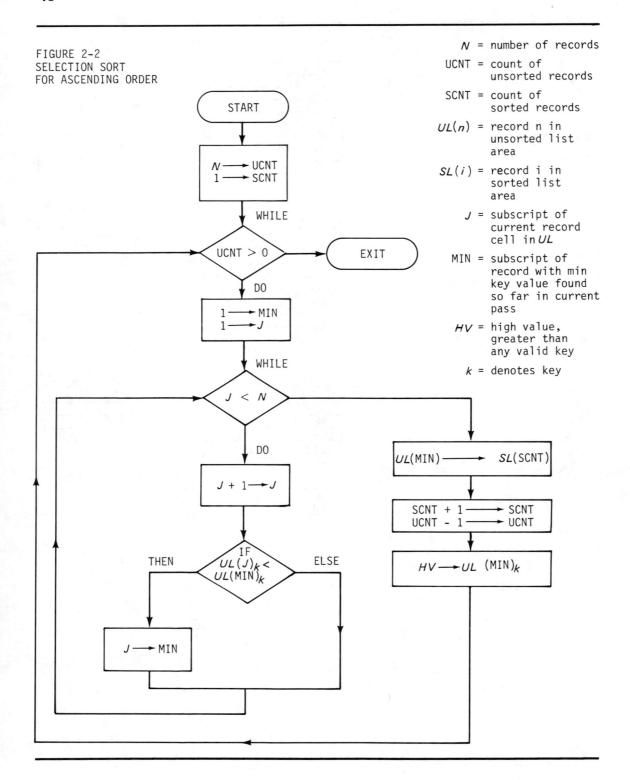

FIGURE 2-2
SELECTION SORT
FOR ASCENDING ORDER

N = number of records
UCNT = count of unsorted records
SCNT = count of sorted records
$UL(n)$ = record n in unsorted list area
$SL(i)$ = record i in sorted list area
J = subscript of current record cell in UL
MIN = subscript of record with min key value found so far in current pass
HV = high value, greater than any valid key
k = denotes key

START

$N \longrightarrow$ UCNT
$1 \longrightarrow$ SCNT

WHILE

UCNT > 0

EXIT

DO

$1 \longrightarrow$ MIN
$1 \longrightarrow J$

WHILE

$J < N$

DO

$J + 1 \longrightarrow J$

IF
$UL(J)_k <$
$UL(MIN)_k$

THEN

ELSE

$J \longrightarrow$ MIN

$UL(MIN) \longrightarrow SL(SCNT)$

SCNT + 1 $\longrightarrow$ SCNT
UCNT - 1 $\longrightarrow$ UCNT

$HV \longrightarrow UL(MIN)_k$

SELECTION SORT   /* N = number of records to be sorted */
FOR ASCENDING ORDER   /* UCNT = count of unsorted records; SCNT = sorted record count */
                         /* UL(J) = record J of unsorted list */
                         /* SL(I) = record I of sorted list */
                         /* J = location of current record in unsorted list */
                         /* MIN = location of record with minimum key for current pass */
                         /* HV = high value, greater than any valid key */
                         /* ULK(J), SLK(I) = key values in respective lists */

```
PROC  SELECT-SORT
    UCNT = N
    SCNT = 1
    WHILE UCNT > 0  DO
        MIN = 1
        J = 1
        WHILE J < N  DO
            J = J + 1
            IF ULK(J) < ULK(MIN)
                THEN  MIN = J
                ELSE  continue
            ENDIF
        ENDDO
        SL(SCNT) = UL(MIN)
        SCNT = SCNT + 1
        UCNT = UCNT - 1
        ULK(MIN) = HV
    ENDDO
END PROC
```

exactly n moves, whereas the second will require at most $n - 1$ exchanges; however, an exchange usually requires three moves. Therefore, we should not, in general, expect a savings with respect to record movement. Figure 2-3 uses the same list as before, and Figure 2-4 gives the algorithm for selection with exchange sort in flowchart form with the equivalent pseudocode following it.

Exchange Sorts: These sorts compare the keys of two records within a list and, if these are out of order with respect to each other, an exchange is made. The number of passes through the list to complete the sort will depend on the specific sort of this type used. The only additional storage required is a work area equal to the size of a record to assist in the exchange.

One of the most common of all exchange sorts is the *bubble sort,* so called because records appear to move up into position through a list much as bubbles move up through water. This sort compares successive pairs of records and requires at most $n - 1$ passes for a list containing n records. If the algorithm starts at the top of the list for each pass, then after the first pass, the

---

FIGURE 2-3 (a) Start; (b) after first pass; (c) after second pass; (d) after third pass (continued)

Key	Data
08	
02	
05	
03	
01	
04	
07	
06	
09	

(a)

	Key	Data
*	01	
	02	
	05	
	03	
*	08	
	04	
	07	
	06	
	09	

(b)

Key	Data
01	
02	
05	
03	
08	
04	
07	
06	
09	

(c)

	Key	Data
	01	
	02	
*	03	
*	05	
	08	
	04	
	07	
	06	
	09	

(d)

last record in the list will be in its true position. After the second pass, the next to last record in the list will be in position, and so on. For this reason, each pass need only examine one less pair than the preceding one.

This means that for a list containing n records, we have the following:

Pass number	Pairs to be examined
1	$n - 1$
2	$n - 2$
3	$n - 3$
.	.
.	.
.	.
$n - 1$	1

Therefore, the maximum number of comparisons or looks will be the average number of pairs per pass times the maximum number of passes, or $L = (n/2)(n - 1) = [(n)(n - 1)]/2$.

This number is half that given for the first selection sort discussed; however, it is the same as the selection with exchange sort. It is worth noting that selection sorts always require the same number of comparisons to sort a

---

FIGURE 2-3 (e) after fourth pass; (f) after fifth pass; (g) after sixth pass. The seventh and eighth passes leave the list unchanged.

(e)

(f)

(g)

Seventh and eighth passes leave the list unchanged.

*denotes exchanged pair of records

52

FIGURE 2-4 SELECTION WITH
EXCHANGE SORT FOR
ASCENDING ORDER

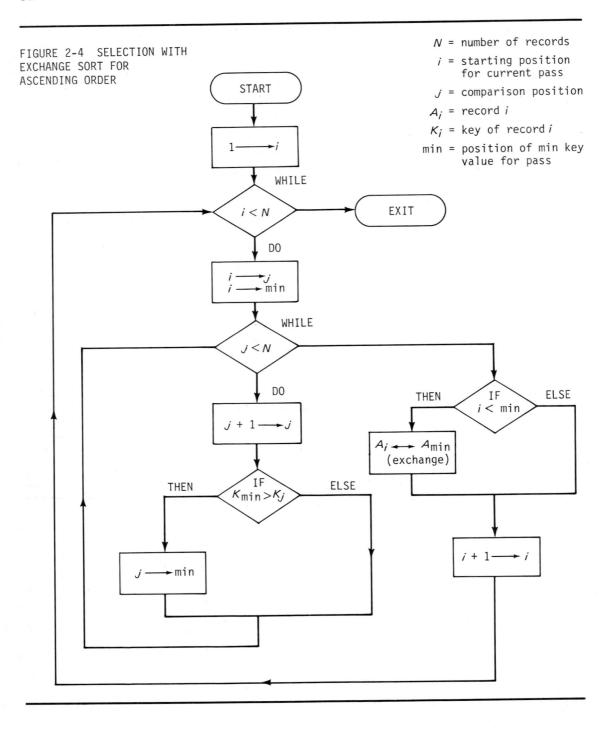

N = number of records
i = starting position
    for current pass
j = comparison position
A_i = record i
K_i = key of record i
min = position of min key
      value for pass

SELECTION WITH
EXCHANGE SORT
FOR ASCENDING ORDER

```
/*  N = number of records to be sorted */
/*  I = starting position for current pass */
/*  J = current record location for comparison */
/*  A(I) = record at location I */
/*  K(I) = key of record at location I */
/*  MIN = position of minimum key value for pass */

PROC   SELEX-SORT
    I = 1
    WHILE I < N   DO
        J = I
        MIN = I
        WHILE J < N   DO
            J = J + 1
            IF   K(MIN) > K(J)
                THEN   MIN = J
                ELSE   next statement
            ENDIF
        ENDDO
        IF I < MIN
            THEN   exchange A(I) and A(MIN)
            ELSE   next statement
        ENDIF
        I = I + 1
    ENDDO
END PROC
```

given list; however, if a check is made during each pass to see if an exchange did occur, the bubble sort can terminate after the first pass in which there is no exchange because at this point the list will be in order. This situation will not affect the number of exchanges performed by the sort, but in some cases it can greatly reduce the number of comparisons and thus improve the performance (see Figure 2-5). Figure 2-6 gives the algorithm for a bubble sort in flowchart form with the equivalent pseudocode following it.

Insertion Sorts: These sorts insert records, one at a time, into an ordered sublist to preserve the desired order until the sublist contains exactly all of the records from the original list. If we want to sort an unordered list using this method, we can either use separate areas for the original list and the evolving ordered sublist, or we can partition the original list into an ordered portion and an unordered portion so that the unordered portion contracts as the ordered portion grows.

First, we examine the method using two list areas where L_1 is the original unordered list containing records $a_1, a_2, \ldots, a_n$, and L_2 is the ordered sublist, which is initially empty. The first step is to copy the first record, a_1, from L_1 to the first position of L_2. At this point, L_2 is ordered by default since it contains only one record. We then move down to a_2 in L_1 and compare this record to the single record in L_2. If a_2 should precede a_1, then a_1 is moved down to the second position in L_2 and a_2 is inserted into the first position. If a_2 should not precede a_1, it is inserted in the second position of L_2. We continue moving down L_1 to the next record and then locate its relative position with respect to the other records in L_2. If necessary, any records that it should precede are moved down one position, and the new record is inserted into its relative position so that order is maintained. This process continues until all records are copied to L_2.

This technique requires n passes of the ordered sublist to sort n records; however, each pass terminates as soon as the insertion position is located and filled. This technique will yield a worst case of comparisons of $L = (n^2 - n)/2$, which is the same as that for the selection sort and the bubble sort, but the nature of this sort is such that as the number of comparisons increases, the

FIGURE 2-5 PERFORMANCE
OF A BUBBLE SORT ON
A SHORT LIST

After Pass	Start	1	2	3	4	
	5	3	3	1	1	
	3	5	1	2	2	
	7	1	2	3	3	
	1	2	4	4	4	
	2	4	5	5	5	
	4	6	6	6	6	
	6	7	7	7	7	Sort
Exchanges		~~1111~~	111	11	0	stops
Compares		~~1111~~ 1	~~1111~~ 1111	1111	111	

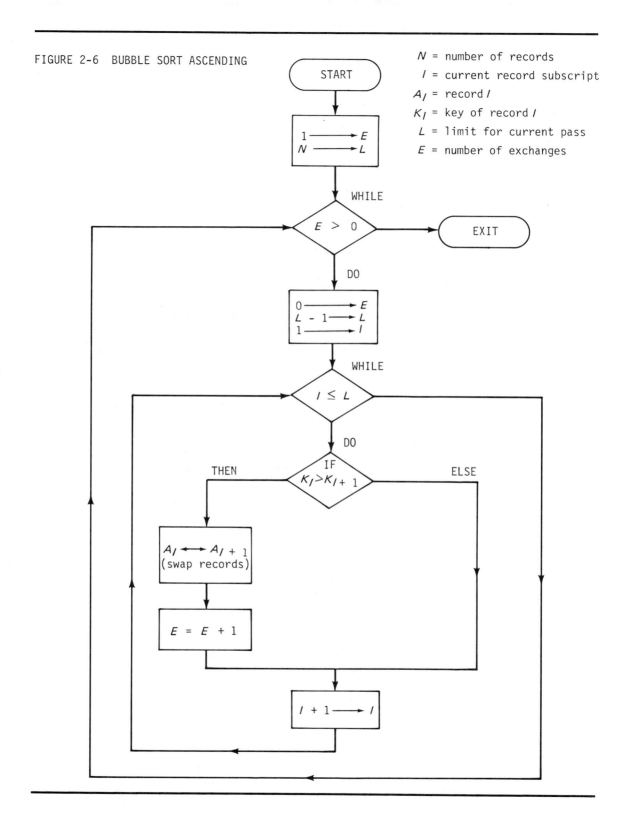

FIGURE 2-6 BUBBLE SORT ASCENDING

N = number of records
I = current record subscript
A_I = record I
K_I = key of record I
L = limit for current pass
E = number of exchanges

BUBBLE SORT ASCENDING

```
/*  N = number of records in list */
/*  I = location (index) of current record */
/*  A(I) = record at location I */
/*  K(I) = key of record at location I */
/*  L = limit for current pass */
/*  E = number of exchanges */

PROC  BUBBLE-SORT
    E = 1
    L = N
    WHILE E > 0    DO
        E = 0
        L = L - 1
        I = 1
        WHILE I ≤ L    DO
            IF K(I) > K(I+1)
                THEN exchange A(I) and A(I+1)
                    E = E + 1
                ELSE next statement
            ENDIF
            I = I + 1
        ENDDO
    ENDDO
END PROC
```

BUBBLE SORT
ROUTINE IN COBOL

```
WORKING-STORAGE SECTION.
     .
     .
     .
77    REC-COUNT    PIC    S9(5)    USAGE IS COMP.
77    I            PIC    S9(5)    USAGE IS COMP.
77    NEXT         PIC    S9(5)    USAGE IS COMP.
77    EXCHANGES    PIC    S9(5)    USAGE IS COMP.
77    LIMIT        PIC    S9(5)    USAGE IS COMP.
     .
     .
     .
01    REC-TABLE.
      02    REC OCCURS _____ n _____ TIMES.
               03 REC-KEY PIC _____.
               03 DATUM PIC _____.
      02    TEMP-REC PIC _____.
     .
     .
     .
PROCEDURE DIVISION.
     .
     .
     .
BUBBLE-SORT-ASCENDING.
     MOVE 1 TO EXCHANGES.
     MOVE REC-COUNT TO LIMIT.
     PERFORM BUBBLE-PASS UNTIL EXCHANGES = 0.
BUBBLE-SORT-EXIT.  EXIT.
     .
     .
     .
BUBBLE-PASS.
     MOVE 0 TO EXCHANGES.
     SUBTRACT 1 FROM LIMIT.
     PERFORM COMPARE-RECS VARYING I FROM 1 BY 1 UNTIL I > LIMIT.
COMPARE-RECS.
     ADD 1, I GIVING NEXT.
     IF REC-KEY (I) > REC-KEY (NEXT)
        THEN MOVE REC (I) TO TEMP-REC
             MOVE REC (NEXT) TO REC (I)
             MOVE TEMP-REC TO REC (NEXT)
             ADD 1 TO EXCHANGES
        ELSE NEXT SENTENCE.
```

number of record moves decreases. Thus, if this sort is attempted on an ordered list, there are $(n^2 - n)/2$ comparisons and n moves (no moves if partitioning is used), but if the list is ordered in reverse, there will be $n - 1$ comparisons and $(n^2 + n)/2$ moves (see Figure 2-7).

A refinement of the insertion sort described here eliminates the need for a second list area. In this method, we separate the list to be sorted, L, into an ordered partition L_1 and an unordered partition L_2. At the start of the sort, L_1 contains the first record of L and $L_2 = L$ minus the first record. At the end of each pass, L_1 is increased by one record and L_2 is decreased by one record until, after the last pass $(n - 1)$, $L_1 = L$ and L_2 is empty. We need to employ a hold area the size of a single record so that we do not overlay any records during the movement of records to accommodate an insertion. Once it has been determined that the top record in the unordered portion of the list is out of order, this record is moved to the hold area. The records that must be displaced are moved down one position each, starting with the bottom of the ordered portion of the list. Then the record in the hold area is moved to its new position. This results in $n - 1$ passes in which an average of $n/2$ records are moved down one position with an additional two moves on each of these $n - 1$ passes to accommodate the holding and insertion of a record, which gives $(n^2 - n)/2 + 2(n - 1) = (n^2 + 3n - 4)/2$ moves.

A slight variation of this partitioned insertion sort occurs when records are presented from the outside world, one at a time, for sorting. In this case, we have only the sorted portion of the list and an empty portion. Records are placed directly into the hold area and then inserted as before into their proper positions. It should be noted that, of the basic sorts, only the insertion sort affords us the opportunity of maintaining a sorted list as records enter the list area without considerable loss of efficiency.

The partitioning refinement not only saves the second list area, it also eliminates the need to move a record that happens to be in place for any particular pass. Since this technique is clearly an improvement over the first technique, we present the logic for it alone (see Figure 2-8). Figure 2-9 shows the algorithm for the insertion sort in flowchart form; the equivalent pseudocode accompanies it.

FIGURE 2-7

Start		Pass I		Pass II		Pass III		Pass IV		Pass V		Pass VI	
L_1	L_2	L_1	L_2	L_1	L_2	L_1	L_2	L_1	L_2	L_1	L_2	L_1	L_2
6	-	6 → 6		6	3	6	3	6	1	6	1	6	1
3	-	3	-	3	6	3	4	3	3	3	3	3	2
4	-	4	-	4	-	4	6	4	4	4	4	4	3
1	-	1	-	1	-	1	-	1	6	1	5	1	4
5	-	5	-	5	-	5	-	5	-	5	6	5	5
2	-	2	-	2	-	2	-	2	-	2	-	2	6

Summary and Comparison of the Basic Sorts: Now that we have studied examples of the three basic sorts, it is natural to ask which is best. Unfortunately, the answer is that it depends on the condition of the list to be sorted. For instance, if you happen to sort a list that is already in order, then the bubble sort is best since it would require exactly one pass of $n - 1$ compares with no record movement. But if the list happens to be ordered in reverse, then the bubble sort is the worst because it then requires $(n^2 - n)/2$ compares with an *exchange for each compare* resulting in $3(n^2 - n)/2$ record moves.

Before proceeding with this comparison, we need to define standards by which any two or more sorts can be compared. The three standards that we use are:

1. Performance

2. Storage requirements

3. Ease of implementation

For a short list, standards 2 and 3 are usually more important if minimum requirements for 1 are met. However, as list size increases, standard 1 is the dominant measure if minimum requirements for 2 and 3 are met. It should be relatively clear what is meant by storage requirements and ease of implementation, but performance needs further discussion. For our purposes, we assume that performance is directly proportional to the number of comparisons and record moves that a sort performs in producing an ordered list.

It has been shown that the theoretical minimum for the number of compares *in the worst case* for any sort is C or $L = \lceil \log_2 N! \rceil$ where N is the number of records in the list. This equation becomes difficult to compute as

FIGURE 2-8

Start L	After Pass I	Pass II	Pass III	Pass IV	Pass V	Pass VI
L_1 4	L_1 ⌈ 3	L_1 ⌈ 3	L_1 ⌈ 2	L_1 ⌈ 2	L_1 ⌈ 1	⌈ 1
3	⌊ 4	⌊ 4	3	3	2	2
5	⌈ 5	⌊ 5	4	L_1 ⌈ 4	3	3
L_2 2	2	⌈ 2	⌊ 5	5	L_1 ⌊ 4	L_1 ⌊ 4
7	L_2 7	L_2 7	7	⌊ 7	5	5
1	1	1	L_2 ⌈ 1	L_2 ⌈ 1	7	6
6	⌊ 6	⌊ 6	⌊ 6	⌊ 6	L_2 ⌊ 6	⌊ 7
Compares	1	2	1	4	1	6 = 15
Moves*	3	0	5	0	7	3 = 18

*For any given pass the number of moves equals the number of records moved down one position plus two moves for the record inserted.

FIGURE 2-9 INSERTION SORT ASCENDING

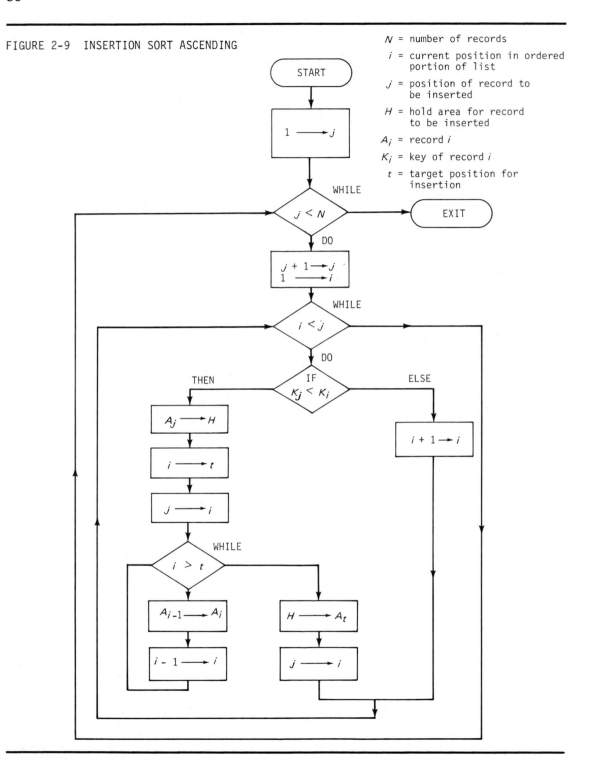

N = number of records
i = current position in ordered portion of list
j = position of record to be inserted
H = hold area for record to be inserted
A_i = record i
K_i = key of record i
t = target position for insertion

START

$1 \longrightarrow j$

WHILE

$j < N$

EXIT

DO

$j + 1 \longrightarrow j$
$1 \longrightarrow i$

WHILE

$i < j$

DO

IF
$K_j < K_i$

THEN

ELSE

$A_j \longrightarrow H$

$i + 1 \longrightarrow i$

$i \longrightarrow t$

$j \longrightarrow i$

WHILE

$i > t$

$A_{i-1} \longrightarrow A_i$

$H \longrightarrow A_t$

$i - 1 \longrightarrow i$

$j \longrightarrow i$

INSERTION SORT
ASCENDING

```
/*  N = number of records in list to be sorted */
/*  I = current position in order portion of list */
/*  J = position of record to be inserted */
/*  H = temporary hold area for record to be inserted */
/*  A(I) = record at location I */
/*  K(I) = key of A(I) */
/*  T = target position for the insertion */


PROC    INSERTION-SORT
    J = 1
    WHILE  J < N  DO
        J = J + 1
        I = 1
        WHILE I < J  DO
            IF K(J) < K(I)
                THEN H = A(J)
                    T = I
                    I = J
                    WHILE I > T  DO
                        A(I) = A(I - 1)
                        I = I - 1
                    ENDDO
                    A(T) = H
                    I = J
                ELSE I = I + 1
            ENDIF
        ENDDO
    ENDDO
END PROC
```

N increases. Therefore, it is common to use the approximation $C = \lceil N \log_2 N \rceil$ as N reaches a value such that the difference between the two is acceptable. Using the information in Figure 2-11, it seems reasonable to use the approximation when $N \geq 64$.

Since no record movement occurs until a compare is made, the worst case with respect to movement is that each compare results in a record move or exchange. We assume that an exchange results in three moves. But, in the case of record movement, we do not have a theoretical minimum that applies to the worst case of every sort as we did with compares. For example, the worst case with respect to movement for any selection sort is N exchanges, but this is certainly not true for insertion or exchange sorts. Therefore, we must evaluate moves on an individual basis. Figure 2-10 summarizes the three basic sorts.

Since each sort in Figure 2-10 has a worst case for comparisons of $(n^2 - n)/2$, we present Figure 2-11 to help in our analysis of performance. Computations for both $\lceil \log_2 n! \rceil$ and its approximation $\lceil n \log_2 n \rceil$ are shown with the percent error that would be incurred from using the approximation for a given value of n. (After $n = 150$, the approximation would seem to suffice.)

We now need to establish some way of estimating whether the number of comparisons or the number of moves has the greatest effect on total performance. Again, we see that the answer depends on properties that are variable.

First of all, we should realize that a compare for any sort actually refers to an iteration through the loop of instructions that describes a pass for the sort and, likewise, a move or exchange refers to the set of instructions required to perform this function apart from the other instructions within the compare loop. Second, we can expect the execution time for a compare to be relatively constant for a particular sort on a particular machine, except for a minor

FIGURE 2-10
SUMMARY OF
THE THREE
BASIC SORTS

Standard \ Sort	Bubble	Selection with Exchange	Insertion (Partitioned)
Comparisons (min,max)	$n - 1$, $\dfrac{n^2 - n}{2}$	$\dfrac{n^2 - n}{2}$, $\dfrac{n^2 - n}{2}$	$n - 1$, $\dfrac{n^2 - n}{2}$
Movement* (min,max)	0, $3\left(\dfrac{n^2 - n}{2}\right)$	0, $3(n - 1)$	0, $\dfrac{n^2 + 3n - 4}{2}$
Storage requirement	same: one list area plus single record area	same	same
Ease of implementation	simple	simple	simple

*One exchange = 3 moves.

variation due to the length of the key, but the execution time for a move will be very much dependent on the length of the record. To illustrate this, Figure 2-12 shows a possible implementation of the bubble sort using IBM 360/370 assembly language. It is not important for readers to understand the particulars of this language to see that the compare loop involves five machine instructions on each iteration, and that the exchange requires four instructions—one for each move and one to count the exchange. The number of instructions seems to imply that an exchange takes slightly less time than a compare except for the fact that a move instruction is more costly than any of the others. A glance at the flowcharts for the selection and exchange and insertion sorts should convince readers that roughly the same situation exists for each of the three basic sorts. A check into the timings for several of the IBM 360/370 machines reveals that an exchange (three moves) requires two or three times the execution time of a compare for short records—20 bytes or less—and eight to ten times as much time by the time records have reached a length of 100 bytes. Therefore, we can conclude that, in general, an exchange takes several times the execution time of a compare, and that for short records a move is roughly equivalent to a compare.

When we examine the flowcharts of the more complex sorts that follow (Shell and quick), it is apparent that a compare is slightly more costly for them than it is for the basic sorts. This fact should be considered when we estimate the point at which one of these more complex sorts is more desirable than one of the basic sorts.

Several authors have suggested that a "good sort" is one whose worst case for comparisons does not exceed $2n \log_2 n$ as the maximum expected value for n records. We might go a step further and say that an *acceptable sort* should not exceed $5n \log_2 n$ as the maximum expected value for n records. This guideline seems reasonable given the number of sorts from which we can choose.

FIGURE 2-11

Number of Records (n)	$\dfrac{n^2 - n}{2}$	Theoretical Limit $\lceil \log_2 n! \rceil$	$\lceil n \log_2 n \rceil$	% error
2	1	1	2	100
4	6	5	8	60
8	28	16	24	50
16	120	45	64	42
32	496	118	160	36
50	1225	215	282	31
64	2016	296	384	29
100	4950	526	665	26
128	8128	719	896	25
150	11,175	876	1084	24
200	19,900		1529	
500	124,750		4484	
1000	499,500		9996	

FIGURE 2-12   IBM 360/370 ASSEMBLY-LANGUAGE IMPLEMENTATION OF A BUBBLE SORT
ASCENDING FOR A TABLE WITH 20 RECORDS

```
                    RECS      DS     20CL100
                    WORKREC   DS     CL100
                               .
                               .
                               .
                              LA     9,19             SET COMPARE COUNTER
                    PASS      LA     6,RECS           R6 POINTS TO 1st REC IN LIST
                              LA     7,100(6)         R7POINTS TO NEXT REC
                              LR     8,9              SET COUNTER FOR INNER LOOP
                              SR     11,11            CLEAR EXCHANGE COUNTER
              ⎧    COMPLOOP   CLC    95(3,6),95(7)    COMPARE KEYS
              ⎪               BNH    CONT1
              ⎪               LA     11,1(11)         ADD 1 TO EXCHANGE COUNTER
  Compare     ⎨               MVC    WORKREC,0(6)     EXCHANGE RECS
  loop for    ⎪               MVC    0(100,6),0(7)
  each pass   ⎪               MVC    0(100,7),WORKREC
              ⎪    CONT1      LA     6,100(6)         INCREMENT R6,R7 TO NEXT
              ⎪               LA     7,100(7)         PAIR OF RECORDS
              ⎩               BCT    8,COMPLOOP       CONTINUE PASS
                              C      11,=F'0'         CHECK FOR NO EXCHANGES
                              BE     DONE             EXIT IF NO EXCHANGES
                              BCT    9,PASS
                    DONE       .
                               .
                               .
```

All of the basic sorts have a worst case for comparisons of $(n^2 - n)/2$. Consequently, we solve for n.

$$\frac{n^2 - n}{2} \leq 2n \log_2 n$$

$$n - 1 \leq 4 \log_2 n$$

$$n - 1 \leq 4 \left[\frac{1}{\ln 2} \ln n \right]$$

$$n - 1 \leq 4 \left[1.4427 \ln n \right] \rightarrow n < 18$$

The solution indicates that any time $n < 18$ records, any of the three basic sorts would be good sorts. A similar calculation or reference to Figure 2-12 should indicate that as long as n does not exceed 50 or 60 records, any of them may still be acceptable, but for $n \geq 100$, another sort clearly is indicated.

As for choosing among the basic sorts, given that they are all acceptable, there is no clear winner. The bubble sort is best when there are no records greatly out of position since it will terminate after a few passes, but it is the worst of the three when the list tends toward reverse order. It will also reach the maximum number of compares any time the record that belongs in the first position of the list begins in the last position.

Selection with exchange will always require the maximum number of comparisons, but it will never require more than $n - 1$ exchanges. Therefore, the selection with exchange is clearly better than the bubble sort when a list is greatly out of order.

The insertion sort reaches its greatest number of comparisons when it is used on a list that is already in order; it reaches its fewest number when the list is ordered in reverse. But in the case of reverse order, the insertion sort requires the maximum number of moves, $(n^2 + 3n - 4)/2$. As the number of compares decreases, the number of moves increases, and vice versa. The insertion sort is best, however, whenever one or several records are being added to a list that is already ordered. This logic extends to a list in which the majority of the list is partially ordered and the unordered portion can be separated and then inserted into the ordered portion.

So, in summary, any of the basic sorts is good for short lists of approximately 20 records or fewer, and any is usually acceptable for lists of up to 50 records. If the list tends toward any of the special conditions just discussed, then one sort may be preferable to the others although savings will not be dramatic. Beyond 50 records, there are better sorts that should be used, and these are discussed in later sections. In fact, even if the choice is purely the aesthetic preference of the user, no significant harm will be done *as long as the list is short.*

The Shell Sort Since we established that the basic sorts are generally good only for short lists, we now study a sort that is, in general, better than the basic sorts for sorting longer lists. This sort is named for

D. L. Shell who first described it in 1959. It is an exchange sort that includes two major refinements over the bubble sort. These refinements are: backup after an exchange has occured and comparisons of records at a diminishing interval from pass to pass. More specifically, the sort works by comparing elements at interval distances that decrease for each pass until this distance is equal to 1 for the last pass. The first distance is $d_0 = \lfloor N/2 \rfloor$ where N is the number of records. Successive distances are calculated as $d_n = \lfloor d_{n-1}/2 \rfloor$.

The progression through the list is from the top, one element at a time, until an exchange occurs or until the end of the list is reached. When an exchange does occur, a check is made to see if the exchange will be propagated back through the list by backing up at intervals of the current value of d until no exchange occurs: then the procedure resumes at the point at which the exchange started. Figure 2-13 and the accompanying pseudocode illustrate the Shell sort.

This process moves records that are greatly out of order into position with fewer compares and exchanges; thus it is faster. The earlier passes refine the list so that all of the records are close to their true position. The last pass is then essentially a bubble sort with backup (sometimes called a *shuttlesort*) and, as we have seen earlier, the bubble sort can perform quite well on a list that is nearly in order.

Exact analysis of the performance of the Shell sort is difficult and has never been established mathematically. However, extensive statistical analysis of test runs with this sort indicate that the number of comparisons in the worst case is proportional to $n^{1.25}$ or $C = kn^{1.25}$. The constant k is dependent on several factors, including the methods by which d is calculated. There is general agreement that d should be kept odd to avoid possible weakness in the sort since an even value for d can cause comparisons made during the current pass to be repeated on the next pass when exchanges occur. A clever method for insuring that d remain odd with a minimum of additional computation was proposed by T. N. Hibbard (1963). He suggested that the original d be chosen as an integral power of 2 minus 1 (for example, 3, 7, 15, 31, and so on). Thus, each succeeding d can be calculated as before $(\lfloor d/2 \rfloor)$ and will remain odd. This property can be readily seen if we express a d meeting the Hibbard criteria as a binary integer such as $31_{10} = 11111_2$ and, therefore, the calculation of $\lfloor d/2 \rfloor$ amounts to a shift to the right of the binary integer by one bit. Hibbard also suggested that this initial d be chosen such that $d < N < 2d$, where N is the number of records in the list to be sorted. This initial d can be calculated by either of the two methods that follow:

1.
LET X $= \lfloor \log_2 N \rfloor$
THEN d $= 2^x - 1$

2. Use an iterative approach if logarithmic or exponential functions are not available or convenient.

Figure 2-14 illustrates Hibbard's refinement of the Shell sort.

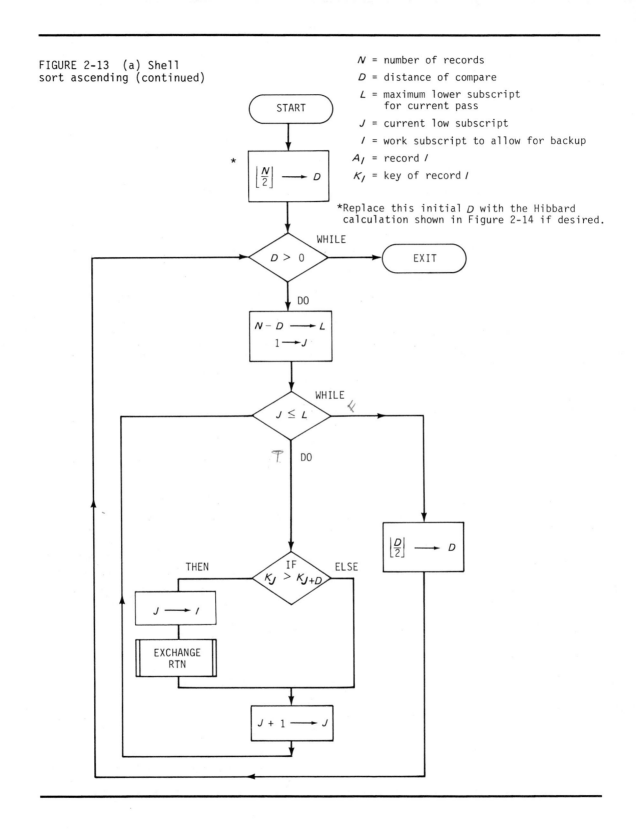

FIGURE 2-13 (a) Shell
sort ascending (continued)

N = number of records

D = distance of compare

L = maximum lower subscript
for current pass

J = current low subscript

I = work subscript to allow for backup

A_I = record I

K_I = key of record I

*Replace this initial D with the Hibbard
calculation shown in Figure 2-14 if desired.

START

* $\left\lfloor \dfrac{N}{2} \right\rfloor \longrightarrow D$

WHILE

D > 0 → EXIT

DO

N − D ⟶ L
1 ⟶ J

WHILE

J ≤ L

DO

$\left\lfloor \dfrac{D}{2} \right\rfloor \longrightarrow D$

THEN   IF   ELSE
$K_J > K_{J+D}$

J ⟶ I

EXCHANGE
RTN

J + 1 ⟶ J

FIGURE 2-13 (b) exchange

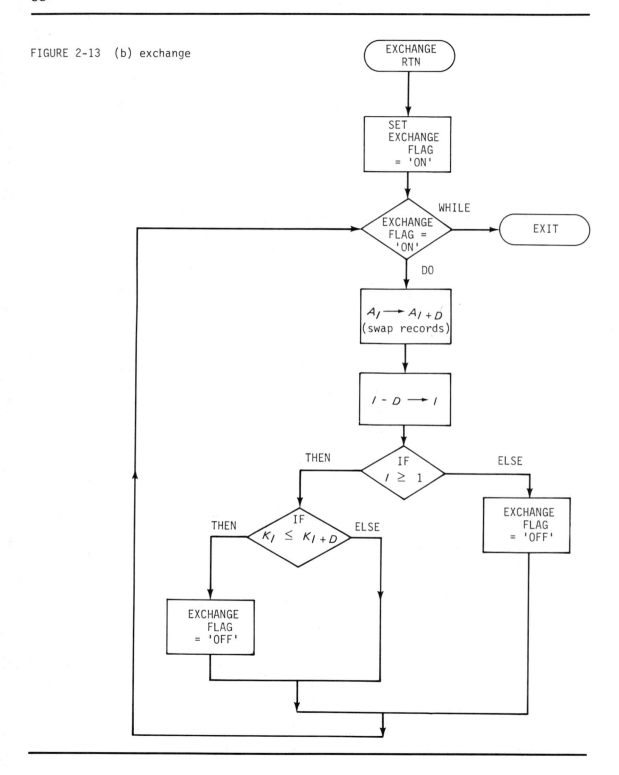

```
SHELL SORT ASCENDING          /*  N = number of records */
                              /*  D = distance of compare (in record positions) */
                              /*  L = limit for current pass */
                              /*  J = current record position */
                              /*  I = work subscript to allow for backup.  Similar to J */
                              /*  A(I) = record at location I */
                              /*  K(I) = key of record at location I */


              PROC    SHELL-SORT
                  BEGIN MAIN
                      D = ⌊N/2⌋
                      WHILE D > 0   DO
                          L = N - D
                          J = 1
                          WHILE J ≤ L   DO
                              IF K(J) > K(J)+D)
                                      THEN⎰I = J
                                           ⎱do EXCHANGE routine
                                          ELSE next statement
                                      ENDIF
                                      J = J + 1
                                  ENDDO
                                  D = ⌊D/2⌋
                          ENDDO
                      END MAIN
                      BEGIN EXCHANGE
              /* EX-FLAG = flag to continue exchange of records */
                          EX-FLAG = 'ON'
                          WHILE EX-FLAG = 'ON'   DO
                              exchange A(I) and A(I+D)
                              I = I - D
                              IF I ≥ 1
                                  THEN IF K(I) ≤ K(I+D)
                                          THEN EX-FLAG = 'OFF'
                                          ELSE next statement
                                      ENDIF
                                  ELSE EX-FLAG = 'OFF'
                              ENDIF
                          ENDDO
                      END EXCHANGE
                  END PROC
```

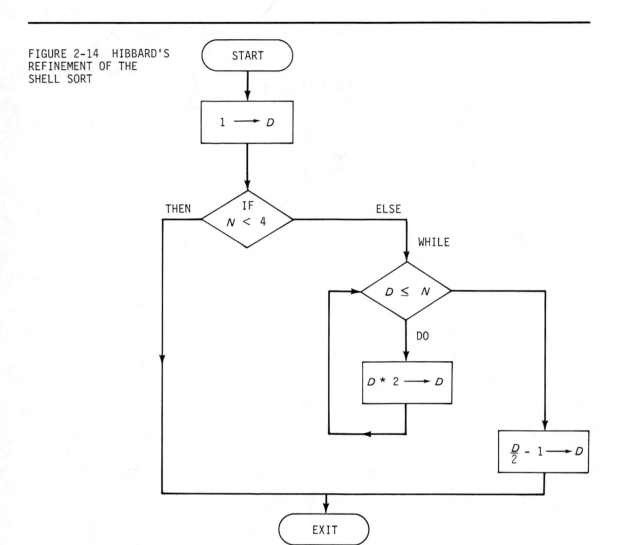

FIGURE 2-14 HIBBARD'S
REFINEMENT OF THE
SHELL SORT

Empirical tests described by such authors as Knuth, Lorin, and Wirth indicate that the Shell sort can be considered a good sort for lists up to a few hundred records and an acceptable sort for lists of up to one or two thousand records.

An example of the performance of a list of 15 records is shown in Figure 2-15. Figure 2-16 on page 72 shows a comparison of the bubble sort on the same list.

END ———————— First Test

The Quick Sort As we have shown, the basic sorts do quite well for short lists, but they become unacceptable as the list length increases. For example, for a list of 10 records, the basic sorts have a worst case for comparisons of $[(10)^2 - 10]/2 = 90/2 = 45$, which is only about twice the theoretical limit of $\lceil \log_2 10! \rceil = 22$, but by the time we have 100 records, the basic sorts have a worst case of $[(100)^2 - 100]/2 = 4950$ while the theoretical limit is only $\lceil \log_2 100! \rceil = 526$.

If we could somehow arrange our list of 100 records so that we had 10 partitions of 10 records each, and if each partition contained records whose keys were all less than the keys of the next partition, then we could simply sort each of our partitions one at a time and the list would be in order.

Using one of the basic sorts then, our worst case for comparisons would be $10[(10^2 - 10)/2] = 10(45) = 450$ comparisons, and this is even better than the theoretical limit for a single list of 100 records. Now we cannot expect

FIGURE 2-15
EXAMPLE OF THE
PERFORMANCE OF
A SHELL SORT ON
A LIST OF 15
RECORDS

	Original List	After Pass I	After Pass II	After Pass III

(table data as shown in figure, with $d = 7$, $d = 3$, $d = 1$ passes)

| | Exchanges | 4 | 11 | 9 | = 24 |
| | Compares | 8 | 21 | 23 | = 52 |

FIGURE 2-16 PERFORMANCE OF A BUBBLE SORT ON THE LIST OF FIGURE 2-15

After Pass	Original List	Pass I	Pass II	Pass III	Pass IV	Pass V	Pass VI	Pass VII	Pass VIII	Pass IX	Pass X	Pass XI
	5	5	5	5 2	2	2	2 1	1	1	1	1	
	11	11 8	8 2	2 5	5 4	4 1	1 2	2	2	2	2	
	15 8	8 11 2	2 8 7	7 4	4 5 1	1 4	4	4	4	4 3	3	
	8 15 2	2 11 7	7 8 4	4 7 1	5	5	5	5	5 3	3 4	4	
	2 15 7	7 11 4	4 8 1	1 7 6	6	6	6	6 3	3 5	5	5	
	7 15 4	4 11 1	1 8 6	6 7	7	7	7 3	3 6	6	6	6	
	4 15 1	1 11 6	6 8	8	8	8 3	3 7	7	7	7	7	
	1 15 6	6 11	11	9	9 3	3 8	8	8	8	8	8	
	6 15 14	14 9	9 11	11 3	3 9	8	9	9	9	9	9	
	14 15 9	9 14 12	12 3	3 11	11 10	10	10	10	10	10	10	
	9 15 12	12 14 3	3 12	12 10	10 11	11	11	11	11	11	11	
	12 15 3	3 14 13	13 10	10 12	12	12	12	12	12	12	12	
	3 15 13	13 14 10	10 13	13	13	13	13	13	13	13	13	
	13 15 10	10 14	14	14	14	14	14	14	14	14	14	
	10 15	15	15	15	15	15	15	15	15	15	15	
Exchanges	12	11	8	6	4	2	2	1	1	1	0	= 48
Compares	14	13	12	11	10	9	8	7	6	5	4	= 99

lists to exist as a series of ordered partitions, but if we can devise an efficient technique that achieves this, then our task of sorting becomes much simpler and quicker. This is exactly what the quick sort does.

The quick sort or one of its variations is the fastest internal sort under general conditions that we will study (see Figure 2-19). It is certainly one of the fastest sorting methods found in the literature, and it approaches the theoretical limit for the speed of any sort under random conditions as n becomes large. The first version of the sort was published by C. A. R. Hoare in 1962, and it has undergone several refinements since then.

The sort works by progressing from both ends of a list and comparing key values to a pivot key that is selected from the list. The values are tested to see if they are greater than or less than the pivot value and then exchanged, if necessary, so that at the end of a pass all records with key values less than the pivot are below it in the list, and all records with key values greater than the pivot are above it in the list. This procedure divides the list into two partitions on either side of the pivot and moves the pivot record into its true position for the final ordered list.

The longer partition is stored in a stack (to be explained in detail later). Then a new pivot is picked from the shorter partition, and the process continues until the smaller sublist reaches a length of 1 or until it reaches a size by which it can be sorted efficiently by a simple method such as the selection with exchange sort or the bubble sort.

The best selection for a pivot is the true median of the list; however, the true median cannot be known immediately, and so an assumed median is chosen. The simplest choice, though not the optimum choice, is the first record in the list. Most variations of this sort vary primarily in the way the pivot is chosen. The example we study here uses the method of selecting the first element as the pivot, which was the original approach. Elements are compared by progressing from one end of the list, element by element, until the pivot is exchanged, and then the progression resumes from the other end of the list (see Figure 2-17).

At this point, record 25 is in its true position. Sublist (12, 17, 06, 08, 22), which is contained in cells 1–5, is stored in the stack, and the process is continued on the sublist in cells 7–10. The stack is implemented simply by storing the beginning and ending cell addresses (see Figure 2-18).

Using the technique for choosing the pivot shown in Figure 2-17, the worst case arises when the pivot turns out to belong in the first position of the list being partitioned. An occasional occurrence of the worst case during a sort will not greatly affect performance, but if a list tends to be nearly in order, then it occurs frequently. Such a frequent occurrence results in many partitionings which only reduce the length of the remaining list by one.

To greatly reduce the likelihood of the preceding worst-case situation, R. C. Singleton proposed selecting the pivot as the median of the first, middle, and last records from the list to be partitioned. This selection immediately eliminates the possibility of choosing a true end point as a pivot, and it allows

FIGURE 2-17

Original List	(25)	17	06	55	22	78	08	45	12	28
Compare										
1	25									28
2	25								12	
X	12								25	
3		17							25	
4			06						25	
5				55					25	
X				25					55	
6				25				45		
7				25			08			
X				08			25			
8					22		25			
9						78	25			
X						25	78			*I = J*
New Order	12	17	06	08	22	(25)	78	45	55	28

I ⟶ Pivot   ⟵ *J*

FIGURE 2-18

Stack

Left	Right
1	5

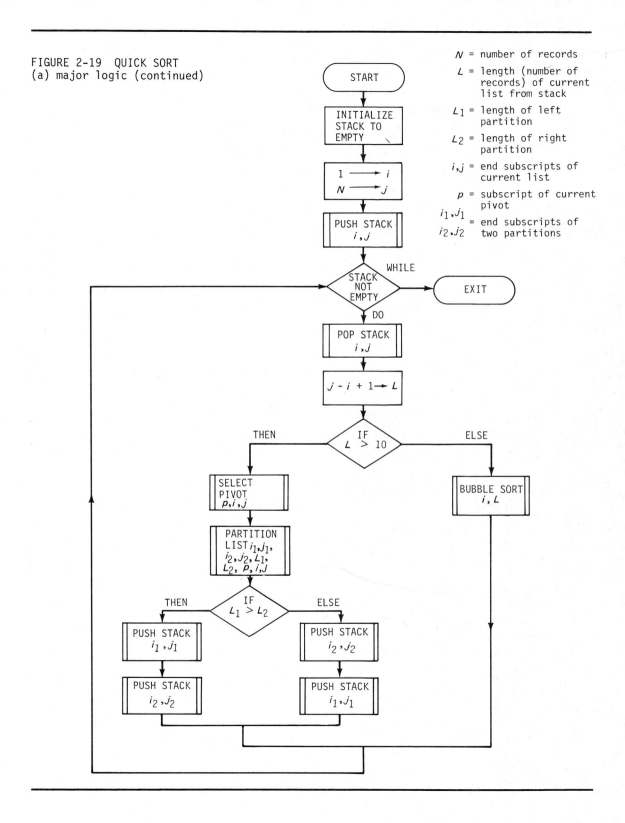

FIGURE 2-19 QUICK SORT
(a) major logic (continued)

N = number of records
L = length (number of records) of current list from stack
L_1 = length of left partition
L_2 = length of right partition
i,j = end subscripts of current list
p = subscript of current pivot
i_1,j_1 = end subscripts of two partitions
i_2,j_2

START

INITIALIZE STACK TO EMPTY

$1 \longrightarrow i$
$N \longrightarrow j$

PUSH STACK
i,j

STACK NOT EMPTY

WHILE

EXIT

DO

POP STACK
i,j

$j - i + 1 \longrightarrow L$

IF $L > 10$

THEN

ELSE

SELECT PIVOT
p,i,j

BUBBLE SORT
i, L

PARTITION LIST $i_1,j_1,$
$i_2,j_2,L_1,$
L_2, p, i, j

IF $L_1 > L_2$

THEN

ELSE

PUSH STACK
i_1,j_1

PUSH STACK
i_2,j_2

PUSH STACK
i_2,j_2

PUSH STACK
i_1,j_1

76

FIGURE 2-19 QUICK SORT
(b) partition list ascending

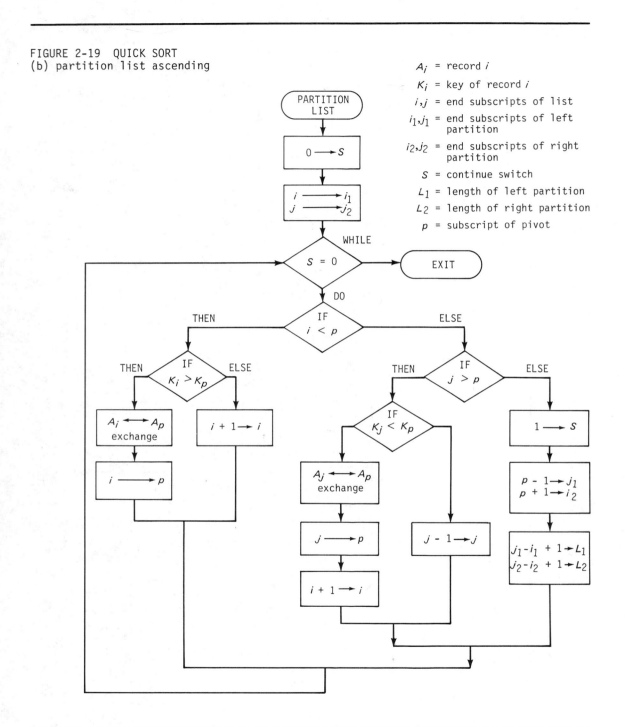

the pivot to be, at worst, a second record from either end, which can occur only if both records from either end of the list are chosen in the sample of three. This worst case cannot occur with any frequency if the list is nearly in order, and it is highly unlikely to occur with any frequency under other conditions. However, readers should remember that highly unlikely does not mean impossible!

The Singleton method of choosing the pivot is used in the quick-sort algorithm shown in Figure 2-20.

In studying the algorithm, readers may find the following notes helpful:

1. The pivot will always be in its true position after a partitioning and is therefore excluded from the two resulting partitions.

2. The pivot will never be a true end point of the list being partitioned, even if duplicate records exist.

3. Should a partitioning yield a partition with a length of 1, its end points i and j will be equal.

4. A call to one of the basic sort routines to sort a list of length 1 will result in an immediate return since the list is already sorted.

5. Both partitions are stacked after each partitioning, with the longer preceding the shorter.

We now reach the point of deciding when to use the quick sort and how to estimate its performance against other sorts. Lorin compared a Singleton version of the quick sort with several other sorts on identical lists of 100, 1000, and 5000 records. The lists were sorted under three initial conditions; ordered, reverse ordered, and random. In his tests, he found that the quick sort used between 1.1 and 1.4 times the theoretical limit approximation of $n \log_2 n$ for comparisons. No other sort did as well on the combination of conditions on any of the list sizes.

When comparing the quick sort to the Shell sort, Lorin's tests showed the quick sort to be two to three times faster than the Shell sort for lists of 5000. Wirth's test showed the quick sort to be two times faster at 256 records and approximately three times faster at 512 records. In the author's own classes, using the algorithms in this book on purely random lists, we found the quick sort to show no advantage at 50 records, a slight advantage at 100 records, and to be approximately two times faster at 400 records. The number of comparisons for the quick sort stayed under $1.5\, n \log_2 n$ for up to 1000 records, which was the longest list tested.

In summary, the quick sort is definitely more complex to implement than the Shell sort, but it requires no additional storage except for the minor amount needed for the stack and the additional code of the algorithm. It is a good sort for any n expected, and it offers a clear performance advantage over

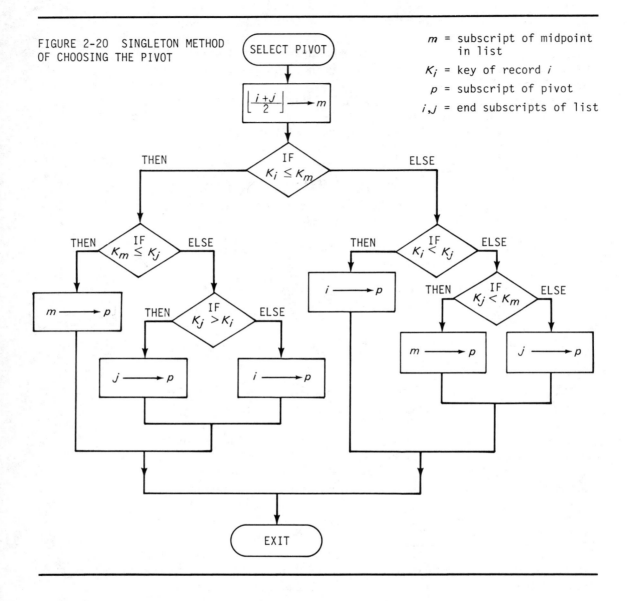

FIGURE 2-20 SINGLETON METHOD OF CHOOSING THE PIVOT

m = subscript of midpoint in list

K_i = key of record i

p = subscript of pivot

i,j = end subscripts of list

QUICK SORT—
MAJOR LOGIC

```
/* N = number of records */
/* L = length (in records) of current list from stack */
/* L₁ = length (in records) of left partition */
/* L₂ = length (in records) of right partition */
/* I,J = left and right end positions of current list */
/* P = location of current pivot */
/* I₁, J₁ and I₂, J₂ = end positions of current two partitions */
/* STACK = stack; each element contain end points for a partition */


PROC  QUICK-SORT
    BEGIN MAIN
        initialize STACK to empty
        I = 1
        J = N
        push I and J into STACK /* First Partition is whole list */
        WHILE STACK NOT empty DO
            pop I and J from STACK
            L = J - I + 1
            IF  L > 10
                THEN do SELECT-PIVOT routine
                    do PARTITION-LIST routine
                    IF L₁ > L₂
                        THEN push I₁,J₁ into STACK
                            push I₂,J₂ into STACK
                        ELSE push I₂,J₂ into STACK
                            push I₁,J₁ into STACK
                    ENDIF
                ELSE  do (basic sort) on list I,J
            ENDIF
        ENDDO
    END MAIN
```

PARTITION LIST
ASCENDING

```
/*  A(I) = record at location I */
/*  K(I) = key of record at location I */
/*  S = continue switch */
/*  other variables same as above */


BEGIN PARTITION-LIST
    S = 0
    I₁ = I    /* left end of left partition = I */
    J₂ = J    /* right end of right partition = J */
    WHILE S=0  DO
        IF I < P
            THEN IF K(I) > K(P)
                    THEN exchange A(I) and A(P)
                        P = I
                    ELSE I = I + 1
                ENDIF
            ELSE IF J > P
                    THEN IF K(J) < K(P)
                            THEN exchange A(J) and A(P)
                                P = J
                                I = I + 1
                            ELSE J = J - 1
                        ENDIF
                    ELSE S = 1
                        J₁ = P - 1
                        I₂ = P + 1
                        L₁ = J₁ - I₁ + 1
                        L₂ = J₂ - I₂ + 1
                    ENDIF
                ENDIF
        ENDDO
    END PARTITION-LIST
```

SINGLETON METHOD
OF CHOOSING
THE PIVOT

```
/*  M = location of median of list to be partitioned */
/*  other variables same as above */


BEGIN SELECT-PIVOT
    M = ⌊(I+J)/2⌋
    IF K(I) ≤ K(M)
        THEN IF K(M) ≤ K(J)
                THEN P = M
                ELSE IF K(J) > K(I)
                        THEN P = J
                        ELSE P = I
                    ENDIF
            ENDIF
        ELSE IF K(I) < K(J)
                THEN P = I
                ELSE IF K(J) < K(M)
                        THEN P = M
                        ELSE P = J
                    ENDIF
            ENDIF
    ENDIF
END SELECT-PIVOT
END PROC
```

the Shell sort, in general, whenever there are more than a few hundred records. However, the Shell sort should still give acceptable performance up to a few thousand records.

A comparison of five of the sorting algorithms presented in this book is shown in Figure 2-21 for lists of 100 records. The same set of 100 records was tested in four arrangements (in order, near ordered, badly ordered, and reverse ordered) for each of the sorts. The in-order arrangement and the reverse-ordered arrangement need no explanation, but the other two terms need clarification. *Nearly ordered* refers to an initial arrangement in which no record is more than 10 positions from its final position. *Badly ordered* refers to an initial arrangement in which the entire list has been scrambled such that many of the records are 50 positions or more out of order, with a worst case of a record 82 positions out of order. These two orderings are shown on page 83.

Other Internal Sorts A number of other good sorts are found in the literature, but they are not covered in this book for several reasons. First, it is not the intent of this book to present sorts in an exhaustive manner, but rather to present the reader with a set of sorts, at least one of which would give

FIGURE 2-21 COMPARATIVE PERFORMANCE OF SORTS ON A LIST OF 100 RECORDS

Sort / Key Arrangement	Bubble		Selection with Exchange		Insertion		Shell		Quick	
	Compares	Moves	Compares	Moves	Compares	Moves	Compares	Moves	Compares	Moves
In order	99	0	4950	0	4950	0	503	0	473	0
Near order (no record more than 10 positions out of place)	945	537	4950	171	4840	317	612	339	610	339
Badly ordered (some records greatly out of position)	4797	7728	4950	297	2465	2758	*939	1488	800	891
Reverse Ordered	4950	14,850	4950	150	99	5148	668	780	1015	444

*Using the Hibbard refinement, this case was reduced to 816 compares with 1203 moves.

FIGURE 2-22
DIAGRAM FOR
ADDRESS
CALCULATION
SORT

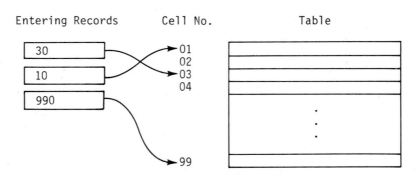

Entering Records   Cell No.   Table

	NEARLY ORDERED		BADLY ORDERED
0800	5600	7100	0300
0600	5300	7200	0400
0100	5900	1900	9800
0200	5700	2000	4500
0500	5800	7400	0500
0400	5950	7500	4600
0060	6300	7600	4700
0700	6000	7700	4800
0050	6100	2100	4900
0300	6200	2200	0050
1800	6800	2300	5100
1000	6400	9400	5200
1100	6500	7800	5300
1200	6600	2400	5400
1300	6700	2500	5500
1400	7400	7900	5600
1500	7500	2600	0000
1600	7650	8000	5700
1700	7700	2700	5800
0900	7800	2900	5900
2300	6900	8100	0600
2000	7000	3000	6000
2100	7100	9600	0700
2200	7200	3100	0800
2400	7300	3200	0900
2500	8000	8200	6300
2600	8800	8300	6100
2700	8100	3300	6200
2800	8200	3400	0100
1900	8300	8400	6400
3600	8700	8500	6500
3200	7950	3500	6600
3300	8600	3600	1000
3400	8400	3700	6700
3500	8500	3800	6800
3700	9300	3900	1100
3800	9900	4000	1200
2900	9100	4200	6900
3000	9800	9900	7000
3100	9200	8600	1300
4400	9400	2800	1400
4800	9500	8700	1500
4100	9700	8800	1600
4000	9000	5900	1700
3900	9600	9000	1800
4200		9100	
4300		9200	
4500		9300	
4600		7300	
4700		9500	
5100		9700	
4900		4100	
5200		4300	
5400		0200	
5500		4400	

FIGURE 2-23   OPERATION OF A RADIX SORT

Original List	Pass I Bin	Content	Collect	Pass II Bin	Content	Collect	Pass III Bin	Content	Collect Final
426	0	empty	951	0	empty	621	0	empty	188
951	1	951,621,391	621	1	empty	426	1	188	342
342	2	342	391	2	621,426	342	2	empty	391
621	3	643	342	3	empty	643	3	342,391	426
577	4	empty	643	4	342,643,649	649	4	426	557
188	5	empty	426	5	951,557	951	5	557,577	577
391	6	426	577	6	empty	557	6	621,643,649	621
643	7	577,557	557	7	577	577	7	empty	643
557	8	188	188	8	188	188	8	empty	649
649	9	649	649	9	391	391	9	951	951

Original List	Pass I	Pass II	Pass III
426	951	621	188
951	621	426	342
342	391	342	391
621	342	643	426
577	643	649	557
188	426	951	577
391	577	557	621
643	557	577	643
557	188	188	649
649	649	391	951

good or acceptable performance under any conditions. Second, some of these sorts require the concepts of logical order, which are not covered until later in the book. Two additional sorts are mentioned briefly.

Address Calculation Sort: This sort calculates the exact location of a given record from its key value and moves it directly into position. This sort is the fastest of all, but it is rarely used because, to be reasonably efficient with respect to storage requirements, the calculation algorithm must provide a 1 to 1 mapping onto a set of consecutive or nearly consecutive integers which preserves the original order. Under all but very special conditions, it is very difficult to find an algorithm that can meet this requirement.

Example: A company with 90 employees has assigned a unique employee number to each employee. The numbers are multiples of 10 between 10 and 990. Employee records are to be read into memory and stored into a table sorted by employee number.

By dividing each key by 10, we obtain a set of values between 1 and 99; this set preserves the order and yields only 9 missing integers within the range (see Figure 2-22). In case of empty cells, we could use a single pass through the table to move records up to leave all empty cells at the bottom. Otherwise, a routine accessing the sorted table would have to check for vacant cells.

Radix Sort: This sort is used by mechanical card-sorting machines. It works on the key field one digit at a time from right to left, least significant to most significant, and it groups the records into sublists that are ordered on the last digit. This sort creates sets of records with a common value in the digit position being compared. There will be a pass for each digit in the key and a sublist for each possible value of a digit in the key. However, some sublists may be empty. That is, if the key consists of decimal digits, there will be 10 sublists—called *bins*—for each pass. As the passes proceed from right to left, a record is not moved unless it is out of position on a digit of higher significance (see Figure 2-23).

EXTERNAL SORTS

As we stated previously, external sorts make use of external work areas on some medium such as tape or disk, and they are needed whenever a list is too long to fit in available main memory. These sorts work by creating ordered sublists from the original list and then merging these sublists to form one ordered list. As one might expect, the sorts differ in the way in which the ordered sublists are created and/or in the way the merge is accomplished. The creation of the ordered sublists usually involves internal sorting, which we have already studied, and so we now examine merging.

Merging   The process of merging combines two or more ordered lists into one similarly ordered list. A merge process will progress down a set of ordered sublists concurrently while keeping a current pointer to each. A

FIGURE 2-24   MERGE OF TWO LISTS, A AND B, CONTAINING FIVE AND SEVEN ELEMENTS, RESPECTIVELY, WITH i = A's POINTER, j = B's POINTER, AND k = L's POINTER

Step	List A	List B	List L	Pointers after Move
				(start)$i = 1$, $j = 1$, $k = 1$
1	2	3	2	$i = 2$, $j = 1$, $k = 2$
2	5	4	3	$i = 2$, $j = 2$, $k = 3$
3	9	8	4	$i = 2$, $j = 3$, $k = 4$
4	12	10	5	$i = 3$, $j = 3$, $k = 5$
5	15	16	8	$i = 3$, $j = 4$, $k = 6$
6		17	9	$i = 4$, $j = 4$, $k = 7$
7		20	10	$i = 4$, $j = 5$, $k = 8$
8			12	$i = 5$, $j = 5$, $k = 9$
9			15	i = end, $j = 5$, $k = 10$
10			16	$j = 6$, $k = 11$
11			17	$j = 7$, $k = 12$
12			20	j = end, k = end

MERGING TWO LISTS
ASCENDING

```
/*  A and B = the two nonempty lists to be merged */
/*  L = the resulting list from A and B */
/*  I and J = the current locations in A and B, respectively */
/*  K(I) = key of record at location I */
/*  S = switch to end merge */
/*  C = current location in L */


PROC    MERGE-TWO
    I = 1
    J = 1
    C = 1
    S = 0
    WHILE  S = 0   DO
        IF  K(I) ≤ K(J)
            THEN   do COPYL to copy record from list A to L
            ELSE   do COPYL to copy record from list B to L
        ENDIF
    ENDDO
END PROC
```

pointer is simply a field or variable that contains the location of a record. In the example shown in Figure 2-24 the pointers are i and j, with i always containing the location of the record in list A, which will be compared to the record in list B that is pointed to by j. After the comparison, the appropriate element is copied from its corresponding sublist to the new list; the current pointer for this sublist is advanced to the next element, and then the current elements are compared again and the process continues until all of the elements from the sublists have been copied to the new list. Figure 2-25 illustrates merging two lists in ascending order.

Natural-Order Sort The *Natural-order sort* uses the natural-ordered sublists or *strings* that occur within any given list, then merges these sublists to form longer ordered sublists until one ordered list is obtained. These naturally ordered sublists are found by progressing down the original list

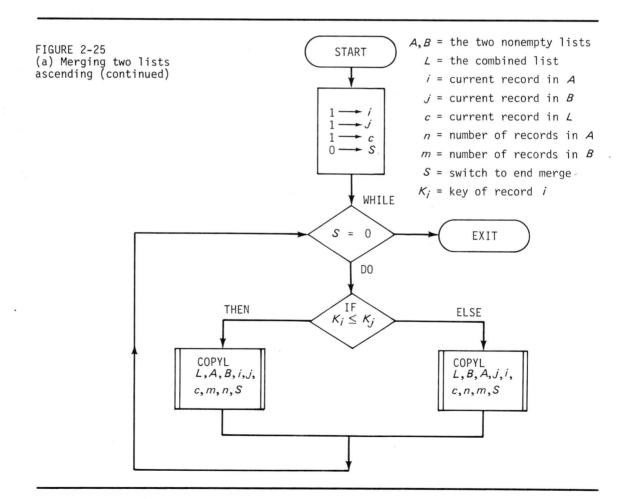

FIGURE 2-25
(a) Merging two lists
ascending (continued)

A, B = the two nonempty lists
L = the combined list
i = current record in A
j = current record in B
c = current record in L
n = number of records in A
m = number of records in B
S = switch to end merge
K_i = key of record i

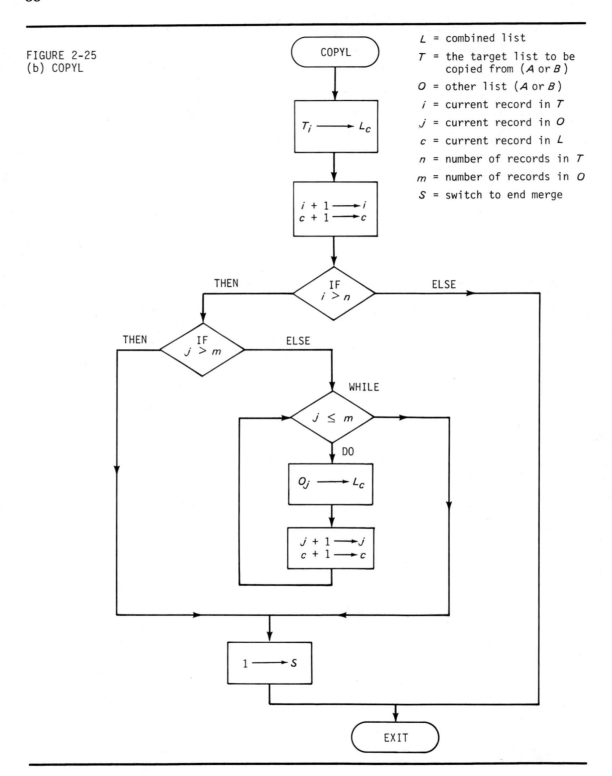

FIGURE 2-25
(b) COPYL

```
                COPYL


        /*  L, C, and S = as before in main merge routine */
        /*  T = the target list from which to copy (either A or B) */
        /*  O = the other list (A or B) to complement T */
        /*  I and J = current records in T and O, respectively */
        /*  N and M = number of records in T and O, respectively */


        PROC    COPYL
            L(C) = T(I)
            I = I+1
            C = C+1
            IF I > N
                THEN IF  J > M
                            THEN    continue
                            ELSE   WHILE J ≤ M  DO
                                        L(C) = O(J)
                                        J = J+1
                                        C = C+1
                                    ENDO
                        ENDIF
                        S = 1
                ELSE   continue
            ENDIF
        END PROC
```

comparing successive keys. As soon as a key is found to be out of order with respect to the one that immediately precedes it, the corresponding record will form the first element in the next sublist.

A minimum of three work areas is needed for this method, although it is more efficient with four or more. The ordered sublists are copied to alternating work areas. New and longer ordered sublists are formed by merging the ordered sublists from the previous work areas to the other work areas not used in the first step, so that we are working with two sets of work areas whose roles exchange for each pass.

Figure 2-26 shows four work areas in addition to the original list. A pass down the original list is made in which strings are written alternately between $W1$ and $W2$. For ascending order, a new string begins when $K_n > K_{n+1}$ where K_n indicates the key of record n. On the second pass, the first string from each of $W1$ and $W2$ is merged onto $W3$, and then the second strings from $W1$ and $W2$ are merged onto $W4$. The process of merging two strings from $W1$

FIGURE 2-26 SORT ASCENDING USING WORK AREAS $W1, W2, W3$, AND $W4$: (a) original list; (b) pass I (distribute sublists); (c) pass II (merge) (continued)

Sublist	Original List
1	14
	25
2	08
	12
	13
3	09
4	05
	11
	18
5	10
	17
	20
	21
6	07
	16

(a)

Pass I (Distribute Sublists)			
$W1$	$W2$	$W3$	$W4$
14	08	not used	
25	12		
09	13		
10	05		
17	11		
20	18		
21	07		
	16		

(b)

Pass II (Merge)			
$W1$	$W2$	$W3$	$W4$
		08	05
Same as		12	09
Pass I, but		13	10
will be		14	11
released for		25	17
work in next		07	18
pass		16	20
			21

(c)

FIGURE 2-26 (d) pass III (merge); (e) pass IV (final merge).

Pass III (Merge)			
W1	W2	W3	W4
05	07		
08	16	Same as	
09		before	
10			
11			
12			
13			
14			
17			
18			
20			
21			
25			

(d)

Pass IV (Final Merge)
Original List or W3
05
07
08
09
10
11
12
13
14
16
17
18
20
21
25

(e)

and W2 alternately to W3 and W4 continues until all of the records reside on W3 or W4. Now we have created longer strings on the second pair of work areas than we had on our first pair, and there are roughly half as many strings as there were before. We continue alternating the roles of the pairs of work areas until one area contains a single string consisting of the entire list.

The advantage of this method is its simplicity, but its weakness is in its unpredictable string lengths. The shorter the strings in the beginning, the more strings produced and, thus, more passes are required to complete the sort since the worst case for passes is $\log_2 n$ where n is the number of strings. It is important to realize that, contrary to internal sorts, external sorts move every record examined on every pass during the merge phase.

If a counter is kept for the number of merges written to each receiving work area for a pass, the final merge will occur after the pass in which no counter exceeds 1.

Balanced Sort   A refinement to the natural-order sort, and one that can assure a desired string length in the beginning, is called a *balanced sort*. A balanced sort is one that uses the same number of input and output work areas during all but the final merge pass and the initial step of creating strings. (This condition is also desirable for the natural-order sort, but it is not a requirement.) In addition, the strings produced are all the same size, which is accomplished by taking n records at a time and using an internal sort on these. This procedure has the effect of multiplying the string length by the number of inputs for each pass, with the possible exception of one string always being shorter than the others due to an initial short string caused because the original list did not contain a multiple of n records.

Basically, after the initial strings are produced, this sort works in the same manner as the natural-order sort. Figure 2-27 shows an example of a balanced sort with four work areas. The balanced sort gains power as the number of work areas (N) increases such that if a file contains S ordered strings the number of passes required to merge the strings is $P = \lceil \log_{N/2} S \rceil$. For example: when there are 6 work areas and 100 strings it will take $P = \lceil \log_3 100 \rceil = 5$ passes to complete the merge.

Polyphase Sort   A disadvantage of the balanced sort is that only half of the work areas can be used for input to the merge on each pass. A sort that improves on this situation is called the polyphase sort. The *polyphase sort* produces fixed-length strings similar to those in the balanced sort, but the strings are distributed very differently. For any given application of this sort, if there are N available work areas, there will be $N - 1$ input areas and 1 output area. The strings are distributed initially across $N - 1$ of the work areas according to a generalized Fibonacci sequence in which each number in the sequence is the sum of the previous $N - 1$ terms. More specifically, the Fibonacci sequence is based on Fibonacci numbers defined as follows:

$$p = \text{the order, or the number of consecutive integers that are added to produce the next integer.}$$

$$F_i^{(p)} = \text{the } i\text{th integer in the sequence of order } p \text{ (for example, } F_0^{(2)} = 0, F_1^{(2)} = 1\text{).}$$

Then
$$F_i^{(p)} = 0 \qquad \text{when } 0 \le i < p - 1$$

$$F_i^{(p)} = 1 \qquad \text{when } i = p - 1$$

$$F_i^{(p)} = F_{i-1}^{(p)} + F_{i-2}^{(p)} + \cdots + F_{i-p}^{(p)} \qquad \text{when } i > p - 1$$

FIGURE 2-27 BALANCED SORT

Original List	After Pass I (includes internal sort)				After Pass II			
$n = 5$	(output)				(input)		(output)	
7	$W1$	$W2$	$W3$	$W4$	$W1$	$W2$	$W3$	$W4$
3	3	1	(not used)		Same as		1	4
15	7	2			Pass I		2	5
8	8	9					3	6
14	14	10					7	11
2	15	16					8	12
1	4	5					9	13
16	6	11					10	17
9	13	12					14	18
10	18	17					15	19
20	20	19					16	20
18								
4					Pass III will merge $W3$ and $W4$ to			
6					the final output area.			
13								
17								
19								
5								
11								
12								

Examples:

For $p = 2$, $F_0^{(2)} = 0$

$F_1^{(2)} = 1$

$F_2^{(2)} = 1 + 0 = 1$

$F_3^{(2)} = 1 + 1 = 2$

$F_4^{(2)} = 2 + 1 = 3$

$F_5^{(2)} = 3 + 2 = 5$

$F_6^{(2)} = 5 + 3 = 8$

For $p = 3$, $F_0^{(3)} = 0$

$F_1^{(3)} = 0$

$F_2^{(3)} = 1$

$F_3^{(3)} = 1 + 0 + 0 = 1$

$F_4^{(3)} = 1 + 1 + 0 = 2$

$F_5^{(3)} = 2 + 1 + 1 = 4$

$F_6^{(3)} = 4 + 2 + 1 = 7$

$F_7^{(3)} = 7 + 4 + 2 = 13$

The distribution of the strings is such that when there are N work areas, we try to achieve a distribution that will behave according to the Fibonacci numbers generated for order $p = N - 1$. There are several variations on the way the Fibonacci sequence is used in distributing the strings to the $N - 1$ work areas. One such technique, called *augmentation*, works as follows.

Given N work areas, with one containing all of the initial input, we distribute strings to the first $N - 1$ work areas according to the first $N - 1$ Fibonacci numbers of order $N - 1$. We choose the maximum number from this group of $N - 1$ numbers and add this number of strings to each of the other work areas, except for the area that contained this maximum. We then choose a new maximum from the next set of $N - 1$ numbers and repeat the process until all strings have been distributed. Thus for each distribution pass we augment each output area by a number of strings that is equivalent to the next term in the appropriate Fibonacci sequence.

Example: We are given four areas—W0, W1, W2, and W3—with W0 being empty or containing the initial 105 strings. The *total* number of strings on each work area after each distribution pass is shown in Figure 2-28.

The merge or collection phase merges each of the $N - 1$ work areas onto the initial empty work area until the work area containing the smallest number of strings is emptied. At this point, the new empty area becomes the new output area, and the process continues until all of the areas have been merged onto one area.

Example: We use the distribution of 105 strings shown in Figure 2-29, each with a length of n records. Figure 2-29 shows the number of strings and their lengths.

FIGURE 2-28
DISTRIBUTION
PHASE OF
POLYPHASE
SORT

Distribution Pass Number	W0	W1	W2	W3	Total Strings Distributed at This Point
1	empty	0	0	1	1
2		1	1	1	3
3		2	1	2	5
4		2	3	4	9
5		6	7	4	17
6		13	7	11	31
7		13	20	24	57
8		37	44	24	105

FIGURE 2-29
COLLECTION PHASE OF
POLYPHASE SORT

After Merge Phase	W0	W1	W2	W3
start	0	$37n$	$44n$	$24n$
1	$24(3n)$	$13n$	$20n$	0
2	$11(3n)$	0	$7n$	$13(5n)$
3	$4(3n)$	$7(9n)$	0	$6(5n)$
4	0	$3(9n)$	$4(17n)$	$2(5n)$
5	$2(31n)$	$1(9n)$	$2(17n)$	0
6	$1(31n)$	0	$1(17n)$	$1(57n)$
7	0	$1(105n)$	0	0

Using the balanced sort with 4 work areas, there are also $\lceil \log_2 105 \rceil = 7$ merge passes, but in the case of the balanced sort, each pass of the merge would copy every record. However, in the polyphase sort, all but the last pass requires less movement than this.

As we mentioned earlier, most major computer vendors supply good external sort-merge packages; so the need to write an external sort is fairly rare among programmers, unless the programmer happens to write software for a vendor or software house. In this case, readers are advised to go beyond this brief presentation before attempting such a task.

Vendor sort-merge packages tend to be quite comprehensive and generate different sorts according to input parameters about the number, size, and physical location (for example, disk or tape) of the records. For instance, the IBM OS sort-merge package will generate one of five different sorts, including the balanced and polyphase sorts, depending on the situation. The Univac OS 1100 provides a similar choice of sorts. Consequently, readers should consider these products very carefully before rejecting them.

SEARCHING

We stated earlier that all file processing involves searching. Indeed, we must search to retrieve a record; we must search to add or delete a record; and we must search to determine whether a record is present or absent from a given file. Given the importance of the process of searching, we now turn to several basic techniques for searching a physically ordered file.

As we study these techniques, we are interested in comparing the relative efficiency of one technique to another. Therefore, for a given file, we consider efficiency to be proportional to the number of record compares (looks) required by one method divided by the number of looks required by the other; that is, efficiency $= C(L_1/L_2)$, where C is a constant based on the ratio of the execution times for a single look in each method. ($E < 1$ means search 1 is faster.)

SEQUENTIAL SEARCH OF AN UNORDERED LIST

The sequential search of an unordered list begins with the first (or last) record in the list and progresses through the list in one direction by moving to the next record in the list until a target record is found or until the end of the list is reached. This technique will take, on the average, $(N + 1)/2$ looks to locate a record within the list. However, it will require N looks to determine that a particular record is absent from the list.

Figure 2-30 gives the algorithm for a sequential search of an unordered list in flowchart form; the equivalent pseudocode accompanies it. The algorithm is simple and straightforward. Since insertions can be made at the end of the list and missing records are not expected at any specific location, the algorithm will suffice for general processing of an unordered list of length

N. The algorithm starts by comparing the key value of the first physical record in the list to an argument. If no match is found, the search progresses down the list in physical sequence, one record at a time, until a match is found or until the end of the list is reached. If a match is found, the termination of the compare loop is forced by setting the loop counter to an appropriate value. If the list is of undetermined length, the search must be modified to check for a special end-of-list record instead of checking for a maximum record.

An interesting alternate algorithm for processing an unordered list of length *N* was proposed by E. Horowitz and S. Sahni. As part of the search initialization, they suggested adding an extra dummy record at the end of the list with a key value equal to the search argument. In this way, the check for the end of the list is eliminated since a key match will always result. However, a missing target record will be recognized by an invalid search index. To find a record within the list, this technique requires the same number of looks as the previous algorithm, plus one additional look to determine a missing record, but the savings in time per look should result in better efficiency in all but very short lists, such as a list where $N = 1$ if key and list index are the same data type and length. The comment about list index being of the same type and length may need clarification. An index is usually (and should be) maintained as a binary integer, which can be compared very quickly by a binary computer. A key, on the other hand, can be any one of a variety of data types and lengths, such as a 20-character name field. Thus, a key compare may require several times the execution time of an index compare, which will affect the exact list size (n) at which a single key compare requires less execution time than repeated index compares. Figure 2-31 shows the alternate algorithm for a sequential search of an unordered list in flowchart form; the equivalent pseudocode accompanies it.

SEQUENTIAL SEARCH OF AN ORDERED LIST

A sequential search of an ordered list is similar to that for an unordered list with one exception. The search of an ordered list will terminate if a key that changes the order relationship to the search argument is found. That is, $K_i > X$ in an ascending-order search.

The average number of looks to find a record in the list is $(N + 1)/2$, as before, but an ordered list also gives us an average of $(N + 1)/2$ looks to determine whether a record is missing—an improvement over the search of an unordered list.

The algorithm for the search appears in Figure 2-32, and the equivalent pseudocode accompanies it. When a no-find condition occurs, the algorithm will return the location of the first record with a key value that exceeds the search argument. If no such key value exists, the location will be equal to the last position in the list. An alternate method using an extra dummy record (similar to the previously cited algorithm of Horowitz and Sahni) is shown in Figure 2-33; the equivalent pseudocode accompanies it.

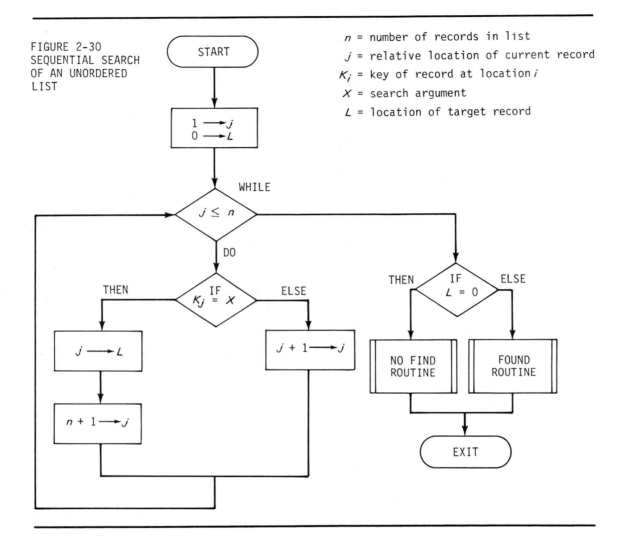

FIGURE 2-30
SEQUENTIAL SEARCH
OF AN UNORDERED
LIST

n = number of records in list
j = relative location of current record
K_i = key of record at location i
X = search argument
L = location of target record

SEQUENTIAL SEARCH
OF AN UNORDERED LIST

```
/*  N = number of records in the list */
/*  J = relative location of current record */
/*  K(I) = key of record at location I */
/*  X = search argument */
/*  L = location of target record */


PROC    SEARCH-LIST-UNORDERED
    J = 1
    L = 0
    WHILE  J ≤ N  DO
        IF  K(J) = X
            THEN  L = J
                  J = N + 1    /* force termination of loop */
            ELSE  J = J + 1
        ENDIF
    ENDDO
    IF  L = 0
        THEN  do no find routine
        ELSE  do found routine
    ENDIF
END PROC
```

100

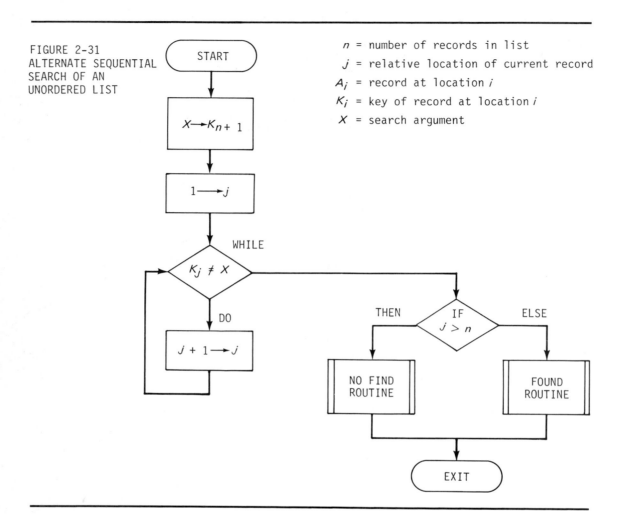

FIGURE 2-31
ALTERNATE SEQUENTIAL
SEARCH OF AN
UNORDERED LIST

n = number of records in list
j = relative location of current record
A_i = record at location i
K_i = key of record at location i
X = search argument

START

$X \longrightarrow K_{n+1}$

$1 \longrightarrow j$

WHILE

$K_j \neq X$

DO

$j + 1 \longrightarrow j$

THEN   IF   ELSE
           $j > n$

NO FIND
ROUTINE

FOUND
ROUTINE

EXIT

ALTERNATE SEQUENTIAL
SEARCH OF AN
UNORDERED LIST

```
/*  N = number of records in list */
/*  J = relative location of current record */
/*  A(I) = record at location I */
/*  K(I) = key of record at location I */

PROC     H-S-SEARCH
    K(N+1) = X
    J = 1
    WHILE  K(J) ≠ X  DO
        J = J + 1
    ENDDO
    IF  J > N
        THEN  do no find routine
        ELSE  do found routine
    ENDIF
END PROC
```

FIGURE 2-32
SEQUENTIAL SEARCH
OF AN ORDERED LIST
ASCENDING

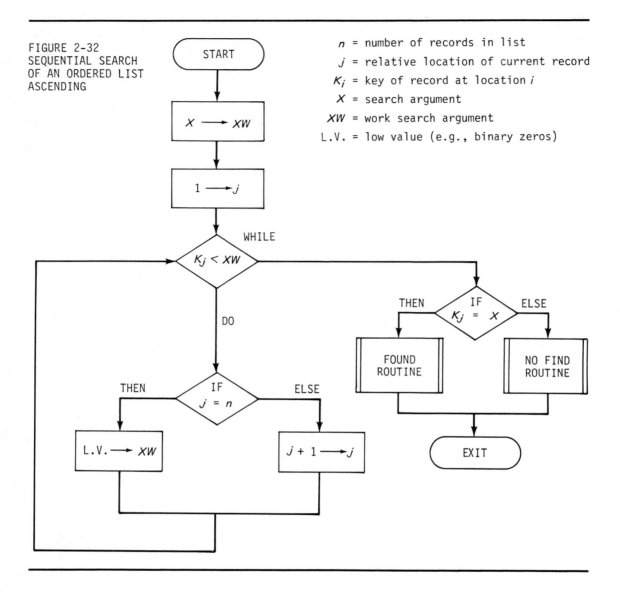

n = number of records in list
j = relative location of current record
K_i = key of record at location i
X = search argument
XW = work search argument
L.V. = low value (e.g., binary zeros)

SEQUENTIAL SEARCH OF
AN ORDERED LIST
ASCENDING

```
/*  N = number of records in list */
/*  J = relative location of current record */
/*  K(I) = key of record at location I */
/*  X = search argument */
/*  XW = temporary work area for copy of search argument */
/*  LV = low value (e.g. binary zeros) */


PROC    SEARCH-LIST-ORDERED
    XW = X
    J = 1
    WHILE  K(J) < XW   DO
        IF  J = N
            THEN  XW = LV  /* END OF LIST */
            ELSE  J = J + 1  /*  CONTINUE SEARCH */
        ENDIF
    ENDDO
    IF  K(J) = X
        THEN  do found routine
        ELSE  do no find routine
    ENDIF
END PROC
```

FIGURE 2-33
ALTERNATE SEQUENTIAL
SEARCH OF AN ORDERED
LIST ASCENDING

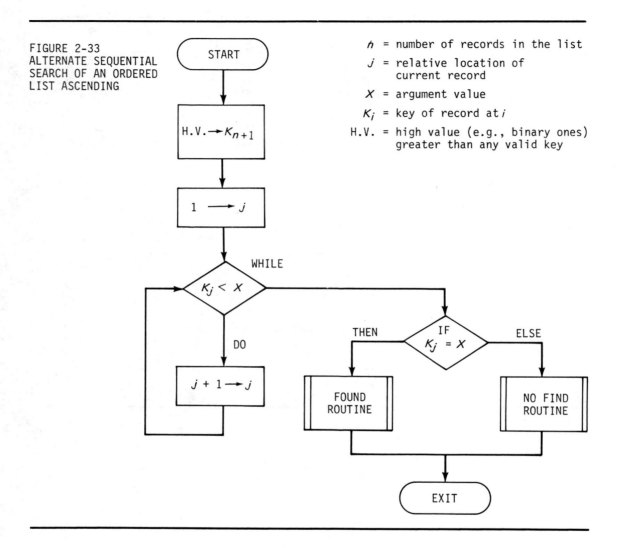

START

$H.V. \rightarrow K_{n+1}$

$1 \rightarrow j$

WHILE

$K_j < X$

DO

$j + 1 \rightarrow j$

THEN

IF
$K_j = X$

ELSE

FOUND
ROUTINE

NO FIND
ROUTINE

EXIT

n = number of records in the list

j = relative location of current record

X = argument value

K_i = key of record at i

H.V. = high value (e.g., binary ones) greater than any valid key

```
ALTERNATE SEQUENTIAL          /*  N = number of records in list */
SEARCH OF AN ORDERED          /*  J = relative location of current record */
LIST ASCENDING                /*  K(I) = key of record at location I */
                              /*  HV = high value (e.g. binary ones) */
                              /*  X = argument value */


PROC    SEARCH-LISTA
    K(N+1) = HV
    J = 1
    WHILE K(J) < X      DO
        J = J + 1
    ENDDO
    IF K(J) = X
            THEN  do found routine
            ELSE  do no find routine
END PROC
```

BINARY SEARCH

A *binary search* is a search technique for an ordered list in which the search population is reduced by half after each look that does not result in a match. When the choice of the search argument is random, the average number of looks or compares is as low as any for a search technique that preserves physical order (see Figure 2-34).

As long as a list contains more than two elements, this technique requires fewer average looks than a sequential search. However, one iteration through a binary search algorithm takes more execution time than an iteration for a sequential search. Therefore, the break-even point between the two search methods depends on the number of records in the list and the respective execution times for an iteration of each method.

The maximum number of looks for a binary search of a list of n records is $N = \lceil \log_2 n \rceil$. The average number of looks is found by summing the number of looks to find each record in a list of size n and then dividing by n. See Figure 2-35 for an example with $n = 100$.

$L_{ave} = 580/100 = 5.8$ where L_{ave} is the average number of looks. Since this method is tedious for large n, we use the approximation $L_{ave} = (\log_2 n) - 1$ for $n > 30$.

If $T_s =$ the average time for a sequential search to search a list of n records, and if $T_b =$ average time for the binary search, then the break-even point occurs when $T_s = T_b$. But $T_s = t_s [(n + 1)/2]$, where t_s is the time for one iteration of the sequential search, and $T_B = t_B [(\log_2 n) - 1]$, where t_B is the time for one iteration of the binary search. When $t_s[(n + 1)/2] = t_B[(\log_2 n) - 1]$, the break-even point can be calculated by solving for n. Likewise, for any given

FIGURE 2-34 TRACING STEPS OF
A BINARY SEARCH TO LOCATE
A TARGET RECORD

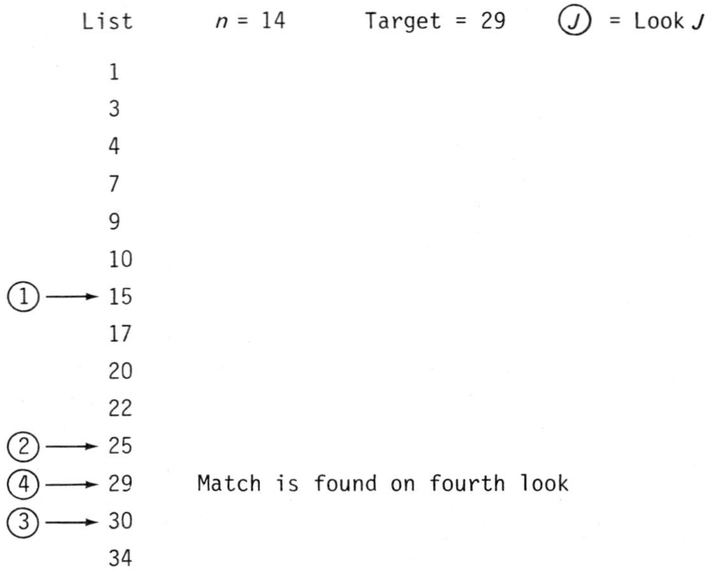

List $n = 14$ Target = 29   ⓙ = Look J

```
              1
              3
              4
              7
              9
             10
  ① ────▶ 15
             17
             20
             22
  ② ────▶ 25
  ④ ────▶ 29      Match is found on fourth look
  ③ ────▶ 30
             34
```

FIGURE 2-35 TABULATION OF
TOTAL LOOKS REQUIRED TO
LOCATE EVERY RECORD IN
A LIST OF 100 RECORDS

Number of Looks	Records Found	Total Looks
1	1	1
2	2	4
3	4	12
4	8	32
5	16	80
6	32	192
7	37	259
Totals	100	580

value of n, if $t_s[(n+1)/2] < t_B[(\log_2 n) - 1]$, the sequential search is faster. See Figure 2-36 for a comparison of binary and sequential searching methods.

Example: Suppose an iteration for the binary method is five times as long as for the sequential method on a given machine for given sequential and binary search algorithms. Therefore, $t_B = 5t_s$. Which method is faster for 32 records?

$$T_s = t_s\left(\frac{n+1}{2}\right) = t_s\left(\frac{32+1}{2}\right) = \underline{16.5t_s}$$
$$T_B = t_b[(\log_2 n) - 1] = 5t_s[(\log_2 32) - 1]$$
$$= 5t_s(5 - 1) = 5t_s(4.0) = \underline{20.0t_s}$$

Therefore, $T_s < T_B$; so the sequential search would be faster.

It is worth noting that if a binary search is used with the insertion sort described earlier, the number of comparisons can be reduced considerably as n becomes large. However, the number of moves will not be affected. Consequently, we can expect this refinement to improve the performance of the insertion sort to the point that it may outperform the other basic sorts on long random lists, but not to the point that it will perform as well as a Shell or quick sort; so we will not pursue it further. Figure 2-37 shows the algorithm for a binary search in flowchart form; the equivalent pseudocode accompanies it.

A slight variation of the binary search is choosing an initial starting position other than the midpoint of a list. This variation is desirable in a case where, for example, the majority of the searches are found in the bottom 10% of the list. In this case, the first look can be made at the point between the bottom 10% and upper 90% of the list. The average number of looks is reduced although the worst case is increased by one look.

The sequential search and the binary search are the only two searching methods that we present for searching physically ordered lists since the proper choice between these two methods should protect the programmer from any gross inefficiencies in searching physically ordered lists. We present additional techniques for searching in the following chapters on logical order, some of which can be easily adapted to work on physically ordered lists should the need arise.

FIGURE 2-36 COMPARISON OF BINARY AND SEQUENTIAL SEARCHING METHODS

Number of Records	Average Looks for Sequential Search	Average Looks for Binary Search
10	5.5	2.9
100	50.5	5.8
1000	500.5	9.0
10000	5000.5	12.4

FIGURE 2-37
BINARY SEARCH

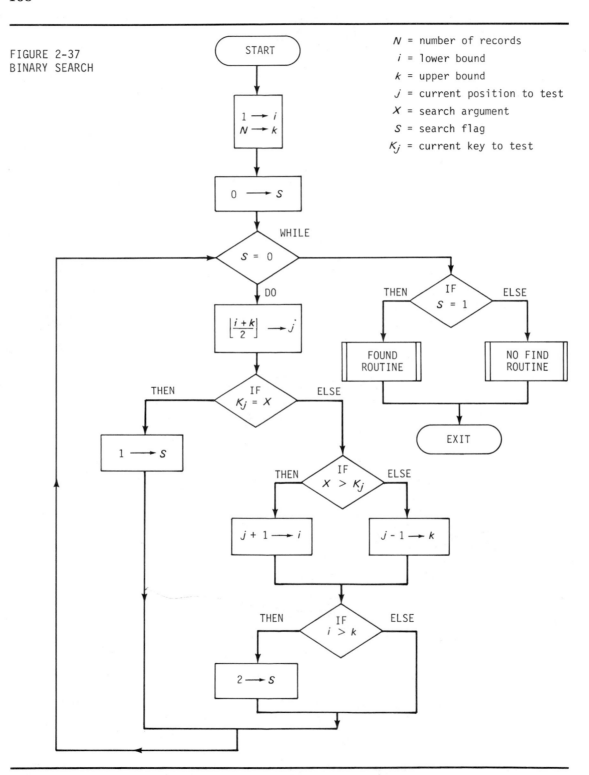

BINARY SEARCH

```
/*  N = number of records in list */
/*  I,K = lower and upper bounds to continue search */
/*  J = current records position to be tested */
/*  X = search argument */
/*  K(J) = key of record at location J */
/*  S = search flag; 0 = continue, 1 = found, 2 = no find */


PROC    BINARY-SEARCH
    I = 1
    K = N
    S = 0
    WHILE  S = 0   DO
        J = ⌊(I+K)/2⌋   /* find midpoint of remaining segment */
        IF   K(J) = X
            THEN  S = 1   /* record found */
            ELSE IF X > K(J)
                    THEN I = J + 1   /* take upper half */
                    ELSE K = J - 1   /* take lower half */
                 ENDIF
                 IF I > K
                    THEN  S = 2  /* record missing */
                    ELSE  continue
                 ENDIF
        ENDIF
    ENDDO
    IF  S = 1
        THEN do found routine
        ELSE do no find routine
    ENDIF
END PROC
```

MAINTAINING A SEQUENTIAL FILE

Once a file has been created, we must make sure that it contains valid information and that it retains its basic characteristics with respect to structure and order. The activities we perform to achieve this goal are commonly referred to as *file maintenance*. For a physically sequential file, maintenance is basically reduced to update activities, namely, posting, adding, and deleting of records.

For a file residing totally in main memory, these activities can be expressed easily in terms of processes that we have already discussed. Posting involves searching to locate the desired record and then changing the appropriate fields directly. Adding can be accomplished by simply adding the new record to the end of the file for an unordered file or, using a slight modification of the partitioned insertion sort algorithm, by inserting the record into its correct position. Deleting can be accomplished by first searching to find the desired record and then moving each of the succeeding records one position forward so that the deleted record is overlaid. The step of overlaying the deleted record can be eliminated from the deletion process if we simply mark the key field of the deleted record as "deleted." However, this choice degrades our search time, as described in Chapter 1.

Maintaining a sequential file stored on an external medium, such as magnetic tape or disk, involves additional considerations. First, all transfer of data to and from such a medium must be performed in complete physical records or blocks. Thus we cannot post individual fields directly as we did with memory-resident files. Second, we cannot conveniently shift record blocks from their original physical positions without recreating the file. Therefore, our addition and deletion procedures again differ from those used with memory-resident files. Each of the maintenance procedures described here requires a sequential search of an external file. This search is essentially the same as for an internal file except that the search algorithm needs to include an I/O step to read each record into memory before it can be examined. This search is included in the posting algorithm in Figure 2-38. (The equivalent pseudocode accompanies this figure.)

Posting of an external sequential file is the simplest of the maintenance procedures and, in most respects, it is quite similar to posting a memory-resident file. The file is read sequentially (searched) until the target record is found, whereupon the appropriate fields are changed in the record image stored in memory, and the entire record is rewritten to the external file to overlay the original record. Thus the major difference is that we replace fields when we post internal files, but we replace records with external files. The algorithm shown in Figure 2-38 for posting an external file treats I/O in a generic fashion. However, the specifics due to I/O procedures in a given language may require a slight adjustment. We show the process for unblocked records since most programming languages perform "logical" I/O operations, whereby the blocking and unblocking of records is handled automatically and is transparent to the programmer.

If several postings are required for a given file, posting efficiency can be

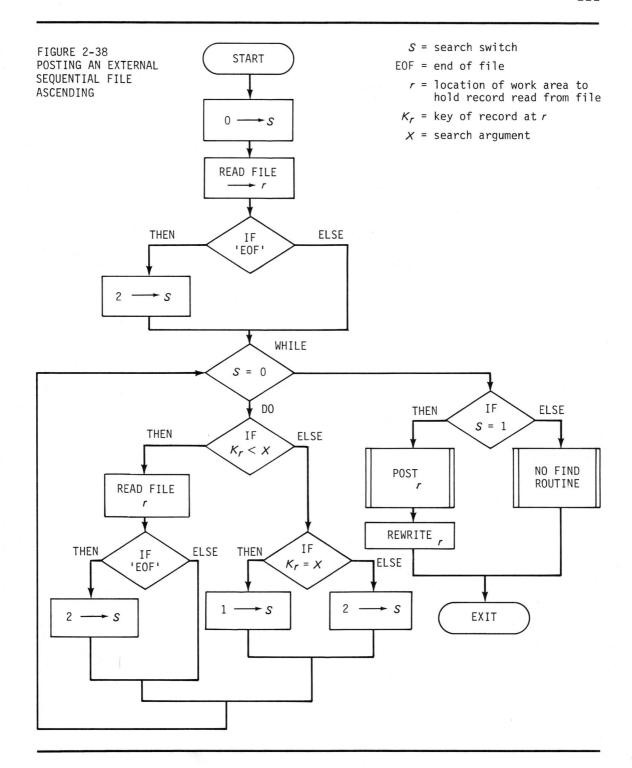

FIGURE 2-38
POSTING AN EXTERNAL
SEQUENTIAL FILE
ASCENDING

S = search switch
EOF = end of file
r = location of work area to hold record read from file
K_r = key of record at r
X = search argument

POSTING AN EXTERNAL
SEQUENTIAL FILE
ASCENDING

```
/*  S = search switch, value as before */
/*  EOF = end of file detected */
/*  R = location of work area to hold record read from file */
/*  K(R) = key of record at R */
/*  X = search argument */


PROC    POST-SEQ-EXTERNAL
    S = 0
    READ FILE, R  /* record read into R */
    IF 'EOF'
        THEN  S = 2
        ELSE  continue
    ENDIF
    WHILE  S = 0  DO
        IF K(R) < X
            THEN  READ FILE, R
                IF 'EOF'
                    THEN S = 2
                    ELSE continue
                ENDIF
            ELSE IF K(R) = X
                THEN S = 1  /* record found */
                ELSE S = 2  /* record missing */
                ENDIF
        ENDIF
    ENDDO
    IF  S = 1
        THEN  post appropriate fields at R
            REWRITE FILE, R
        ELSE  do no find routine
    ENDIF
END PROC
```

improved by creating a sequential "posting file" sorted in the same order as the target file. This posting file will allow all posting to be accomplished in one pass of the target file.

As we have seen, posting does not affect the physical structure of a sequential file. However, addition and deletion of records to a file does affect its structure, and procedures designed to accomplish these functions must maintain the basic characteristics of a sequential file.

We mentioned before that the most convenient way to handle addition and deletion of records to an external file is to recreate the file. This recreation is necessary because of the small repertory of I/O commands that we have at our disposal in most programming languages, and because repeated sequential searching of a file can quickly lead to an unacceptable number of I/O operations.

The process is usually achieved by creating an update file consisting of one record for each update operation. The update records contain all of the information needed in the respective update operation and an update code to identify the type of operation (that is, addition or deletion, as well as posting if desired). The update file is sorted according to the same order as the target file so that the update session can be accomplished in one pass of both files. The two files are processed concurrently much in the fashion of the two-way merge discussed earlier. In fact, the merge can be viewed as a special case of updating in which all records in the update file are additions. However, in general updating we must provide a choice of actions when processing the records from the update file: namely, deletion is treated as omitting a record from the original file, posting will change a record from the file, and addition will cause a new record to be merged into the new file.

The systems flowchart in Figure 2-39 depicts the process. The tape symbol is used simply to emphasize the physical sequential nature of the file.

FIGURE 2-39 SYSTEMS FLOWCHART
OF UPDATING A FILE BY RECREATION

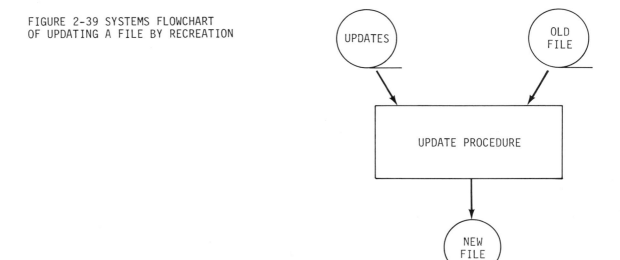

REVIEW EXERCISES

1. Explain briefly:

   (a) Insertion sort
   (b) Polyphase sort
   (c) Address calculation sort
   (d) Difference between internal and external sorts
   (e) A good sort and an acceptable sort

2. Compare the three basic sorts and explain under which conditions one would be preferable to another.

3. Compare the bubble, Shell, and quick sorts and explain under which conditions one would be preferable to the others.

4. Explain the basic technique for sorting a list that is too long to fit into memory.

5. Given the following data, show how they appear after each pass for (a) a bubble sort, (b) a selection and exchange sort, and then (c) a Shell sort. Count the number of compares and exchanges for each pass and total them for each sort.

Start Bubble

```
4
7
1
5
3
2
6
```

Compares _____

Exchanges _____

Start Selection

4
7
1
5
3
2
6

Compares _____

Exchanges _____

Start Shell

4
7
1
5
3
2
6

Compares _____

Exchanges _____

6. Explain how the quick sort works using the following example:
   47 17 25 15 88 85 66 33 55 11 67 57 13 79 54 56

7. Complete Figure 2-40 to compare sequential and binary search techniques on an ordered list to find a record in the list. You can round to the nearest look for binary.

FIGURE 2-40

Number of Records	Average Looks for Sequential	Average Looks for Binary
10		
25		
50		
100		

8. If an iteration for a given binary search takes three times as long as an iteration for a given sequential search, determine which method is faster for a list of 25 records. (Show your work.)

PROGRAMMING ASSIGNMENTS

1. Write a program that will compare two of the basic sorting methods (bubble, selection with exchange, insertion) with the Shell sort by counting numbers of compares and record moves as each sort in turn sorts a common list of more-or-less randomly ordered records. The program should:

   (a) Accommodate up to 100 records of the following format

PART NO.	QUANTITY
4 bytes	4 bytes

   where both part number and quantity are stored as binary numbers after being read in from cards.

   (b) Print the unsorted list once, and then print the sorted list after each sort with the count of compares and moves for that sort. Note that an exchange normally requires three moves.

2. Using the record format of programming assignment 1, compare the relative performances of the Shell and quick sorts on identical lists of 50, 100, and 200 records. As before, count the number of compares and exchanges for each sort, and print these totals along with the unordered list and sorted list in each case.

3. LOGICALLY ORDERED LISTS

An unordered list must be sorted to make it physically ordered. When the list is updated through addition or deletion of records, it must be sorted again to regain its physical order. Actually, if the update involves only deletions, sorting can be avoided by simply marking records as deleted, but this would increase search time because each record would have to be tested for a null case before it could be used in a comparison, and cells containing deleted or null records are wasted. So, in general, if a list is to be updated, it must be resorted after each update session. An *update session* is defined as a period in which updating is in process and normal retrievals from the list are inhibited.

If a list is relatively static with respect to updates, there is generally little concern over the occasional resorting that is required. But if the list is volatile or if dynamic updating (that is, an update session is equivalent to one addition or deletion) is required, then the overhead due to sorting can very easily exceed all other processing performed against the list.

Fortunately, a list can be ordered logically without being ordered physically and, by using search routines based on this logical order, we can eliminate or greatly reduce the need for sorting after the list has been created. Logical order is achieved by the addition of pointer fields, called *links*, to each record. These links indicate the location of the next record or group of records in a particular ordering scheme.

LINKED LISTS

The simplest logical structure is the linear linked list or simply linked list for short. A *linked list* is a list in which each record points to its successor, except for the last record, which has an end-of-list indicator in its pointer field. Most other logical structures are extentions of the concept of a linked list. Since pointer fields tend to be rather short—usually 1 to 4 bytes in length—the addition of a pointer field to a record is normally a quite acceptable, if not minor, amount of space overhead. Nonetheless, any overhead must be considered and evaluated in the creation of records. See the example in Figure 3-1.

Notice that Figure 3-1 shows a special pointer called LISTPTR. This pointer occupies a fixed location and always indicates where the first logical record in the list begins. This indication is necessary since, as in this figure, there is no requirement that the first logical record reside in the first physical cell of the list.

CREATION OF A LINKED LIST

Although Figure 3-1 shows that there can be a wide discrepancy between the physical positions of the records and their logical order, it is often the case that when the linked list is first created, the physical and logical order are identical, and only after updating does this relationship disappear.

This case is true because one of the simplest ways to create a linked list is to sort the list and then pass through the list once, inserting in the pointer field of each record the next physical location in the list. See Figure 3-2 for an example. Figure 3-3 shows an algorithm of the creation of a linked list from an existing unordered list; the equivalent pseudocode accompanies it.

FIGURE 3-1
LINKED LIST
ORDERED LOGICALLY

LISTPTR	Location	Key	Other Data	Link
6	1	50		3
	2	25		4
	3	63		7
	4	38		8
	5	82		*end
	6	16		2
	7	72		5
	8	48		1

Record

"End" may equal a special character such as "" or a special value such as 999 or 0.

FIGURE 3-2
LINKED LIST
ORDERED LOGICALLY
AND PHYSICALLY

LISTPTR	Location	Key	Link
1	1	ABLE	2
	2	BAKER	3
	3	BROWN	4
	4	GREEN	5
	5	SMITH	end

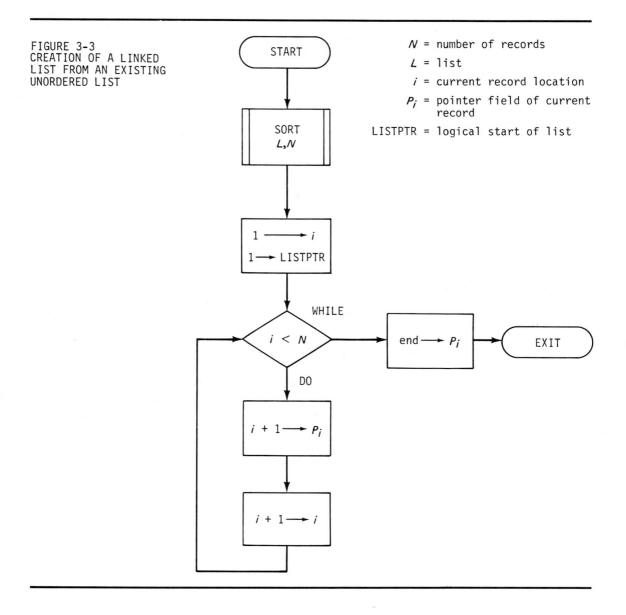

FIGURE 3-3
CREATION OF A LINKED
LIST FROM AN EXISTING
UNORDERED LIST

N = number of records

L = list

i = current record location

P_i = pointer field of current record

LISTPTR = logical start of list

CREATION OF
A LINKED LIST
FROM AN EXISTING
UNORDERED LIST

```
/*  N = number of records */
/*  L = unordered list */
/*  I = current record location */
/*  P(I) = pointer field of current record */
/*  LISTPTR = logical starting position of linked list */

PROC      CREATE-LNKLIST
    sort the unordered list
    I = 1               /* relative physical beginning of sorted list */
    LISTPTR = 1 /* initially, logical and physical start are same */
    WHILE I < N   DO
        P(I) = I + 1
        I = I + 1
    ENDDO
    P(I) = end                /* mark pointer of last logical record */
END PROC
```

SEQUENTIAL SEARCHING OF A LINKED LIST

Sequential searching involves simply assigning the pointer or link value of the current record as the location of the next record to be accessed. Other than that, it is the same as a sequential searching of a linear list.

The simple sequential-search algorithm must be augmented slightly if it is to be used in the process of adding or deleting records, since in both cases the location of the record that precedes the added or deleted record must be saved. These additional steps are included and marked in the algorithm in Figure 3-4 so that the logic will not need to be repeated later.

ADDITION AND DELETION TO A LINKED LIST

We said before that updating of linked lists does not necessitate additional sorting. This condition is true because, in adding records to or deleting records from a linked list, we can preserve order by altering the pointers of the one or two records that are affected by the update.

Deletion is accomplished by moving the pointer field value of the record to be deleted to the pointer field of its predecessor record. See Figure 3-5 for an example. By following the pointer chain, record C will be excluded from the search sequence. Addition is accomplished by placing the new record in whatever cell is most convenient, copying the pointer field value from the predecessor record into the pointer field of the new record, and, finally, modifying the pointer field of the predecessor to point to the new record (see Figure 3-6).

COBOL IMPLEMENTATION
OF CREATION OF A
LINKED LIST

```
                                         .
                                         .
                                         .
                    WORKING-STORAGE SECTION.
                    01   COUNTER-AND-POINTERS.
                         02   REC-COUNT PIC S9(4) COMP.
                         02   I         PIC S9(4) COMP.
                         02   LISTPTR   PIC S9(4) COMP.
                         02   NEXT-REC  PIC S9(4) COMP.
                         02   END-LST   PIC S9(4) COMP VALUE 9999.
                                         .
                                         .
                                         .
                    01   LIST-AREA.
                         02   LIST-REC OCCURS 100.
                              03   REC-KEY PIC_____.
                              (other data fields)
                              03   REC-PTR PIC  S9(4)  USAGE COMP.
                                         .
                                         .
                                         .
                    PROCEDURE DIVISION.
                                         .
                                         .
                                         .
                    BUILD-LINKED-LIST.
                         CALL 'SORTLST' USING LIST-AREA, REC-COUNT.
                         MOVE 1 TO LISTPTR.
                         PERFORM SET-LINKS VARYING I FROM 1 BY 1
                             UNTIL I = REC-COUNT
                         MOVE END-LST TO REC-PTR(I).
                    BUILD-LINKED-LIST-EXIT. EXIT.
                                         .
                                         .
                                         .
                    SET-LINKS.
                         ADD 1 TO I GIVING NEXT-REC.
                         MOVE NEXT-REC TO REC-PTR(I).
```

122

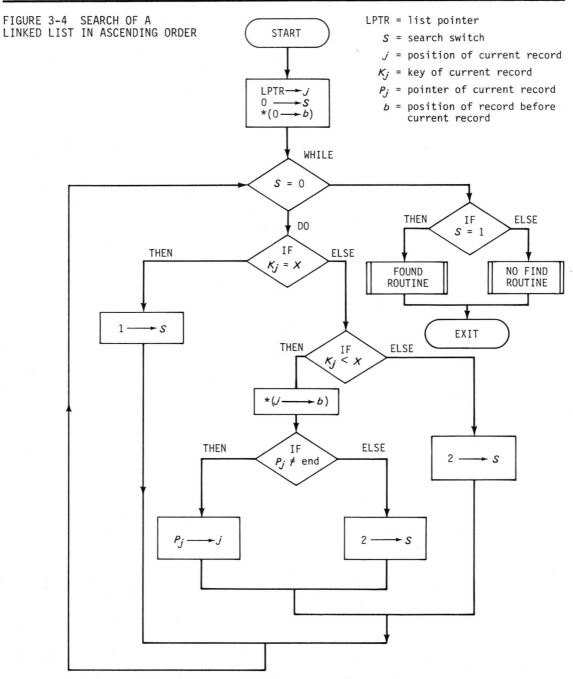

FIGURE 3-4 SEARCH OF A
LINKED LIST IN ASCENDING ORDER

LPTR = list pointer
S = search switch
j = position of current record
K_j = key of current record
P_j = pointer of current record
b = position of record before
current record

START

LPTR $\longrightarrow j$
$0 \longrightarrow S$
$*(0 \longrightarrow b)$

WHILE

$S = 0$

DO

IF
$K_j = X$

THEN   ELSE

$1 \longrightarrow S$

THEN   IF   ELSE
$S = 1$

FOUND
ROUTINE

NO FIND
ROUTINE

EXIT

THEN   IF   ELSE
$K_j < X$

$*(j \longrightarrow b)$

THEN   IF   ELSE
$P_j \neq$ end

$2 \longrightarrow S$

$P_j \longrightarrow j$

$2 \longrightarrow S$

*If this search is to be used to add or delete to the list, then
the location of the previous record must be saved. If the search
reaches the end of the list with $K_j < X$, $b = j$ will be returned.

SEARCH OF
A LINKED LIST
IN ASCENDING ORDER

```
/*  LPTR = list pointer */
/*  S = search switch; 0 = continue, 1 = record found,
    2 = record missing */
/*  J,K(J),P(J) = location, key, and pointer of
    current record */
/*  B = position of record before current record;
    need for update */
/*  statements shown as *(  ) are needed in
    updating only */


PROC         SEARCH-LNKLIST
    J = LPTR
    S = 0
    *(B = 0)
    WHILE  S = 0  DO
        IF  K(J) = X
            THEN S = 1                        /* record found */
            ELSE IF  K(J) < X
                    THEN *(B = J)
                        IF  P(J) ≠ end
                            THEN  J = P(J)
                            ELSE S = 2
                        ENDIF
                    ELSE  S = 2               /* record missing */
                ENDIF
        ENDIF
    ENDDO
    IF  S = 1
        THEN  do found routine
        ELSE  do no find routine
    ENDIF
END PROC
```

Applications of linked lists are many and varied. Those presented here are typical but in no way cover the gamut of possibilities.

For our first example, suppose that we have a program that maintains a list of valid users that are to have access to the program and its accompanying data files. We want the list to be in ascending order according to user identification number, and we expect a rather active number of additions and deletions to the list. We can build a new entry (record) in any location that is convenient and insert this entry into the list without disturbing the other entries, except for the adjustment in the pointer field of the record that now precedes our new entry. Similarly, deletion of an entry also requires only that we adjust the pointer of one record.

This brings us to our next example, which is memory management. In the preceding example, we sidestepped this issue simply by saying that a new entry would be built in a convenient location. One method of finding such a location is available if our linked list resides in a contiguous area that can be viewed as a vector with elements equal in size to the records of the list. All "free" elements (that is, those not assigned to the linked list) can be marked as free so that the vector can be sequentially searched to find an available space. Deleted records can also be marked as free so that they can be reused when needed.

FIGURE 3-5
DELETION OF AN
ELEMENT FROM A
LINKED LIST

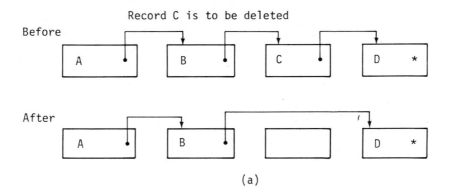

(a)

(b)

A generally better solution is to create a second linked list of all available free locations. When a location is needed to build a new entry for our primary list, it is taken from the list of free space. When a record is deleted from our primary list, its space is appended to the free-space list for reassignment and, thus, we not only solve our problem of memory management with respect to our list elements but also eliminate the requirement for our elements to reside within the confines of a single vector.

The use of linked lists in the memory management example brings us to our next two applications of linked lists: stacks and queues.

STACKS AND QUEUES AS LINKED LISTS

STACKS

In Chapter 1, stacks were presented as physically organized structures, but a stack can also be implemented as a linked list in which all additions and deletions are made to the first position in the list. We now have an ideal structure for the free-space list described in the memory management application. The example in Figure 3-7 illustrates the way the stack is employed as a space list to assist in the memory management of the primary data list.

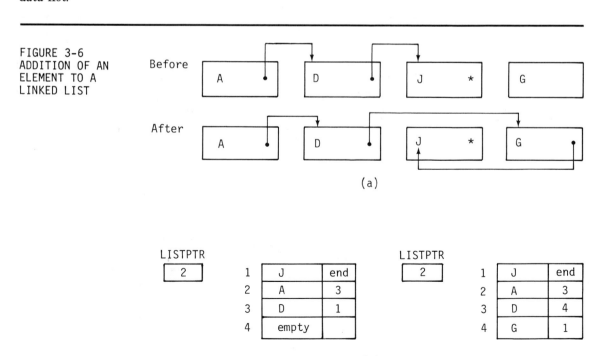

FIGURE 3-6
ADDITION OF AN
ELEMENT TO A
LINKED LIST

(a)

(b)

The algorithm for the manipulation of a stack as a linked list appears in flowchart form in Figure 3-8 (the equivalent pseudocode accompanies it). This algorithm is simply the combination of special cases for the addition and deletion algorithms for a linked list. An additional variable is included to determine which action is needed, push or pop. This variable can be in any convenient form, but a single-digit-integer variable is as good as any. If we attempt to pop an empty list, an end-of-list value is returned. There is no possibility of attempting to push an element into a full list using this algorithm since space for the new element must be acquired before invoking the procedure, and the physical location of the new element will not affect its insertion into a linked list.

We now return to our application example of adding and deleting records within a linked list using a space list in the form of a stack. The algorithms for

FIGURE 3-7
UPDATING A
LINKED LIST
WITH A STACK
AS A SPACE
LIST

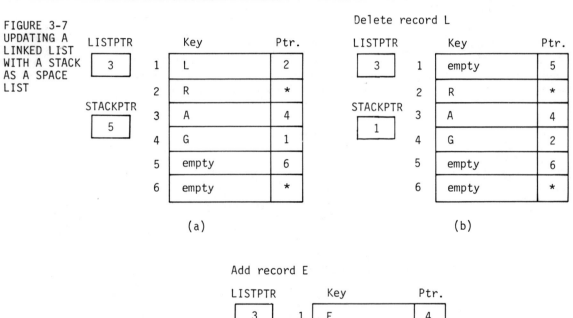

(a)

(b)

(c)

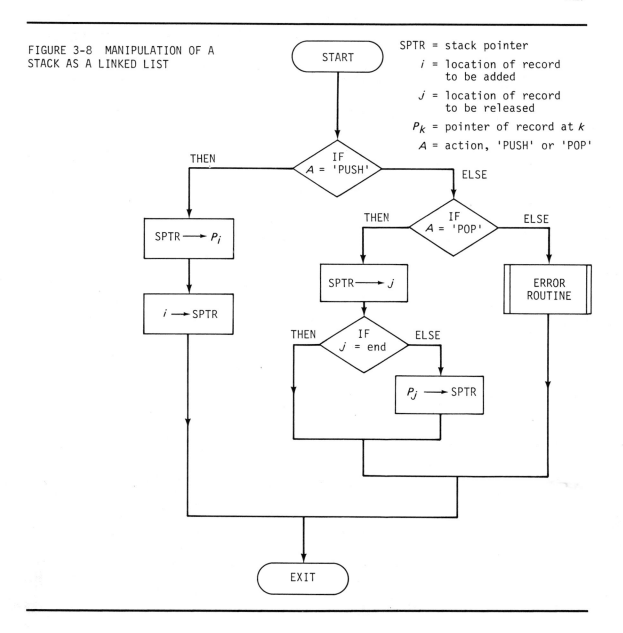

FIGURE 3-8 MANIPULATION OF A
STACK AS A LINKED LIST

MANIPULATION OF
A STACK AS A
LINKED LIST

```
/*  SPTR = stack pointer; always point to top element */
/*  I = location of record to be added (pushed) */
/*  J = location of record to be released (popped) */
/*  P(K) = pointer of record at location K */
/*  A = action, PUSH or POP */


PROC    STACK-LNKLST
    IF A = PUSH
        THEN P(I) = SPTR
            SPTR = I
        ELSE IF A = POP
                THEN J = SPTR
                    IF J = end
                        THEN   continue
                        ELSE   SPTR = P(J)
                    ENDIF
                ELSE  error routine for invalid action
            ENDIF
    ENDIF
END PROC
```

performing the functions of addition and deletion are presented in Figures 3-9 and 3-10. (Pseudocodes accompany them.) Both algorithms make use of the previously defined algorithms for searching a linked list and manipulation of a stack. However, the addition algorithm is slightly more involved because two "error" conditions can occur in addition: no space for a new record (the space stack is empty) and a duplicate record is found. (The latter condition may not be an error, but it must be handled separately.) In deletion, the only error condition that occurs is an attempt to delete a record that does not exist. Also, we must build a record in the newly acquired cell from the space list before we can add it, whereas, in deletion, we need not remove any data to append the deleted record cell to the space list.

In both algorithms, recall that if the variable b has a value of 0, then the search algorithm has positioned us to the first record in the list, and the predecessor of the first element is always the list pointer.

An alternate method of creating a linked list is now available without the use of a sort. If records enter the system one at a time after the decision to link the list has been made, or if a duplicate list area is available, the final list area can be placed in a space list (stack), and then the creation process is achieved by inserting each record in the list according to the method described.

129

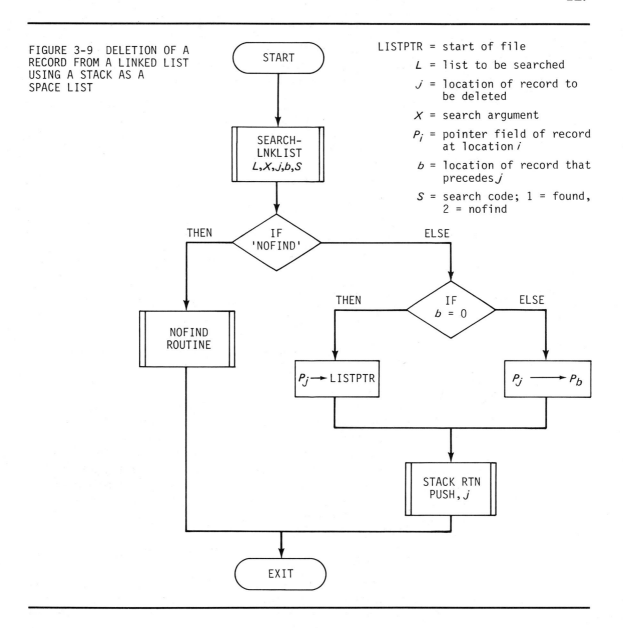

FIGURE 3-9 DELETION OF A
RECORD FROM A LINKED LIST
USING A STACK AS A
SPACE LIST

LISTPTR = start of file
L = list to be searched
j = location of record to
be deleted
X = search argument
P_i = pointer field of record
at location i
b = location of record that
precedes j
S = search code; 1 = found,
2 = nofind

DELETION OF A RECORD   /* L = list to be searched */
FROM A LINKED LIST   /* J = location of record in L to be deleted */
USING A STACK AS   /* X = search argument */
A SPACE LIST   /* P(I) = pointer of record at location I */
                        /* B = location of record that precedes J */
                        /* S = search code; 1 = found, 2 = no find */

```
PROC    DELET-LIST-SK
        do search of L; send X return J, B, S
        IF  S = no find
            THEN  do no find routine
            ELSE  IF  B = 0                    */ check for deletion
                      THEN  LISTPTR = P(J)        of 1st record */
                      ELSE  P(B) = P(J)
                  ENDIF
                  do stack routine; send PUSH,J
        ENDIF
END PROC
```

QUEUES

A queue can be implemented as a linked list with two fixed-position pointers, one pointing to the head where deletions are made and one pointing to the tail where additions are made. Figure 3-11 shows an example.

The algorithm for the manipulation of a queue as a linked list is given in Figure 3-12. (The equivalent pseudocode accompanies it.) In a manner similar to the manipulation of a stack as a linked list, this algorithm is once again a combination of a special case for addition to a linked list (always at the end) and a special case of deletion from a linked list (always at the beginning).

Please note that while addition usually involves a change to only the tail pointer, and deletion usually involves a change to only the head pointer, if we add an element to an empty queue of if we delete the last element from a queue, both pointers are involved. In the event that the queue is empty, both the head and the tail pointers contain an end-of-list indicator.

The advantages in the implementation of a queue as a linked list are the same general advantages that we discussed in connection with linked lists: namely, we don't need to move elements physically to maintain a desired order (logical ordering) and convenience in memory management (free cells available for records can move to and from an associated space list). These advantages are amplified in a dynamic process, such as presenting jobs to an operating system for execution. The operating system can initially place the jobs on a queue and then initiate their execution on a FIFO basis. In this case, the queue entries are maintained in a very limited area so that it is highly

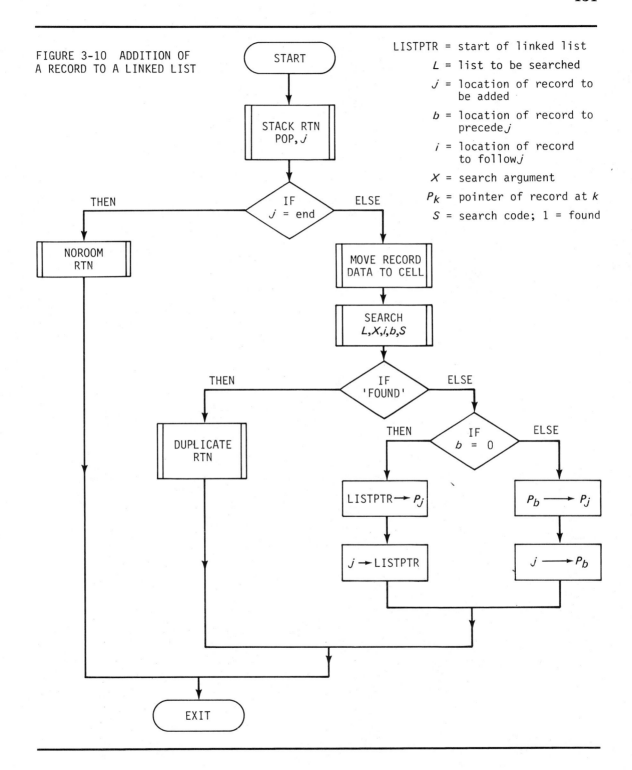

FIGURE 3-10 ADDITION OF A RECORD TO A LINKED LIST

ADDITION OF A RECORD
TO A LINKED LIST

```
/*  L = linked list to receive new record */
/*  J = location of record to be added to L */
/*  B = location of record to precede J */
/*  I = location of record to follow J */
/*  X = search argument */
/*  P(K) = pointer of record at location K */
/*  S = search code; 1 = found */


PROC        ADD-LNKLIST
        do stack routine; send POP, return J
        IF J = end
            THEN  do no room routine
            ELSE  post data into element at J
                  do search list routine; send X,L return I,B,S
                  IF S = found
                      THEN  do duplicate routine
                      ELSE  IF B = 0
                                THEN  P(J) = LISTPTR
                                      LISTPTR = J
                                ELSE  P(J) = P(B)
                                      P(B) = J
                                ENDIF
                  ENDIF
        ENDIF
END PROC
```

desirable to keep wasted space to a minimum. If we use a stack to keep up with all free space in this area once a queue entry has been serviced, its space can be placed in the stack for reassignment to the next job that enters the queue. This complementary interaction between a queue and a stack is a very satisfactory technique for a variety of situations similar to the one just described. An example of this queue and stack interaction on a common area is illustrated in Figure 3-13. The queue area is divided into equal-sized blocks, of which three are initially assigned to the job queue and the rest placed in a stack that serves as a free-space list.

ADDITIONAL APPLICATIONS OF LINKED LISTS

CIRCULARLY LINKED LISTS

A *circularly linked list* or *ring* is a linked list in which the last element points back to the first. This structure is very useful if it is possible to enter the list at more than one point since we can still access every record in the list. See Figure 3-14 for an example.

To search a ring, we need to check to see if we have returned to the point at which we began instead of looking for an end-of-list marker. If we mistakenly apply the search algorithm for a simple linked list to a ring, we can be caught in an infinite loop.

A case in which we might want to enter a linked list at more than one point occurs when records are members of more than one linked list. An example of this is given under the section titled Multilinked Lists.

FIGURE 3-11
UPDATING A
QUEUE

Start
HEADPTR

1

TAILPTR

4

1	B	2
2	0	3
3	A	4
4	T	*
5	empty	

Add record S
HEADPTR

1

TAILPTR

5

1	B	2
2	0	3
3	A	4
4	T	5
5	S	*

Remove record B
HEADPTR

2

TAILPTR

5

1	empty	
2	0	3
3	A	4
4	T	5
5	S	*

134

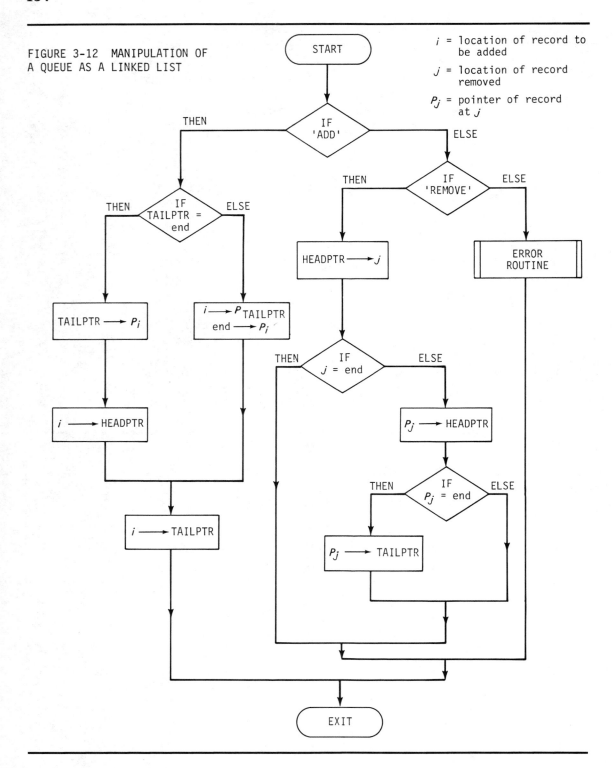

FIGURE 3-12 MANIPULATION OF
A QUEUE AS A LINKED LIST

MANIPULATION
OF A QUEUE
AS A LINKED LIST

```
/*  J = location of record that was removed */
/*  I = location of record to be added */
/*  P(K) = pointer of record at location K */
/*  HEAD, TAIL = beginning and ending locations of queue */
/*  A = action taken; add or remove */


PROC    QUEUE-LNKLIST
    IF  A = add
        THEN IF TAIL = end                      /* check for empty
                THEN  P(I) = TAIL                   queue */
                      HEAD = I
                ELSE P(TAIL) = I
                      P(I) = end
            ENDIF
            TAIL = I
        ELSE IF A = remove
                THEN  J = HEAD
                      IF  J = end                   /* return end
                          THEN  continue               indicator */
                          ELSE  HEAD = P(J)
                                IF P(J) = end
                                    THEN  TAIL = P(J)
                                    ELSE  continue
                                ENDIF
                      ENDIF
            ELSE  do error routine
            ENDIF
    ENDIF
END PROC
```

DOUBLY LINKED LISTS

A *doubly linked list* is a linked list that has both forward and backward pointers. This feature allows us to backtrack in a list without having to start over at the beginning. This list is essentially two linked lists with the same elements in which the order of one is exactly the reverse of the other.

To search this structure, in general we need to call the search algorithm with two different link parameters. See Figure 3-15 for an example. One application of this structure is to have the capability of printing out a list in either ascending or descending order without sorting.

FIGURE 3-13   QUEUE AND STACK INTERACTION: (a) start; (b) after adding JOBS D and E; (c) after deleting JOB A

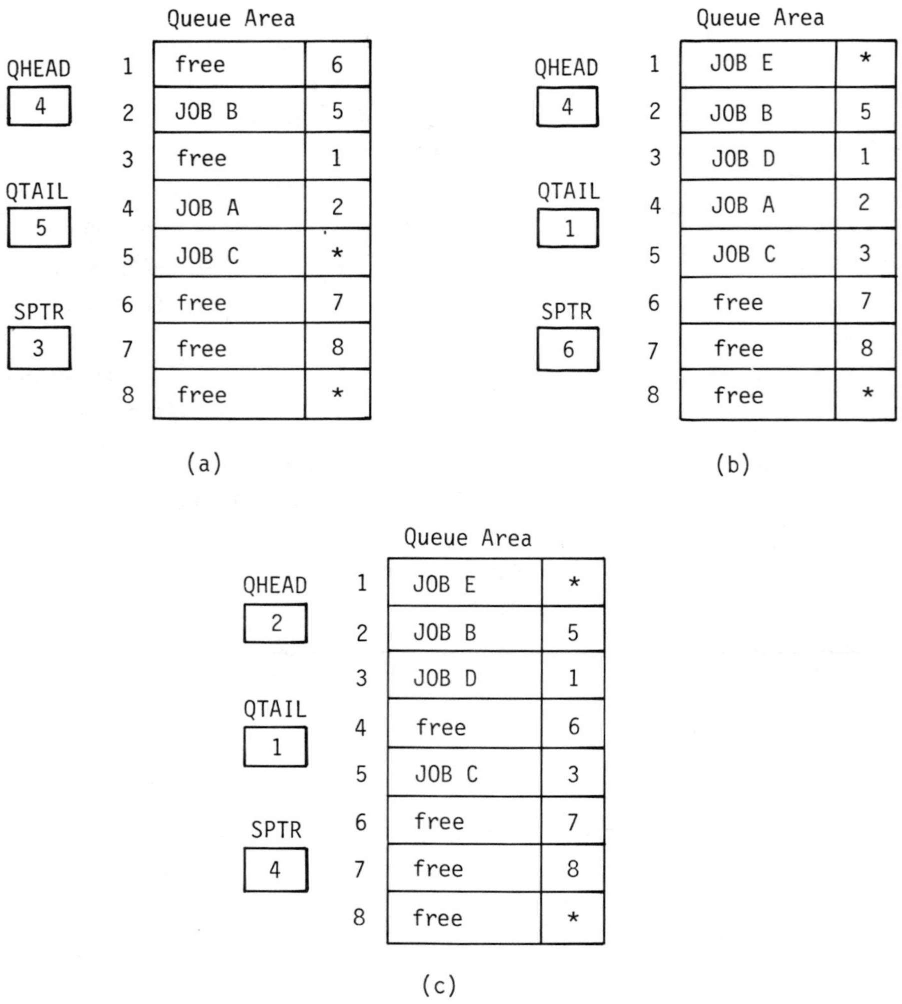

(a)

(b)

(c)

DEQUES

A _deque_ is a double-ended queue. This is a structure in which elements can be added or deleted from either end. The deque can be implemented as a doubly linked list with head and tail pointers. See Figure 3-16 for an example. For an example of the use of a deque in an application, consider the following.

A program is written to service requests from a number of terminal users. Requests are periodically made faster than they can be handled and, when this occurs, requests from all users except one are placed in a ready queue for FIFO servicing. This special user is privileged (for whatever reason) and is treated such that any request from this user is placed at the front of the queue for immediate handling. Should the ready queue be full when a privileged request is made, the last entry will be bumped (deleted) to a standby queue and reentered when size permits. This condition results in a structure in which:

1. Additions of regular requests are made to the TAIL.

2. Additions of privileged requests are made to the HEAD.

3. Deletions of both types of requests are made from the HEAD.

4. Deletion due to bumping is made at the TAIL.

Thus, we have a deque.

FIGURE 3-14 CIRCULARLY
LINKED LIST.

LPTR

1

1	VERDI	2
2	PUCCINI	3
3	WAGNER	4
4	MOZART	5
5	STRAUSS	1

FIGURE 3-15 DOUBLY
LINKED LIST.

FLSTPTR

1

BLSTPTR

5

			Fwd	Bkwd
1	60	FUDD	2	*
2	72	SMITH	3	1
3	80	BROWN	4	2
4	88	JONES	5	3
5	94	GREEN	*	4

MULTILINKED LISTS

A *multilinked list* is a list in which each element has two or more pointers. This structure is useful if we want to order a set of records on more than one key field. For instance, suppose that we want to order a set of records containing information about an organization's members by the names of the members and their social security numbers. There is no direct relationship between these two orderings, but the multilinked structure allows us to accomplish this goal (see Figure 3-17). Note the difference between this structure and the doubly linked list structure.

Another type of multilinked list involves a list in which at least one of the pointer fields defines two or more linked sublists. For example, a group of employees is ordered alphabetically by name. In addition, all employees with the same job title form a linked sublist (see Figure 3-18). The list is shown in this figure with circularly linked lists for the occupations sublists to insure that each person for a particular occupation can be located without the use of a directory.

When directories are presented, readers will see that it is a simple matter to substitute a simple linked sublist. Likewise, when we discuss inverted files, readers will see how we can search directly by categories.

FIGURE 3-16 DEQUE

HEADPTR			
4			

4	B	5	*
5	A	6	4
6	C	7	5
7	H	*	6

TAILPTR

7

FIGURE 3-17
MULTILINKED LIST,
TYPE 1

LSTPTR1

1

LSTPTR2

6

			Ptr1	Ptr2
1	ABLE	425645132	2	7
2	BAKER	743116402	3	*
3	FROST	242443346	4	5
4	HANDEL	410447338	5	1
5	MUNIZ	305442311	6	4
6	PERRIER	108520233	7	3
7	SNERD	551530534	*	2

FIGURE 3-18
MULTILINKED LIST,
TYPE 2

LSTPTR

1

1	ADAMS	SALESPERSON	2	5
2	BENTLEY	PRESIDENT	4	2(*)
3	TATE	SECRETARY	12	6
4	COOK	CLERK	5	8
5	CUEVAS	SALESPERSON	6	7
6	DIAZ	SECRETARY	7	11
7	ELLIOT	SALESPERSON	9	15
8	MCQUIRE	CLERK	15	12
9	GOOCH	ACCOUNTANT	10	9(*)
10	LARSON	MANAGER	8	13
11	SCHILLING	SECRETARY	14	3(*)
12	WILLIAMS	CLERK	13	14
13	YATES	MANAGER	*	10(*)
14	SMITH	CLERK	3	4(*)
15	MILLER	SALESPERSON	11	1(*)

REVIEW EXERCISES

1. Explain briefly:

   (a) stack   (d) doubly linked list
   (b) queue   (e) circular list (ring)
   (c) linked list   (f) multilinked list

2. (a) Complete the following as a linked list in ascending order based on name.

Location	Name	Grade	
1	JOHNSON, JOHN	85	
2	TUCKER, JANE	94	
3	STRAUSS, LEVI	90	
4	ANDERSON, MARY	72	
5	MCGILL, GARY	68	

   (b) Draw a flowchart of the routine to search a linked list $R_1, R_2, R_3, \ldots, R_n$ for a record with a key value equal to an argument value X.

PROGRAMMING ASSIGNMENTS

1. Create a linked list with a space list to facilitate adds and deletes. Input from which the list is to be built has the following format:

   Card Columns

1-4	Key
5-8	Data
9-10	Filler
11-30	Name
31-80	Filler

After the list is built, print it out by following the links. Elements should have the following format:

Key	Data	Name	Link
1 – 4	5 – 8	9 – 28	29 – 32

2. Process adds and deletes and print out the list again. Update cards have the following format:

Card Columns

1–4	Key
5–8	Data
9–10	Filler
11–30	Name
31–79	Filler
80	Code (1 for add, 0 for delete)

4. EXTENDING LOGICAL ORDER

In the preceding chapter, we saw that we could use a linked list to achieve an ordered sequential list without requiring that the list be physically ordered. This fact allowed us to perform all of the sequential processing operations we had used on physically ordered lists before without having to physically move records to perform additions or deletions.

Searching a linked list sequentially is simple enough. However, as the length of the list increases, we need to develop other techniques for searching that will improve our searching efficiency with respect to the number of keys that must be examined before we can locate a given record or position. The binary search algorithm developed in Chapter 2 requires that the list be physically ordered. Therefore, it is inappropriate for use with logically ordered lists. (We readdress the possibility of a binary search on a logically ordered list in Chapter 5.) One way to improve searching performance is to use directories. We should emphasize that although the following discussion concentrates on using directories with logically ordered lists, they can be used in similar fashion with physically ordered lists as well.

DIRECTORIES

A *directory* or *index* is a list (usually ordered) that has the following relationship to an associated file. Each element in the directory is composed of, as a minimum, a key field and a location field. The key field contains a key value for a record from the associated file. The location field contains one of:
(1) the location of the record in the file that is identified by the key value;
(2) the location of the beginning of the sublist that contains this record;
or (3) the location of a lower level directory associated with a segment of the file that contains this record.

If we want to use a directory to process a file, then access to the file will progress first through the directory and then to the file. Thus the file and its directory must be maintained together so that the preceding relationship remains valid. Additions and deletions to a file can cause alterations to directory entries as well, as in the case of deleting a record whose key value is contained in a directory entry. Therefore, all processing of a file or list that involves additions or deletions must take into consideration the possible effects on an associated directory, regardless of whether the file was accessed through the directory.

TOTAL DIRECTORIES

A *total directory* is a directory that has an entry for each key value in a given file; that is, there is a one-to-one relationship between the directory and the key values in the file. When there are no duplicate key values, we have a one-to-one relationship with directory entries and records in the file (see Figure 4-1).

The total directory is useful in a number of circumstances, such as those that follow:

1. The directory may fit in memory when the list will not. The directory normally requires much less storage than the file. Therefore, search time can be improved considerably if a memory-resident directory can be searched instead of repeated reads to the file to find a record. A variation occurs when the directory is segmented and brought into memory a segment at a time. Since the directory segment normally contains more entries in a given amount of space than a segment of records from the file, search time is improved.

2. The file may contain variable-length records such that the beginning location of a record is not a fixed boundary. There are basically three choices: use a record length field in each record, use a pointer field in a fixed location of each record, or use a directory.

3. We can maintain an ordered directory without ordering the file. In the case of logical order, the main advantage to the total

FIGURE 4-1
TOTAL DIRECTORY
WITH AN ORDERED FILE

Directory

ADAMS	1
BRAUN	2
JOHNS	3
KRAUS	4
ZICK	5

File

1	ADAMS	42	M	160
2	BRAUN	25	F	120
3	JOHNS	55	M	180
4	KRAUS	36	F	115
5	ZICK	28	M	155

directory is it compactness. In the case of physical order, only the directory need be sorted. Sorting only the directory usually takes less time since the directory entries are usually shorter. And, if the directory is long enough to warrant it, a simple binary search can be used. This also applies to the case of a file containing variable-length records. If appropriate, the binary search can be used on the associated directory (see Figure 4-2).

The creation of the directory is relatively straightforward and can be done concurrently with the creation of the file or during a single pass after the file has been created. Adding and deleting to the file requires adds and deletes to the corresponding directory entries on a one-to-one basis. The process can be treated as the identical but independent manipulation of two linear lists.

ONE-LEVEL DIRECTORIES

A *one-level directory* is a directory in which each entry points to a sublist in the primary list or file. The sublist may contain only a single record, but it usually contains more and should be treated as a one-to-many relationship (see Figure 4-3). In Figure 4-3, each element in the directory contains the key value of the highest key in the corresponding sublist and the location of the beginning of that sublist.

The directory can be viewed as an ordered set of list pointers that replaces the single list pointer used previously. The directory can itself be implemented as a linked list, and in this case a directory pointer is needed just as it is with any other linked list.

The primary list can be created as a series of disjoint linked sublists or simply as one continuous linked list. If the single linked list is used, care must be taken not to continue a search beyond the desired sublist inadvertently. The advantage in using disjoint sublists is simplicity of maintenance. All access to the file progresses through the directory to the file. The addition or deletion of a record will only affect the sublist to which it belongs and possibly its associated directory entry. The advantage in creating the file as one continuous linked list is that the file can be accessed either through the directory or as a single sequential file. However, in this case we are maintaining

FIGURE 4-2
TOTAL DIRECTORY
WITH AN UNORDERED
FILE

ADAMS	5
BRAUN	1
JOHNS	4
KRAUS	2
ZICK	3

1	BRAUN	25	F	120
2	KRAUS	36	F	115
3	ZICK	28	M	155
4	JOHNS	55	M	180
5	ADAMS	42	M	160

a file for two modes of access, and the addition or deletion of a record in either mode must also accommodate its effect on the other. For example, if we access the file through the directory and delete the first record in one of the sublists, we must adjust the link in the last record in the preceding sublist so that the continuous linked list is maintained. Referring to the file just illustrated, if we delete the LETTUCE record, we must adjust the pointer in the CORN record to point to LIMAS. This accommodation can be accomplished by always saving the location of the previous directory entry as we precede with our search routine or by creating the file as a doubly linked list.

Continuing with our illustration, a search for OKRA would progress down the key values in the directory to PARSLEY since this is the first value for which OKRA ≤ PARSLEY. Then the search transfers to location 9 in the primary list and continues its sequential search until OKRA is found or until a key that has a value greater than OKRA is found. This particular example

FIGURE 4-3
LIST WITH
ONE-LEVEL
DIRECTORY

Directory

Key	Ptr.
BROCCOLI	1
CORN	5
PARSLEY	9
TOMATOES	14

Directory Element Format

High key in sublist	Beginning addr. of sublist

List

	Key	Data	Link
1	ASPARAGUS		2
2	BEANS		3
3	BEETS		18
4	POTATOES		16
5	CABBAGE		6
6	CARROTS		8
7	SQUASH		17
8	CORN		*(9)
9	LETTUCE		10
10	LIMAS		11
11	OKRA		12
12	ONIONS		13
13	PARSLEY		*(14)
14	PEAS		15
15	PEPPERS		4
16	SPINACH		7
17	TOMATOES		*
18	BROCCOLI		*(5)

using the directory used only six looks to find OKRA instead of the eleven that would have been required in a sequential search of the list.

Since we have seen that by using a directory we are able to reduce the number of looks necessary to find a record, it is appropriate to ask the question: "What is the optimum number relationship between a directory and a list?"

To gain an intuitive feel for the answer, consider a list of 100 records. A sequential search of this list would require 50.5 looks on an average. If we use a directory of two entries, we divide the list into 50 record sublists and a search would, on the average, require 1.5 looks in the directory plus 25.5 looks in the corresponding sublist or 27 looks total. Using this technique we can construct Figure 4-4.

Inspection of this figure should tell us that the optimum size for the directory is between 8 and 16.[*] The exact optimum can be obtained using differential calculus in the following manner.

Let N = number of elements in the list.

Let X = number of elements in a sublist.

Then N/X = total number of sublists, and, therefore, the number of entries in the directory.

$\frac{1}{2}(X + 1)$ = average number of looks in a sublist.

$\frac{1}{2}\left(\frac{N}{X} + 1\right)$ = average number of looks in the directory.

L = total number of looks.

$$L = \frac{1}{2}(X + 1) + \frac{1}{2}\left(\frac{N}{X} + 1\right) = \frac{1}{2}\left(X + \frac{N}{X} + 2\right)$$

---

[*]If the readers are unfamiliar with calculus, they can omit this derivation of optimum list size and still understand the results.

FIGURE 4-4
RELATIONSHIP OF
DIRECTORY AND
SUBLIST SIZE TO
SEARCH EFFICIENCY

Directory Size	Sublist Size	Total Average Looks
1	100	51.5
2	50	27.0
4	25	15.5
8	12 or 13	11.3
10	10	11.0
16	6 or 7	12.1
20	5	13.5
32	3 or 4	18.5
50	2	27.0

By differentiating this equation with respect to X and setting $dL/dX = 0$, we can find the minimum value for L.

Thus
$$L = \frac{X}{2} + \frac{N}{2X} + 1$$

$$\frac{dL}{dX} = \frac{1}{2} - \frac{N}{2X^2}$$

When $dL/dX = 0$,

$$\frac{1}{2} - \frac{N}{2X^2} = 0$$

$$\frac{1}{2} = \frac{N}{2X^2}$$

$$X^2 = N$$

$X = \sqrt{N}$ for optimum sublist size, but the directory size is

$$\frac{N}{X} = \frac{N}{\sqrt{N}} = \sqrt{N} \quad \text{also.}$$

Thus the optimum search condition for a search using a one-level directory occurs when the directory size equals the sublist size.

In this example, when $N = 100$, then the directory and each sublist should contain $\sqrt{100}$ or 10 elements each.

When we study multiple-level directories, the same question arises concerning optimum directory and sublist size. Since the current-level directory and next lower level can be viewed as a repetition of the one-level directory case at any level of the directory structure, it therefore follows that the optimum situation occurs when the highest-level directory, each lower-level subdirectory, and each sublist are the same size.

This means that to calculate this size, we take the R root of the number of records N where $R =$ number of levels plus 1. For example, for a one-level directory, $R = 1 + 1 = 2$. Therefore, we take the square root. For a two-level directory, $R = 2 + 1 = 3$, and we take the cube root.

Since we have determined that for a single-level directory the optimum searching efficiency occurs when the number of elements in the directory is the same as the number of records in each sublist, we can now turn to the question of how many records a list must contain before we can gain a search advantage by using a directory instead of a sequential search; that is, if N is the number of records in a list, at which values of N will the number of looks for a one-level directory search be less than the number of looks required for a sequential search?

$$\text{Directory looks} = L_1 = \tfrac{1}{2}(\sqrt{N} + 1 + \sqrt{N} + 1) = \sqrt{N} + 1$$

$$\text{Sequential looks} = L_2 = \tfrac{1}{2}(N + 1)$$

Therefore the directory requires fewer looks when

$$L_1 < L_2$$

or when $\qquad \sqrt{N} + 1 < \tfrac{1}{2}(N + 1)$

Thus $\qquad 2\sqrt{N} + 2 < N + 1$

$$2\sqrt{N} < N - 1$$

$$4N < N^2 - 2N + 1 \qquad \text{and} \qquad 0 < N^2 - 6N + 1$$

or $\qquad N^2 - 6N + 1 > 0$

Using the quadratic formula, we find that for $N > 5.8$ or $N < 0.2$, the directory will require fewer looks. However, $N < 0.2$ would be an empty list, and since N must be a nonnegative integer, we conclude that for $N \geq 6$ the directory will, on the average, require fewer looks. Figure 4-5 illustrates this conclusion.

Figures 4-6 and 4-7 and their accompanying pseudocodes show the creation and searching of a file with a single-level directory. The creation algorithm begins by first creating a single linked list of the records in the file in either ascending or descending order. The number of records to be assigned to each sublist, and therefore to each directory entry, is determined by taking the square root of the number of records in the file and assigning this to the variable M. Next we progress down the file linked list and create a directory entry for each set of M records encountered, and we provide for the possibility of creating one short sublist for the last entry in the directory. If we want disjoint sublists, then we set the pointer field in the last record in each sublist to "end" as soon as its directory entry is created. We link the directory entries at the end to facilitate addition and deletion of directory entries should it be needed as the result of heavy update activity in the file.

FIGURE 4-5 COMPARISON OF
SEQUENTIAL AND ONE-LEVEL
DIRECTORY SEARCH TECHNIQUES

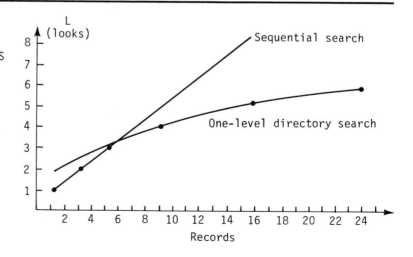

150

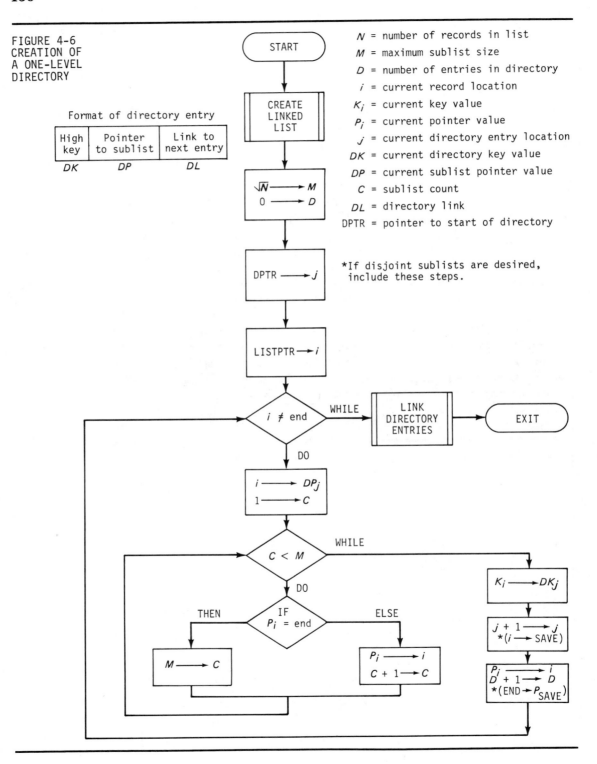

FIGURE 4-6
CREATION OF
A ONE-LEVEL
DIRECTORY

Format of directory entry

High key	Pointer to sublist	Link to next entry
DK	DP	DL

START

CREATE LINKED LIST

$\sqrt{N} \longrightarrow M$
$0 \longrightarrow D$

$DPTR \longrightarrow j$

$LISTPTR \longrightarrow i$

$i \neq end$ — WHILE → LINK DIRECTORY ENTRIES → EXIT

DO

$i \longrightarrow DP_j$
$1 \longrightarrow C$

$C < M$ — WHILE

DO

IF $P_i = end$

THEN   ELSE

$M \longrightarrow C$

$P_i \longrightarrow i$
$C + 1 \longrightarrow C$

$K_i \longrightarrow DK_j$

$j + 1 \longrightarrow j$
$*(i \longrightarrow SAVE)$

$P_i \longrightarrow i$
$D + 1 \longrightarrow D$
$*(END \longrightarrow P_{SAVE})$

N = number of records in list
M = maximum sublist size
D = number of entries in directory
i = current record location
K_i = current key value
P_i = current pointer value
j = current directory entry location
DK = current directory key value
DP = current sublist pointer value
C = sublist count
DL = directory link
$DPTR$ = pointer to start of directory

*If disjoint sublists are desired, include these steps.

CREATION OF
A ONE-LEVEL
DIRECTORY

```
/*  LISTPTR = start of primary list */
/*  N = number of records in primary list */
/*  M = maximum sublist size */
/*  D = number of entries in directory */
/*  I,K(I),P(I) = location, key, and pointer of
    record at I */
/*  J = current directory entry location */
/*  DK,DP,DL = key, pointer, and link of current
    directory entry */
/*  C = count of elements in current sublist */
/*  DPTR = pointer to start of directory */


PROC          DIRECTORY-CREATE
    do creation of linked list
    M = √N
    D = 0
    J = DPTR
    I = LISTPTR
    WHILE I ≠ end  DO
        DP(J) = I
        C = 1
        WHILE  C < M   DO
            IF  P(I) = end
                THEN  C = M
                ELSE  I = P(I)
                        C = C + 1
            ENDIF
        ENDDO
        DK(J) = K(I)
        J = J + 1
        *(SAVE = I)          /* needed if disjoint sublists are desired */
        I = P(I)
        D = D + 1
        *(P(SAVE) = end)   /* needed if disjoint sublists are desired */
    ENDDO
    do linking of directory entries
END PROC
```

FIGURE 4-7 SEARCH OF A
LINKED LIST USING A
ONE-LEVEL DIRECTORY

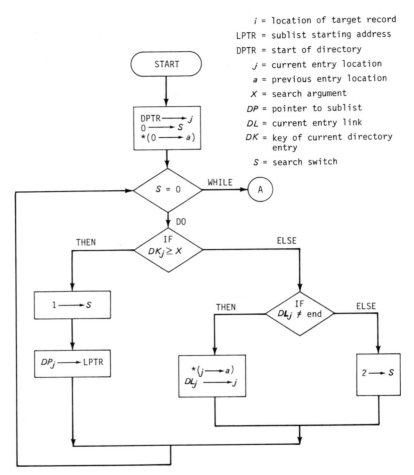

i = location of target record
LPTR = sublist starting address
DPTR = start of directory
j = current entry location
a = previous entry location
X = search argument
DP = pointer to sublist
DL = current entry link
DK = key of current directory entry
S = search switch

*If this routine is to accommodate deletion in the list, then the previous
directory entry must be saved in case a directory entry is also deleted.
It is also useful in maintaining a file that is a single linked list.

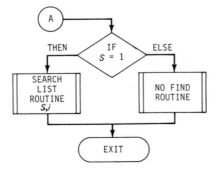

SEARCH OF A LINKED
LIST USING A
ONE-LEVEL DIRECTORY

```
/*  DPTR = pointer to start of directory */
/*  LPTR = pointer to start of target sublist */
/*  J = location of current entry in directory */
/*  A = location of previous entry in directory */
/*  X = search argument */
/*  DK,DP,DL = key, pointer, and link of current
    directory entry */
/*  S = search switch */
/*  I = location of target record in list */
/*  steps marked *(   ) are needed if search is
    used to update */


PROC     DIRECTORY-SEARCH
    J = DPTR
    S = 0
    *(A = 0)
    WHILE S = 0   DO
        IF   DK(J) ≥ X
            THEN   S = 1
                     LPTR = DP(J)
            ELSE
                IF   DL(J) ≠ end
                    THEN *(A = J)
                           J = DL(J)
                    ELSE   S = 2          /* record missing */
                ENDIF
        ENDIF
    ENDDO
    IF   S = 1
        THEN   do SEARCH-LNKLIST; send DP(J), X return S,I
        ELSE   do nofind routine
    ENDIF
END PROC
```

The search algorithm assumes that we are searching a file created in ascending order, using a directory created in the manner just described. It is quite similar to the search of a linked list described in Chapter 3 except that it returns the value of the starting location of the corresponding sublist instead of the value of the location of the target record.

We have already mentioned that additions and deletions to a linked list can affect the values in a directory entry. Therefore, the add and delete routines must check to see if the beginning or ending element in a sublist is involved. Changing the first element in a sublist causes the location field of its corresponding directory entry to change value, and changing the last entry in a sublist affects the value of the key field in the corresponding directory entry.

Additions to a list that is accompanied by a directory does not affect the number of entries in the directory as long as we are willing to accept the possibility that one or more of the sublists may become considerably longer than the others. On the other hand, repeated deletions to a particular sublist can result in an empty sublist, which would cause its corresponding entry to be eliminated from the directory. This is accomplished by deleting the entry from the directory as we suggested earlier by creating the directory as a linked list, or by setting the key field in the entry to a null value. However, if null values are used, then a search of the directory must check for this before each key compare is made. In either case, a relatively high activity of adding and/or deleting records from a list can cause sublists of widely differing lengths. We can usually keep this problem from becoming severe by recreating the list or file and its accompanying directory after regular intervals of update activity; this practice is refered to as file *reorganization*.

MULTILEVEL DIRECTORIES

Multilevel directories are directories that are organized in a hierarchical structure such that only the lowest-level directory entries have pointers to sublists in the file. All other levels have entries that point to a subdirectory. Each level, however, covers the range of the entire file. As we will see later, a directory is a special case of a tree structure.

The simplest form of a multilevel directory is a two-level directory. In this case, there is a master directory at the highest level in which each entry points to a directory of a portion of the file (subdirectory) (see Figure 4-8).

A search for DAVID starts, as all searches start, with the master directory at location 200. The second entry has a key value greater than DAVID; therefore, the search moves to the subdirectory at location 60. The first entry in the subdirectory has a key value greater than DAVID; so the search moves to the sublist starting at location 11 at which the links are followed to DAVID.

Considerations in adding to and deleting from a file with a multilevel directory are similar to those for updating a single-level directory, except that provisions must be made for changes to either end of a sublist that can propagate changes through more than one level in the directory.

Creation of a multilevel directory is essentially iterations of the procedure

FIGURE 4-8 DIAGRAM OF
TWO-LEVEL DIRECTORY

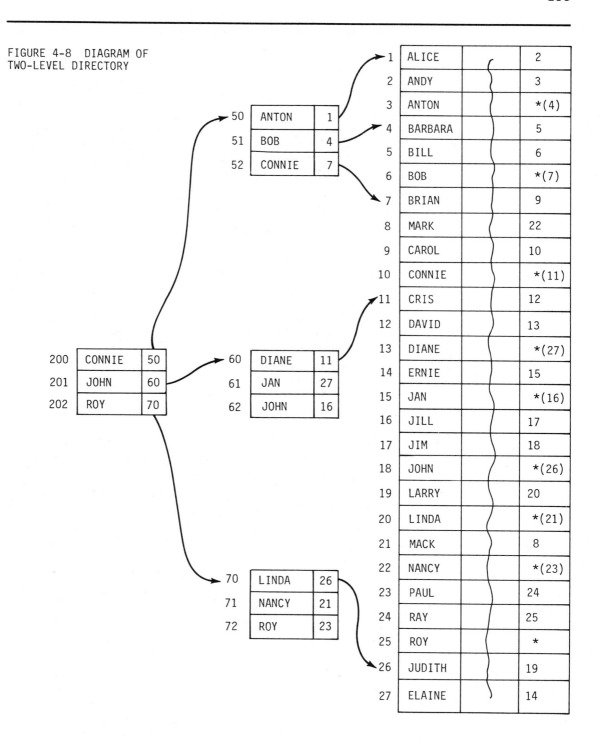

to create a single-level directory with provisions that the upper-level directory location fields point to other directories instead of to a sublist in the file.

Since the main purpose of using a directory is usually to increase searching efficiency, it is appropriate to compare the relative efficiencies of the search techniques discussed so far. This comparison is shown in Figure 4-9. In each case where directories are involved, the optimum size for sublists and directories is used. This optimum size is achieved when the sublist and each directory or subdirectory have the same number of elements. When there is no integer for which this is true, a slight compromise must be made. If we use the technique described earlier, in which R = directory levels + 1 and sublist size was calculated as $\lfloor \sqrt[R]{N} \rfloor$, we have one shortened sublist at each level of our structure except at the highest level of the directory, which contains one or slightly more additional entries.

In Figure 4-9, the average number of looks using any of the directories is calculated as:

$$L = \frac{R(\sqrt[R]{N} + 1)}{2}$$

This formula for the average number of looks follows from the rationale that for a given optimum directory + list structure, we must, on the average, examine half of R lists each having a length of $\sqrt[R]{N}$ elements. The formula is exact when $\sqrt[R]{N}$ is an integer and will otherwise yield a value within 0.5 looks from the true value (for $N \geq 10$).

FIGURE 4-9   COMPARISON OF THE RELATIVE EFFICIENCIES OF VARIOUS SEARCH TECHNIQUES

Search Method ⟶

Number of Records	Sequential Search	Binary Search	One-Level Directory	Two-Level Directory	Three-Level Directory
10	5.5	2.9	4.2	4.7	5.6
50	25.5	4.7	8.1	7.0	7.3
100	50.5	5.8	11.0	8.5	8.3
500	250.5	8.0	23.4	13.4	11.5
1,000	500.5	9.0	32.6	16.5	13.2
5,000	2,500.5	11.3	71.7	27.1	18.8
10,000	5,000.5	12.4	101.0	33.8	22.0
100,000	50,000.5	15.6	317.2	71.1	37.6
1,000,000	500,000.5	18.9	1,001.0	151.5	65.2

Average Number of Looks (L)

Example: To calculate the optimum average number of looks for a list of 5000 records with a two-level directory, we have:

$$L = \frac{3(\sqrt[3]{5000} + 1)}{2}$$

$$= \frac{3(17.10 + 1)}{2}$$

$$= 27.1 \text{ looks}$$

It should be evident from our discussion that directories can offer a considerable advantage over sequential searching as list length increases. By employing multiple levels, directories can provide us with search times close to those that would be obtained with a binary search. These comparative search times for directories and binary searches are even closer than Figure 4-9 indicates since a look for a binary search may take twice as much time as a look with a directory. Directories also offer the advantage of flexible file organization.

The main disadvantages to the use of directories are storage overhead for the directories and the fact that file maintenance causes similar maintenance to the directories, but these disadvantages are often quite acceptable when weighed against the benefits.

FURTHER APPLICATIONS OF DIRECTORIES TO FILES

In our previous discussion, we saw how directories can be used to improve searching efficiency on files that have been implemented as linear lists when we want to access records in an order other than their natural sequential one.

We need to emphasize here that although directories can greatly improve average access times when we process a file in a more-or-less random fashion, the use of directories to process a list according to its sequential order greatly increases average access times. There are basically two reasons for this. First, sequential processing saves the overhead of the directory search routine for each record. It is much easier and quicker to simply move to the next sequential record than to search through, on the average, half of the directory entries of each corresponding subdirectory at each level and then search half of the corresponding sublist before we access our record. For example, for a file of 1000 records using a two-level directory, we need 16.5 looks to find the next record instead of one look to access it sequentially. Second, if a file with a two-level directory resides on a disk drive, a typical arrangement is to use the top-level directory to position us to the proper cylinder, and the corresponding lower-level directory will reside on this cylinder to position us to the proper track. (The rationale for this arrangement is explained later.) This means that in the preceding arrangement we have to perform three I/O operations to access any record in the file—one for each level of the directory and one for the block containing our record. Since we cannot expect the disk heads to be positioned over the top-level directory at the beginning of the access, we normally experience head movement (seeks) before the first two I/O operations. On the other hand, sequential access of a record requires an I/O operation only when a new record block is needed. If we choose to block our records, it could result in a much smaller percentage of I/O operations to process a file. However, even if we do not block our records, we still require only one I/O operation per record access with very infrequent head movement since head movement is required only when we move to the next cylinder.

The reason that we deviated from our original conclusion about the optimum sizes of directories, subdirectories, and sublists when we stored a file on magnetic disk is that the physical characteristics of the disk drive outweigh the considerations of ideal directory and sublist lengths; that is, on a disk, all looks are definitely not equal, because it usually takes more time to perform a seek than to scan an entire disk track. Therefore, we arrange our directories to minimize head movement and I/O operations. (At this point, readers may want to review disk characteristics presented in Chapter 1.)

In summary, we conclude that directories are desirable if we want to process a list in a random fashion, but they are undesirable if we want to process it sequentially.

It so happens that there are many applications in which we sometimes want to process a file randomly, and at other times we want to process it sequentially. One such example is a large payroll file. Information concerning an individual's pay status is retrieved and updated throughout the month in a purely random, or at least unpredictable, manner. In this case, directories can greatly facilitate rapid access times to individual records. Yet, at the end of the month, every employee is paid according to information in the payroll records; so it is desirable in this instance to process the file sequentially.

Another such example is the file of student records at a university. Class grade reports require random entry of information into individual student records, but after all grades have been posted, individual grade reports for each student are printed sequentially.

Files that are organized as lists with accompanying directories so that they can be processed sequentially or randomly are frequently referred to as *indexed sequential files*. The desirability of processing a file in this manner is so commonplace in computer applications that most major vendors supply data management software or access methods that support the creation and processing of such files.

IBM has long supported such files through its Indexed Sequential Access Method (ISAM) which we describe here. Similar capabilities are found with other vendors; however, some specifics may differ slightly. IBM and other vendors choose to use the term "index" instead of "directory" when referring to computing and data-processing activities, but, in this book, we use directory to avoid ambiguity due to other uses of the word "index" in computing literature.

ISAM files consist of three major components: indexes (directories), the prime data area, and overflow. There are two levels of indexes for each ISAM file, with an optional third level if desired. The two required levels correspond closely to the two-level arrangement just described; that is, there is a cylinder index with an entry for each cylinder in the file and a track index located on each corresponding cylinder. Should the cylinder index become large, then a master index that contains an entry for each track in the cylinder index can be created. All index entries are formatted using the count-key-data option described in Chapter 1, so that only one I/O operation is needed for each level of index that is scanned.

The master index entries are formatted so that the key block for each entry contains the high key value for the corresponding track in the cylinder index, and the data block for the entry contains the physical address of the track.

The cylinder index is formatted in a similar fashion such that, for each entry, the key block contains the high key value for the corresponding track index, and the data block contains the physical address of this track index.

The track index is a bit more involved; there are two count-key-data entries for each prime data track used in this cylinder. The first entry, called the *normal entry*, contains the high key of all records physically residing on the track, followed by the physical location of the track, in the same count-key-data format used before. The second entry, called the *overflow entry*, contains the high key for records that have overflowed from this track, followed by the physical address of the first record in the linked list of records that have overflowed from the track. If there are no overflow records for a track, the key block of the overflow entry is identical to the corresponding normal entry and the data block (location) carries a special value (see Figure 4-10).

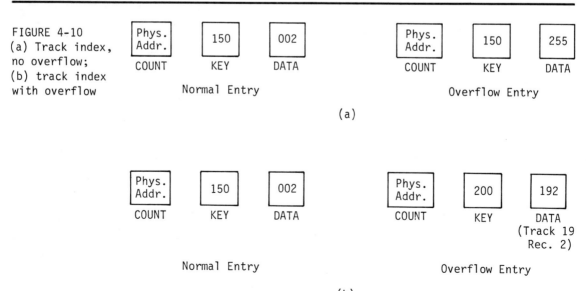

FIGURE 4-10
(a) Track index, no overflow;
(b) track index with overflow

The prime data area contains data records from the file in sequential order stored in count-key-data format. When the file is first created, all data records are contained in the prime data area and, except for the possibility of flaw tracks, these records are in physically sequential order; the records may be blocked or unblocked.

A record is added to the first track whose high key is greater than the key being added such that the physical sequential order of the track is maintained. Should the added record cause an overflow condition, then the new record is inserted into its proper position, and the previous high record on the track is placed in an overflow area. Additional overflow records from the track become part of the linked list of overflow records associated with the corresponding prime data track. In this way, the logical sequential order of the file is maintained even though the physical order of the file has now been broken (see Figure 4-11).

Deleted records are simply marked as deleted, and their space is lost for reuse until the file is reorganized. However, a deleted record cell is not sent to overflow as a result of a record addition.

There are two types of overflow areas, cylinder and independent. *Cylinder overflow* is allocated by tracks on each cylinder of the file, and it is more efficient with respect to access time because additional seeks are not required once the track index has been read. However, cylinder overflow can cause wasted disk storage if overflow does not occur more or less uniformly throughout the file. *Independent overflow* refers to one common or global overflow area that can serve all cylinders. This type of overflow area can be more efficient with respect to space utilization, but it can cause access time to increase due to additional seeks.

FIGURE 4-11 SEQUENCE OF
OVERFLOW FOR A TRACK;
ONLY RECORD KEYS ARE SHOWN

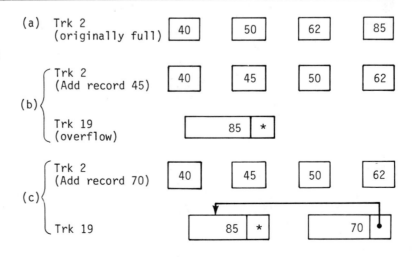

A common arrangement is to provide the bulk of the overflow as cylinder overflow with a small independent overflow for exceptional conditions. In either case, once records are sent to overflow, the corresponding linked list must be read by following the links, which requires a separate I/O operation for each look. This causes access time to degrade considerably. Therefore, a file reorganization should be planned so that the percentage of records residing in overflow for any length of time is kept to a minimum.

INVERTED FILES

An inverted file is a file that has associated with it at least one total directory ordered on a field from the file other than the primary key on which the file is ordered. If such a directory exists for every field in the file, the file is said to be *totally inverted*. Otherwise an inverted file is said to be *partially inverted*. The secondary directories for an inverted file are referred to as *inverted indices.*

The term *inverted file* comes from the concept that the roles of a record and one of its attributes are inverted. Normally we locate a record to determine the value of one of it attributes, but in this case we use the attribute value to locate the record.

The entries in an inverted index contain values from the field in the main file on which the index is ordered and identifiers (or locations) of records in the main file that correspond to these values.

ONE-TO-ONE INVERSION

When there exists a one-to-one relationship between records in the main file and order field values in the inverted index, the order field is a secondary key. This situation is quite common. For instance, suppose that we have an employee file that we wish to search by social security number or by employee name. We can order the file on the field for which we make the majority of our searches and create an inverted index for searching on the secondary key (see Figures 4-12 and 4-13).

There are good reasons for using either of the techniques shown in Figure 4-13. Using an inverted index that contains the location of a record allows us to go directly to the record without performing another search on the main file using the record identifier. Consequently, it is, in general, slightly faster. However, if there is any movement of records in the main file, the corresponding locations in the inverted index must be updated accordingly.

There is also the possibility that there may not be a convenient way of determining the location of the records directly. This is usually the case when records are stored on external media, such as magnetic disks, and we are creating inverted indices at the applications level using vendor supplied access methods, such as indexed sequential routines. In this case, using the identifier with the inverted index is not only more convenient, it is also the only practical choice.

FIGURE 4-12
PRIMARY FILE

	S.S. Number	Name	Division	Pay Grade	Years Service
1	242533209	SMITH, JOHN E	SALES	12	10
2	284627452	BAKER, JOSEPHUS	SUPPLY	8	3
3	322113789	JOHNSON, MARY L.	SALES	10	3
4	357821603	EMORY, JAMES R.	SUPPLY	7	1
5	379428917	WASHINGTON, JUDY H.	D.P.	8	1
6	426720412	ORACLE, DALEY D.	D.P.	11	4
7	448536821	YOKUM, ABNER	SALES	10	5
8	484696353	BRAUN, FRITZ R.	PERSONNEL	8	2
9	512128256	LANE, LOIS	PERSONNEL	9	6
10	569032184	CALDWELL, KAREN	D.P.	9	2

FIGURE 4-13
INVERTED INDEX
(a) Using identifier;
(b) using location

BAKER, JOSEPHUS	284627452
BRAUN, FRITZ R.	484696353
CALDWELL, KAREN	569032184
EMORY, JAMES R.	357821603
JOHNSON, MARY L.	322113789
LANE, LOIS	512128256
ORACLE, DALEY D.	426720412
SMITH, JOHN E.	242533209
WASHINGTON, JUDY H.	379428917
YOKUM, ABNER	448536821

(a)

BAKER, JOSEPHUS	2
BRAUN, FRITZ R.	8
CALDWELL, KAREN	10
EMORY, JAMES R.	4
JOHNSON, MARY L.	3
LANE, LOIS	9
ORACLE, DALEY D.	6
SMITH, JOHN E.	1
WASHINGTON, JUDY	5
YOKUM, ABNER	7

(b)

It is worth noting that an inverted index is still simply a directory, and any procedures that normally apply to the use of a directory, such as binary searching or level directories, also apply to it (see Figure 4-14).

ONE-TO-MANY INVERSION

We also want to build inverted indices for fields that do not contain unique values. This presents us with a one-to-many relationship between the inverted index and the file.

This type of situation arises when, using the employee file from the previous section, we want to find all employees who work in a particular division (see Figure 4-15).

MULTILISTS

The variable number of locations (or identifiers) can present a problem if the file is large and if the order field has relatively few values. In this case, an alternative is to create an index that points to only the first record for a particular field value and then create a linked sublist of other records with the same value. This structure is called a *multilist*; namely, there is a separate linked list for each value of a given attribute (see Figure 4-16).

It should be evident by now that the advantage of using inverted files is the flexibility we have in searching on different attributes or fields within a record. We can conveniently process such questions as "List all employees at pay grade 10." The disadvantage in using inverted files is storage overhead, which is the same disadvantage as when we use directories of any sort, but the problem is compounded with inverted files.

In some cases, a partial solution to this problem is practical. If all or nearly all inquiries (searches) that use a particular field in a record are based on the value of that field, then the field can be stored only in the inverted index and not stored in the main file itself.

Example: Suppose we want to associate a parking-space number with each employee in the employee file of the previous section. However, the only time we need this value is when we want additional information about the individual who uses this parking space, such as name, division, and so on. Therefore, we do not include a parking-space field in the main file, and we create the inverted index shown in Figure 4-17. If we want to find out who belongs in space M-8 and where he or she works, we proceed from the inverted index to the record with an ID value of 379428917, and we find that this space is assigned to JUDY WASHINGTON of D.P.

Of course, this technique is very inefficient, with respect to search time, if we abstract from the main file fields that are needed routinely for searches that do not initiate through the inverted index in which we store them.

FIGURE 4-14 SEARCHING A FILE WITH A SINGLE INVERTED INDEX (SECONDARY KEY) USING
A RECORD IDENTIFIER

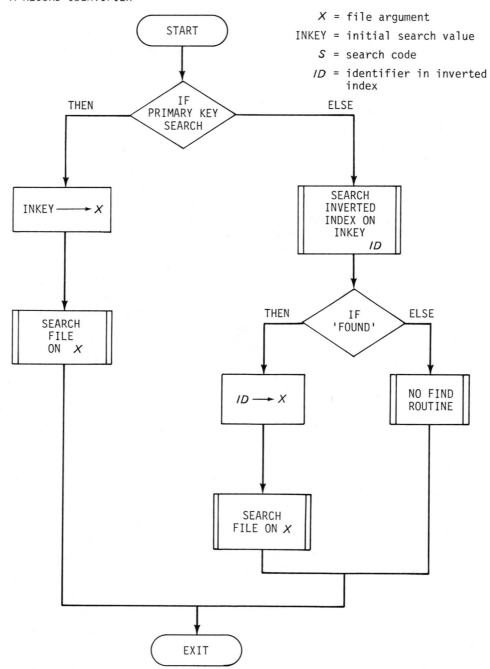

FIGURE 4-15
INVERTED INDEX
ON DIVISION

Division	Locations
D.P.	5,6,10
PERSONNEL	8,9
SALES	1,3,7
SUPPLY	2,4

FIGURE 4-16
MULTILIST

Division	First Location	Link
D.P.	5	20
PERSONNEL	8	22
SALES	1	23
SUPPLY	2	25

Record Location		Link
20	6	21
21	10	*
22	9	*
23	3	24
24	7	*
25	4	*

FIGURE 4-17 INVERTED
INDEX ON PARKING SPACE

Parking Space Number	ID
M-1	242533209
M-2	426720412
M-3	448536821
M-4	322113789
M-5	512128256
M-6	569032184
M-7	484696353
M-8	379428917
W-1	284627452
W-2	357821603

HASHING

In previous sections, we used directories of one or more levels to quickly bring our search to a relatively short sublist that contains or should contain our target record. In his book *Data Structure and Management* (1970), Ivan Flores called this process—and any other technique that quickly isolates a record to a small subset of a list—"neighborhood locatability," which is quite descriptive of the process. As you recall, the greatest disadvantage to the use of directories is storage overhead. Another method of achieving neighborhood locatability, which can lessen this storage overhead and often improve search time, is called hashing.

Hashing is a many-to-one mapping that does not usually preserve order performed on the keys of a list. Hashing is achieved by deriving a *hash value* from the key that indicates to which sublist or neighborhood a record belongs. This sublist is sometimes called a *bucket* when the sublist is limited to a fixed number of records. It is worth mentioning here that the greatest disadvantage of hashing is the difficulty in producing a relatively uniform number of records in the sublists. This problem does not cause storage overhead when the primary list is contained totally in main memory since the sublists can be created as linked lists, all residing within a single host vector with elements being assigned to the sublists from a common space list. However, when the list resides on an external medium, such as magnetic disk, a nonuniform mapping of records results in wasted storage or overflow problems. Regardless of where the list resides, a nonuniform distribution of records can generate a long, worst-case search time, and this worst-case situation is amplified when the list is on an external medium.

Several terms that are commonly used to discuss hashing are given here. *Synonyms* are records whose keys hash to the same value and, thus, as just described, these records belong to the same sublist or bucket. A *collision* occurs when the keys of two records hash to the same value. In other words, when we hash synonyms, we get collisions. Collision handling is fundamental to hashing applications and must be provided for. In the case of sublists that are created as linked lists (described earlier), the result of a collision is simply the insertion of the given record with the rest of its synonyms into an appropriate linked list. But, in the case of buckets, repeated collisions cause a bucket to overflow, and additional steps must be taken. *Overflow* is defined as the condition of assigning more records to a given area than it can accommodate. One way of lessening the likelihood of bucket overflow is to place the list or file into an area that is divided into buckets that are larger than the expected number of records (synonyms) they must accommodate. We define the *loading factor* as the predicted ratio of the average amount of space that will be used in a bucket to the amount of space that is available; it is calculated as L.F. $= n/bk$, where n is the number of records in the file, b is the number of buckets, and k is the number of records that will fit in one bucket. We examine the problem of overflow more fully later in this section.

Although hashing can reduce storage requirements when a relatively uniform distribution of records is possible, its most desirable feature is that, under these conditions, it is usually faster than the directory approach since the hashing will yield the desired primary sublist or neighborhood in one operation, without having to search through the various levels of a directory. This search-time advantage is amplified when the choice involves both records and directories stored on disk because, in this case, an I/O operation is normally required for each level of the directory and again for the target record. With hashing, only one I/O is usually required. Therefore, under random-search requirements, hashing is usually faster than directories as long as the hashing algorithm yields a relatively uniform distribution.

Hashing is not desirable when there is also a requirement to process a list in logical, sequential order. In this case, it is important to employ a technique that preserves logical order, such as is the case with directories, so that the list can be processed as an ordered sequential list. With hashing, every record must be accessed as an independent random search, which can greatly increase sequential processing time if records reside on magnetic disk, since logical order usually bears no relation to physical locations or neighborhoods.

HASHING TECHNIQUES

The selection of a good hashing technique is extremely important to overall search performance, as well as to storage utilization, yet it is sometimes difficult to predict which algorithm will give a more uniform distribution of records. In this case, it may be wise to test empirically those algorithms under consideration. This testing can be done by taking a large random sample of keys from the file, or the whole file if this is practical, and tabulating the frequency of the possible hash values.

There are many possible hashing techniques, and programmers are free to choose from these or make up their own techniques as long as they produce a mapping that is acceptably uniform. A comparison of a number of techniques was published in the *Communications of the ACM* by Lum, Yuen, and Dodd in April 1971. Anyone desiring a fuller treatment of hashing techniques is directed there, as well as to the treatment of the subject by Knuth in volume 3 of *The Art of Computer Programming*. Here we treat three techniques that are commonly used, simple to implement, and perform well under general conditions.

Division There seems to be a consensus among those who have studied hashing algorithms that the division method is the best general-purpose algorithm known so far. This method does not produce the most uniform distribution under all cases, but *when used properly*, it usually gives a good if not near uniform distribution. It rarely gives a poor distribution, and it is extremely simple to implement. Figure 4-18 shows hash value by division.

The method works by dividing a key by the number of sublists or buckets desired and assigning the record to the sublist that is associated with each possible value of the remainder. For instance, suppose that a key consists of 4 numerical digits, and it is decided that there should be 23 sublists. (The number of sublists depends on the desired average sublist size.) Then the hash value is:

$$HASHVAL = (KEY(mod\ 23)) + 1.$$

Example:

```
if KEY = 1234
then HASHVAL = (1234(mod 23)) + 1
      HASHVAL = (15) + 1 = 16
```

and the record would be assigned to sublist (bucket) number 16.

```
if KEY = 2550
then HASHVAL = (2550(mod 23)) + 1
            = (20) + 1 = 21
```

and the record would be assigned to sublist number 21.

```
if KEY = 2300
then HASHVAL = (2300(mod 23)) + 1
            = (0) + 1 = 1
```

and the record would be assigned to sublist number 1.

Several considerations can affect the efficiency of this method. First, we need to consider how many sublists to use. Basically, we decide on the maximum number of records that a sublist should hold and divide that number into the total number of records in the file $(b = N/k$, where b is the number of sublists or buckets, N is the number of records in the file, and k is the desired sublist size).

FIGURE 4-18 HASH VALUE BY DIVISION

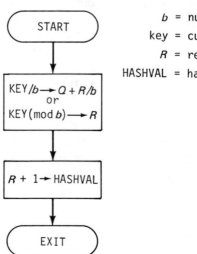

b = number of sublists
key = current key value
R = remainder
HASHVAL = hash value

If the key values form a dense set of values (in other words, if there is a record with a key value for every possible key value in the key range), and if there are no duplicates, then any choice of b will give as nearly perfect a uniform distribution as can be obtained (exactly uniform if N is a multiple of b). If the key values do not form a dense set and cannot easily be transformed into a dense set, then the choice of b deserves more thought.

One must obviously take care not to divide by a value of b that contains a factor that divides into most of the key values. For instance, if all key values are even numbers and one divides by an even number, there are no odd remainders and only half of the sublists can be used.

In fact, the choice of an even number for b is not a good choice any time you have significantly less than a dense set of key values, because division by an even number preserves an even-or-odd property of the dividend in the remainder; that is, if most of the key values are odd, then most of the remainders will be odd.

Much of the literature suggests that b should be the first prime number that equals or exceeds the $b = N/k$ described earlier. This was borne out by tests of Lum, Yuen, and Dodd, but they also found that choosing the first odd number equal to or greater than $b = N/k$ works almost as well.

Division seems to imply that the keys are all numeric, so what happens when they are not? One choice is to treat the bits of the key, or a set portion of the keys, as a binary number and proceed as above.

Example: A high-fidelity warehouse uses a code identifier as a key for all equipment in stock. The key is five bytes long and has the format shown in Figure 4-19. The fifth speaker stocked by the Pioneer Company has a key value of SPI05; in EBCDIC, this is $E2D7C9F0F5_{16}$. This can now be treated as a binary number and divided directly or, if a packing feature is available, the value can be packed first and then divided.

Packing on an IBM 360/370 yields 27905F. This number can now be treated as a packed decimal number and divided by another packed decimal representation of b. If a binary divide is desired, the rightmost character 'F' should be truncated before the divide to remove the repetitive bits, or we can simply divide by 16 and then b to produce the same effect.

When a fixed portion of a key is chosen for division, care must be taken to choose a portion that contains a minimum of repeated values.

Folding   Another method commonly used is called *folding*. In this technique, a key is divided into segments, usually roughly equal to the sublist size, and these segments are added to produce a hash value.

FIGURE 4-19

type	manufacturer	sequence no.
1 byte	2 bytes	2 bytes

Example: Given 9-digit keys that will be assigned to 1000 buckets, if

$$KEY = 242 \quad 786 \quad 473$$

then we add

$$
\begin{array}{r}
242 \\
786 \\
473 \\
\hline
1501
\end{array}
$$

We truncate the high-order digit and assign the record to bucket number 501. Care should be taken to assure that wraparound accounts for roughly an even multiple of buckets (b) so that truncation does not cause a skewing of record assignments.

Mid-square The mid-square technique involves squaring the key or a fixed portion of it and selecting a central portion of the square for sublist assignment.

Example: Given a file with 4-digit keys to be assigned to 100 buckets, if a

$$KEY = 4573$$
$$(KEY)^2 = 20912329$$

by selecting the central two digits and adding 1 to account for a value of 00, we assign the record to bucket number 13.

AN IMPLEMENTATION USING HASHING

To implement a hashing application, we must consider three things: the creation of the sublist through hashing, the search process, and updating. The creation and searching process are so similar that as soon as we design one, the other is a trivial modification. The update employs the search process to get the desired sublist and, at that point, the process is reduced to the updating of a linked list. Therefore, once we solve the creation problem, the rest is quite simple.

The design that we use contains three main features: a hashing algorithm that produces a hash value, a hash table that consists of pointers to each of the sublists, and a list or file containing exactly one sublist for each unique hash value produced by the hashing algorithm. At this point, the hash table may need further explanation.

The hash table contains an entry for each possible hash value that can be produced by the hashing algorithm. The hash value provides the displacement into the table, and a table entry contains the starting address of the corresponding sublist in the main list area. If an entry in the hash table corresponds to a hash value that was not produced by the hashing algorithm, then it will contain an end-of-list or null value. The hash table is simply a set of list pointers such that each pointer corresponds to a particular hash value (see Figure 4-20).

In the creation algorithm in Figure 4-21, we assume that records have been placed in contiguous locations of the list area or host vector and are in no particular order. The hash table has been initialized such that all entries contain end-of-list indicators. We proceed through the entire list one record at a time, hashing each key to determine to which sublist it belongs. This is achieved by using the hash value of the key as a displacement into the hash table. If the corresponding hash-table entry is "end," then we must start a new linked sublist by placing the location of the current record in the hash table. Otherwise, we append the current record to the sublist referenced by the hash table. When we reach the end of the original list, we have a set of linked sublists such that the elements of each sublist are synonyms for the particular hashing algorithm used. Hopefully, we will have approximately the same number of records in each sublist, or at least the distribution will be acceptable for our application. The distribution does depend on the hashing technique used and not on any other part of the creation algorithm. Therefore, if the distribution is unacceptable, we simply change the hashing technique and nothing else.

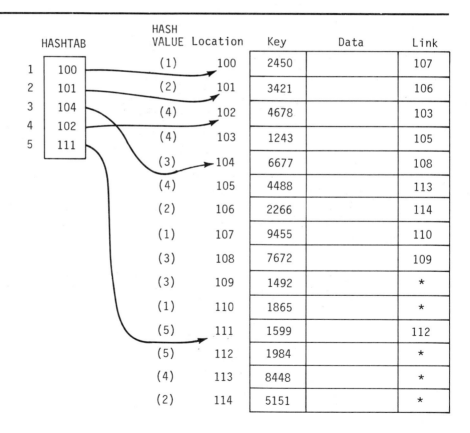

FIGURE 4-20
HASH TABLE

FIGURE 4-21 CREATION OF A
LIST FOR SEARCH
THROUGH HASHING

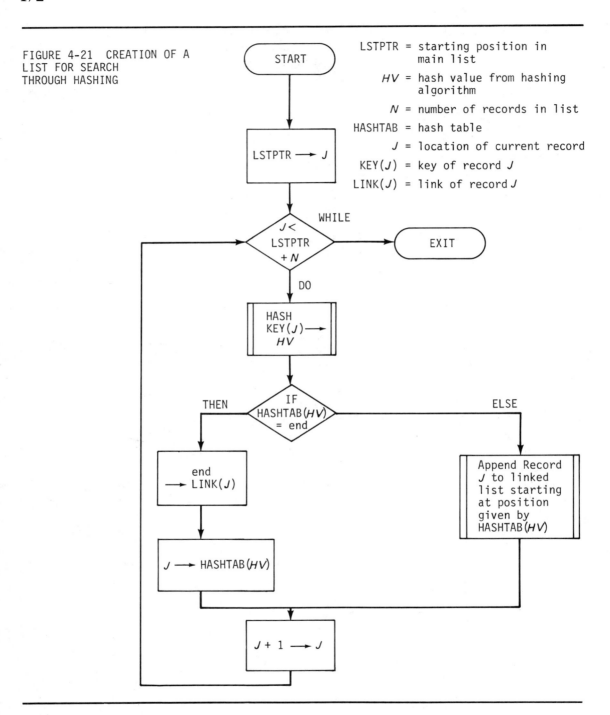

LSTPTR = starting position in
main list

HV = hash value from hashing
algorithm

N = number of records in list

HASHTAB = hash table

J = location of current record

KEY(J) = key of record J

LINK(J) = link of record J

CREATION OF A LIST
FOR SEARCH THROUGH
HASHING

```
/*   LSTPTR = starting position in main list */
/*   HV = hash value from hashing algorithm */
/*   N = number of records in list */
/*   HASHTAB = hash table; one pointer entry for each
     possible HV */
/*   J = location of current record in list */
/*   KEY(J),LINK(J) = key and link of record at J */


PROC    CREATE-HLIST
    J = LSTPTR
    WHILE  J < LSTPTR + N    DO
        do hashing routine; send KEY(J), return HV
        IF HASHTAB(HV) = end
            THEN LINK(J) = end
                HASHTAB(HV) = J
            ELSE do insert record at J to linked sublist
                    starting at position given by HASHTAB(HV)
        ENDIF
        J = J + 1
    ENDDO
END PROC
```

The search algorithm in Figure 4-22 is basically a slight modification of the creation algorithm. We hash a desired key value and proceed to the hash table. If no sublist exists for this hash value, we have a no find condition. Otherwise, the search is reduced to searching a simple linked list as we have done before.

An alternative to the use of a hash table is using the hash value as a displacement into the list area. Suppose we select a hashing algorithm that produces m possible hash values for a set of keys. We initially reserve the first m record locations of our list area for the first record of each of the m possible sublists, and we load the records into the list area one at a time as they are hashed for sublist assignment instead of placing them into the list area before hashing. If a key is hashed to a value that has not been encountered yet, the record is placed in the corresponding record location in the reserved portion of the list, and a new sublist is started. Otherwise, it is placed in the first available location after the first m positions and linked to its existing sublist of synonyms. This technique is illustrated in Figure 4-23, given that HASHVAL = KEY(MOD 3) + 1.

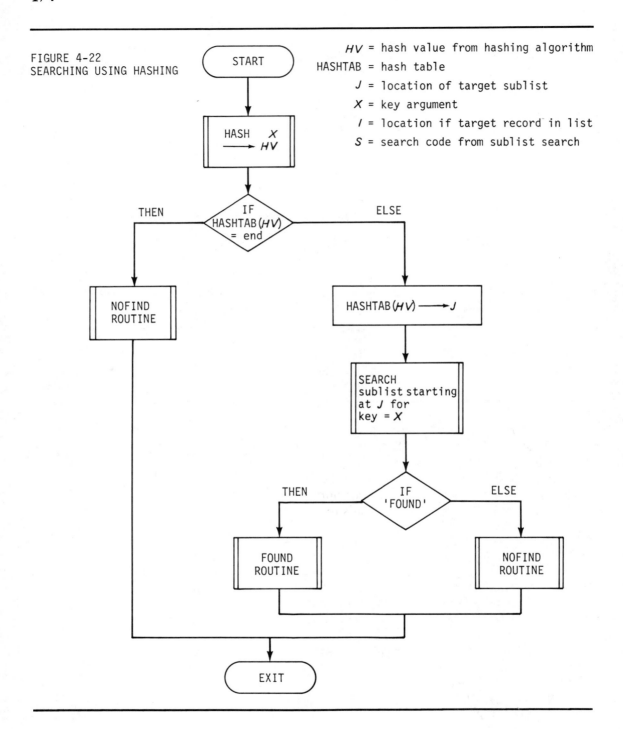

FIGURE 4-22
SEARCHING USING HASHING

SEARCHING USING HASHING

```
/*  S = search code */
/*  HV = hash value from hashing algorithm */
/*  HASHTAB = hash table */
/*  J = location of target sublist */
/*  X = key argument */
/*  I = location of target record in list */


PROC      HASH-SEARCH
     do hashing routine; send  X   return HV
     IF  HASHTAB(HV) = end
          THEN  do nofind routine
          ELSE  J = HASHTAB(HV)
                do search of sublist starting at J;
                send J, X     return I, S
                IF  found
                     THEN  do found routine
                     ELSE  do nofind routine
                ENDIF
     ENDIF
END PROC
```

This technique has the advantages of eliminating the space required by the hash table and eliminating the extra step of obtaining the starting address of a sublist from the hash table instead of directly from the hashing algorithm. However, in this case we must reserve a starting record cell for each possible sublist. Since record cells are normally much larger than a hash-table entry, if the hashing algorithm fails to produce several of the possible hash values, we could waste more space than we save. Also, since this technique requires that the first record in each sublist reside in one of the first m positions, we need to require that records be assigned to their respective sublists as they enter the list area because of the effect on their physical location. While the first technique is totally flexible with respect to records' physical locations so that the sublists can be created at any time it is convenient. This second technique is similar to basic techniques that are explained next for processing disk files through hashing.

USING HASHING TO PROCESS DISK FILES
When organizing a file for storage on a device external to main memory, we must consider physical characteristics of the device that are different from main memory to minimize access time. The characteristics of a disk drive were discussed in detail in Chapter 1, and they have been mentioned in

specific applications at other points in the book; so it should be clear at this point that to minimize access time, we have two considerations beyond the length of the respective sublists. These are: to minimize head movements and to minimize the number of physical reads required to obtain our target record.

The head-movement problem can be solved by using buckets that consist of a single track or a set of contiguous tracks within the same cylinder. The hashing algorithm can then produce the relative bucket number in the manner just described, and this relative bucket number can be converted into a physical track address. Once the physical track address is calculated, the read/write heads can be positioned with a single seek operation.

This bucket arrangement also helps us to minimize the number of physical reads required, since most full-sized computers will possess I/O hardware that can search a track or set of contiguous tracks for a match on a desired key or physical address, so that only one physical read operation is required to fetch the target record or block of records into main memory. Small computers without sophisticated I/O hardware have to resort to reading each record in the corresponding sublist until a match is found; so in this case bucket size should be limited to a single track if it is at all practical.

Our bucket arrangement using a single track or set of contiguous tracks seems to meet all of our needs but, by using buckets, we confine each sublist to a small fixed portion of our total file space; so the likelihood of overflow records is greatly increased. In dealing with overflow records, we still face the same constraints as with our regular lists; we need to employ techniques that will minimize head movement and keep the number of physical reads to a minimum. Head movement is not increased if the overflow from a given bucket is placed within the same cylinder as the bucket. Therefore, we always

FIGURE 4-23

	Location	Key	Data	Link	Order in which records entered list
Reserved for start of sublists	1	06		5	35
	2	01		6	01
	3	35		4	17
	4	17		9	06
	5	15		7	15
	6	07		8	07
	7	27		10	27
	8	16		*	16
	9	14		*	14
	10	09		*	09

attempt to place the overflow record first in the same cylinder as the sublist to which it belongs. If there is no more room in the cylinder, then some sort of secondary or global overflow area can be used, but it is normally better to reorganize or recreate the file at this point. We restrict our discussion of overflow to cylinder or primary overflow since secondary overflow is an immediate extension of this process.

There are two basic techniques for placing overflow records: open addressing and chaining (linking). With *open addressing*, once a bucket has overflowed, the cylinder or primary area is *probed*—meaning scanned according to some predetermined scheme—until an available location is found and the record is placed there.

The simplest type of probe is called a *linear probe*. In this technique, a track, or set of tracks that is adjacent to the track that overflowed, is scanned for placement of the overflow record. Retrieval of the record is performed in exactly the way the record is stored. First, the primary bucket is scanned, and then the adjacent tracks are scanned until the record is found or until a partially filled track is scanned without success. One major problem with this technique is the deletion of records. For the search procedure just described to work, deleted records must remain in the buckets or we must resort to a more complex procedure to move overflow records back into deleted record positions so that the search does not terminate prematurely. Another problem with linear probing is that overflow tends to cause clustering of records, so that portions of the file area become more dense than others and are thus much more likely to cause additional overflow.

The clustering problem can be improved with random probing. In this technique, the overflow records are assigned to other tracks according to a sequence of pseudorandom numbers that can be generated according to several algorithms found in the literature. However, this technique still does not take care of the problem with deletion of records.

The deletion problem is better handled through *chaining*. In chaining, the overflow records are attached to the primary bucket as a linked list. The bucket will carry one special record that contains a pointer (link) to the first overflow record from that bucket. If a bucket is scanned without success, the link record is read and then a series of reads begins along the linked list until the record is found or an end-of-list condition is encountered. With chaining, one or two tracks can be reserved on each cylinder to accommodate overflow from all of the buckets in that cylinder. The main disadvantage with chaining is that it may cause more physical reads than probing.

In conclusion, when we consider overflow techniques for disk files, probing is most likely preferred if the number of deletions is very low. Chaining is generally preferred otherwise. Fortunately for most application programmers, overflow techniques for disk files are built into most operating system software, and we need not pursue it further. Those requiring more information on the subject are directed to Knuth's *Sorting and Searching* and to *An Introduction to Data Structures with Applications* by J. Tremblay and P. Sorenson (1976).

COMPARISON WITH OTHER SEARCH METHODS

The following comparison is based strictly on the number of looks required to find a given record and does not account for the additional considerations that arise due to a specific file organization on a particular external device. These considerations can be treated as they were in the previous section. The comparison of hashing with other search techniques is not quite as straightforward as the comparisons among the methods studied previously, but a rough comparison can be obtained by first considering a perfect uniform distribution and then assuming that a good distribution should yield an average search time no worse than twice the optimum. If a better estimate is needed, then statistical methods can be used with random samples of keys to predict the resulting distribution of a given hashing algorithm.

Figure 4-24 illustrates optimum conditions, such as a perfect uniform distribution of records in corresponding sublists. It indicates that as long as enough sublists are available, search time can be held to a minimal if not constant value. Of course, as the number of sublists increases, so does the size of the hash table, if one is used. For a given number of records, a smaller sublist size can lessen the likelihood of a good distribution. Also it should be noted that average search time is no indication of worst-case searches. Indeed, with hashing, a worst-case search can be many times the predicted average search time; so, if there is a requirement to minimize the worst-case search, then binary searches, directories, and any other balanced tree-type search are much more reliable.

In summary, hashing is the likely choice for a search technique when the following conditions exist:

1. There is a need to search a list in a random manner very quickly.

2. The list is large enough so that the difference in search time between hashing and other methods is significant.

3. There is very little or no requirement to process the file in a sequential fashion.

4. A relatively long worst-case search time is acceptable.

FIGURE 4-24

Number of Records	Number of Sublists	Number of Looks + Hashing H
1000	50	H + 10.5
1000	100	H + 5.5
10,000	100	H + 50.5
10,000	500	H + 10.5
100,000	1000	H + 50.5
100,000	5000	H + 10.5

REVIEW EXERCISES

1. (a) Compare the number of compares (looks) for the following search methods. You may round to the nearest compare.

Number of Records (N)	Average Number of Looks			
	Sequential	Binary Search	One-level Directory	Two-level Directory
100				
1000				

   (b) When should you use an inverted file?

2. Should directories ever be used with the inverted indices of an inverted file? If so, when? If not, why not?

3. Show an inverted file structure which provides ordered access by major for the following student file. Notice that major is not unique among the students.

Name	ID	Major	Sem. Hr.	GPA
BAKER, ALICE	77325	PE	96	2.48
BROOK, JOHN	01420	MUS	120	3.80
CARSON, DAVID	78122	BUS	100	2.95
DAVIS, JAMES	63527	LAW	145	3.10
FILLMORE, MILLARD	40000	LAW	160	2.80
GREEN, JOE	25255	MUS	130	3.96
KNUTH, DONALD	69555	CS	136	4.00
MASON, PERRY	67777	LAW	150	3.92
SHELL, DONALD	71234	CS	130	3.40
SMITH, MELINDA	74526	CS	125	3.50

4. Match for best fit:

_____ stack	(a)	pointer
_____ queue	(b)	basic structure for logical order
_____ directory	(c)	structure with access to one end only
_____ linked list	(d)	provides order on a secondary key
_____ doubly linked list	(e)	each element has two or more pointers
_____ link	(f)	index
_____ circular list	(g)	provides reverse orderings within a given list
_____ multilinked list	(h)	requires at least three looks to find a record
_____ inverted file	(i)	is useful when there is more than one entry point
_____ two-level directory	(j)	FIFO

5. What is hashing?

6. Under what conditions should hashing be considered a good choice for a search technique?

7. Describe one common hashing technique.

8. (a) What is the greatest advantage of using hashing?
   (b) What is the greatest disadvantage of using hashing?

9. Choose a hashing algorithm and show how it could be used to create a file to be searched through hashing. Explain your algorithm briefly and show your hash table and any required pointers needed. The raw records follow.

Location	Key	
100	155	
110	230	
120	048	
130	425	
150	360	
160	782	
170	237	
180	243	
190	120	
200	529	
210	448	

PROGRAMMING ASSIGNMENTS

1. (a) Build a 100-element list composed of linked sublists. Use a directory that is itself a linked list to access the list. The directory entries should contain the address of the first record in the corresponding sublist and the key of the highest record in that sublist.

   (b) Use a space list for aiding adds and deletes.

   (c) Your program should be able to delete each of the following:
   - the first record in a sublist
   - the last record in a sublist
   - an interior record in a sublist

   (d) Your program should be able to add each of the following:
   - an interior record in a sublist
   - a new last record in a sublist
   - the first record in a sublist

   (e) List the directory and sublists in physical order before the adds and deletes are processed.

   (f) Input data will be supplied and will have the following format.

   ```
   cc
    1 -  4     Key
    5 -  8     Data
    9 - 10     Filler
   11 - 30     Name
   31 - 80     Filler
   ```

   (g) Data for adds and deletes have the same format except for a code in position 80 whose values indicate:

   ```
   cc
   80     1-ADD
          0-DELETE
   ```

   (h) After all additions and deletions have been made, the directory and sublist should be printed in logical sequential order as follows:

   ```
   DIRECTORY                ENTRY
         SUBLIST FOR THIS
         ENTRY
   ```

2. Using the data from the file-build portion of problem 1, write a program that allows a search of the file on either key or name.

   (a) Build a file just as you did in problem 1, but replace the directory with a hash table that points to appropriate sublists. Print out the physical hash table and list area to show that they are created properly.

(b) Build an inverted file on the name field in ascending order. *Write* a binary search to search the inverted file. Do not use a canned search provided by the language. Print out the inverted file to show that it was also created properly.

(c) After the file is built, a series of data cards are to be processed for file accessing. These cards have the following format. Print out a log of the transactions indicating what action was taken or what error condition was found.

```
Col                    Col
1-4    Key             80   'K'
1-20   Name            80   'N'
```

Error checking should provide:
- invalid search request, neither 'K' nor 'N'
- key not numeric for a 'K' search
- record missing for no such key
- name missing for no such name

Remember this program *does not* process adds or deletes.

5. TREES

Tree structures are as important as any other nonlinear structure we find in computer applications and, indeed, the study of these structures can provide us with a basis for studying more general structures later. Examples of tree structures are numerous. For instance, the file structure using level directories is a tree structure, and the arrangement of the modules in a top-down designed structured program forms a tree structure. Many others will soon become apparent.

To study trees, we must first define them. An intuitive approach to a definition defines a *tree* as a top-down or hierarchical arrangement of elements or nodes such that there is one node called the *root* from which the hierarchy emanates, and this node resides at level 1. All other nodes, if any, are arranged in levels such that each node is related to exactly one node, called its *parent*, in the level immediately preceding it.

Levels are numbered 1, 2, . . . , n starting with the root and progressing down through the hierarchy. Although all nodes, except the root, are related to exactly one node at the level above it, a node N at level j may be related to many nodes at level $j + 1$; these nodes are referred to as *children* of N. Any node lying on the path between a given node N and the root is called an *ancestor* of N, while any node along any path emanating from N is a *descendant* of N. A node may have no children and, in this case, it is called a *leaf node*. A node with no parent is, of course, the root. A *branch* of a tree consists of the ancestor chain of nodes from a leaf to the root. The *height* of a tree is the number of nodes in the longest branch of the tree.

If B is a node other than the root, then B together with all its descendants and their relationships are said to be a *subtree* of the original tree. To carry this one step further, if A is a node in a tree, with two children B and C, such that its left pointer points to B and its right pointer points to C, then B with all its descendants and their relationships form the *left subtree* of A, while C together with all its descendants and their relationships form the *right subtree* of A. In Figure 5-1, node 1 is the root of the tree; it consists of four levels or has a height of four. Examples of branches are nodes 1, 2, 5, 12 or 1, 3, 8. Node 2 is the parent of node 5, while node 8 is the child of node 3. Node 4 is an ancestor of node 18, and the root is an ancestor of every other node in the tree.

In the implementation of a file as a tree structure, nodes represent records, and relations represent links or pointers.

BINARY TREES

A *binary tree* is a tree in which each node has at most two children. A binary tree is said to be *balanced* if, from any node, the height of the left subtree differs from the height of the right subtree by no more than 1. The tree is *optimally balanced* if the length of each branch in the tree differs from the length of any other branch by no more than 1.

The 12-node tree shown in Figure 5-2 is optimally balanced since the height of branch 1, 3, 7 is three and the height of every other branch is four. However, if we add node 13 as the left subtree of node 8, we obtain a tree that is balanced but not optimally balanced. This is true because, at each node within the tree, the heights of the left and right subtrees differ by no more than 1, yet the tree contains one branch of height five (1, 2, 4, 8, 13) and another branch of height three (1, 3, 7), which can be seen in Figure 5-3.

When a binary tree is implemented in memory, each node consists of a data portion and left and right pointers, as shown in Figure 5-4. A slight variation of this format replaces the data portion with its corresponding key value and a pointer to the complete data. This variation is most appropriate when we use the tree as a directory or index.

FIGURE 5-1   TREE DIAGRAM

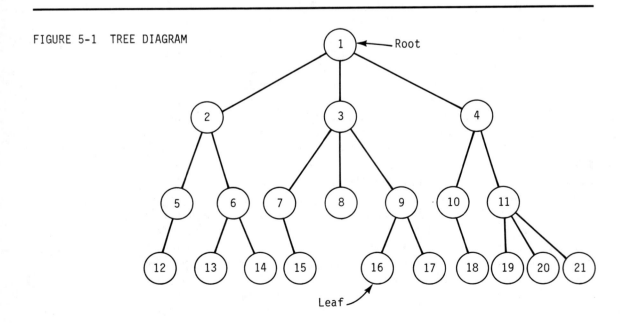

If the node numbers in the diagram of the binary tree in Figure 5-2 are taken to be locations, we have what is shown in Figure 5-5. In memory, we would find what is shown in Figure 5-6.

CREATION

The creation of a binary tree can be accomplished in several ways. One way is to use a balanced insertion starting with an empty tree. This method is discussed later in the section on balancing. Another technique that is less elegant but still produces an optimally balanced binary tree is described here.

First, all of the tree nodes are built in contiguous cells with null or empty left and right pointer fields. These are then sorted on keys placing the nodes in physical order. A variation of the binary search algorithm can now be used to determine the values for the left and right pointer fields and thus complete the tree.

FIGURE 5-2   OPTIMALLY BALANCED BINARY TREE

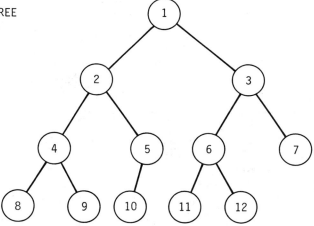

FIGURE 5-3   BALANCED BUT NOT OPTIMALLY BALANCED TREE

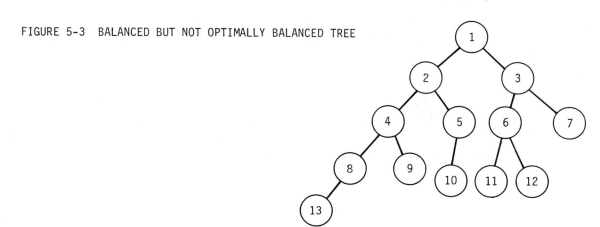

The algorithm shown in Figure 5-7 creates the tree by always taking the left branch of a parent node and stacking the right pointer along with bounds of the subtree belonging to this node. When a leaf node is reached, the stack is popped and the process continues until the stack is empty. When the process is complete, we have an optimally balanced binary tree that is ordered for searching starting at the root. A tree that is ordered in this fashion is also referred to as a *binary search tree*.

Using the algorithm described in Figure 5-7, a 12-node tree would be created in the order indicated in the tree diagram in Figure 5-8. In memory, the tree would appear as shown in Figure 5-9.

SEARCHING

The searching of the binary tree created in Figure 5-8 and, indeed, the searching of any ordered binary tree is simply a logical extension of the binary search algorithm in which we replace the calculation of the physical address to find the next record with the following of a pointer to find the next record. By now it should be obvious that a branch of a tree is defined by a linked list from the root to a leaf. The only difference between searching down a branch of a tree and searching a simple linked list is that, at each node in the branch, we have a possible choice of links.

The algorithm in Figure 5-10 is appropriate to search any ordered binary tree in which the order is established such that, for any node, all nodes in its

FIGURE 5-4
BINARY TREE
NODE FORMAT

| LEFT PTR | DATA | RIGHT PTR |

or

| DATA | LEFT PTR | RIGHT PTR |

FIGURE 5-5 EXPANDED
NODE VIEW OF TREE IN
FIGURE 5-2

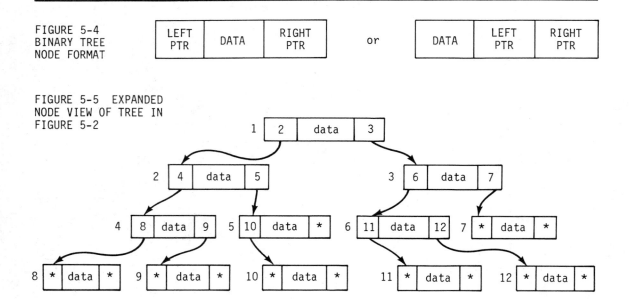

left subtree bear the same order relationship to it (that is, all less than or all greater than), and all nodes in its right subtree bear the same order relationship to it, whether it is balanced or not. If the tree is optimally balanced, this search is equivalent to a binary search of a list without requiring that the list be in physical order.

Searching an optimally balanced binary tree that is ordered is even faster than using a binary search on a physically ordered list, because the tree search involves only one additional compare instruction over the process for a look in the search of a linked list. The binary search requires this same additional compare plus the computation of a new midpoint for each look. Therefore, the binary search tree not only offers the convenience of logical order over physical order but also offers improved search efficiency.

FIGURE 5-6 MEMORY
REPRESENTATION OF
TREE IN FIGURE 5-2

ROOTPTR		DATA	LEFT PTR	RIGHT PTR
1	1	(	2	3
	2		4	5
	3		6	7
	4		8	9
	5		10	*
	6		11	12
	7		*	*
	8		*	*
	9		*	*
	10		*	*
	11		*	*
	12	)	*	*

FIGURE 5-7 CREATION
OF AN OPTIMALLY
BALANCED ORDERED
BINARY TREE

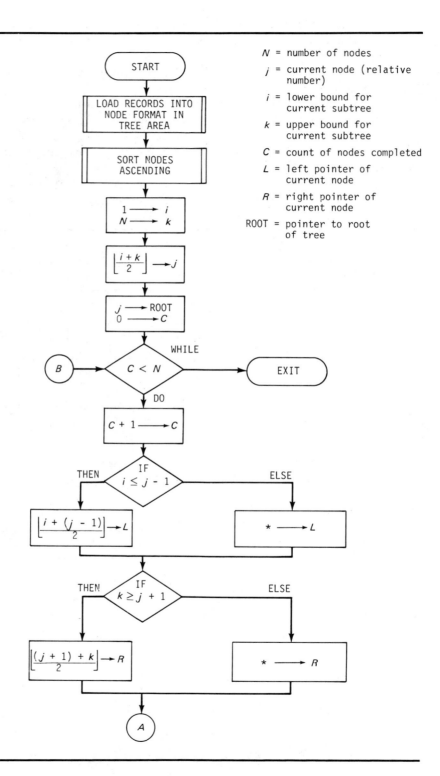

N = number of nodes

j = current node (relative number)

i = lower bound for current subtree

k = upper bound for current subtree

C = count of nodes completed

L = left pointer of current node

R = right pointer of current node

ROOT = pointer to root of tree

FIGURE 5-7 (continued)

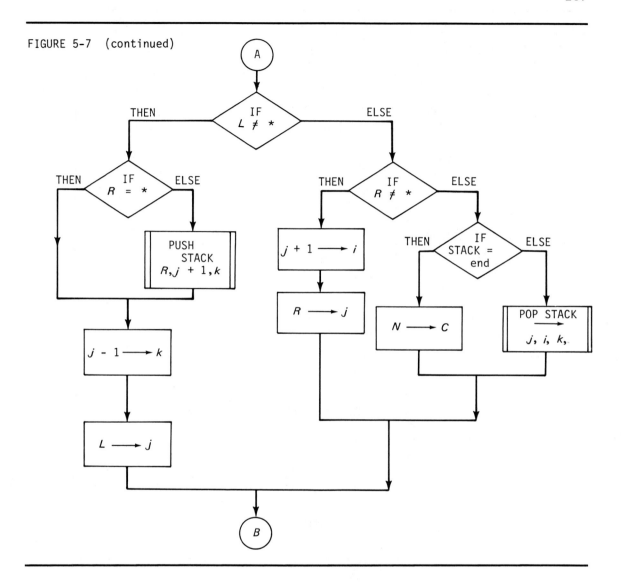

CREATION OF AN
OPTIMALLY BALANCED
ORDERED BINARY TREE

```
/*  N = number of nodes in tree;  J = location of
    current node */
/*  I,K = lower and upper bounds of current subtree */
/*  C = count of nodes completed */
/*  L,R = left and right pointers of current node */
/*  ROOT = pointer to root of tree */

PROC   CREATE-TREE
    do routine to load records into node format in tree area
    do sort nodes in ascending order
    I = 1
    K = N
    J = ⌊(I + K) / 2⌋
    ROOT = J
    C = 0
    WHILE  C < N    DO
        C = C + 1
        IF  I ≤ J - 1
            THEN  L = ⌊(I + (J - 1)) /2⌋
            ELSE  L = end
        ENDIF
        IF  K ≥ J + 1
            THEN  R = ⌊((J + 1) + K) /2⌋
            ELSE  R = end
        ENDIF
        IF  L ≠ end
            THEN  IF  R = end
                      THEN   continue
                      ELSE   PUSH STACK send R, J+1, K
                  ENDIF
                  K = J - 1
                  J = L
            ELSE  IF  R ≠ end
                      THEN  I = J + 1
                            J = R
                      ELSE  IF  STACK = end
                                THEN  C = N     /* check error */
                                ELSE  POP STACK return J,I,K
                            ENDIF
                  ENDIF
        ENDIF
    ENDDO
END PROC
```

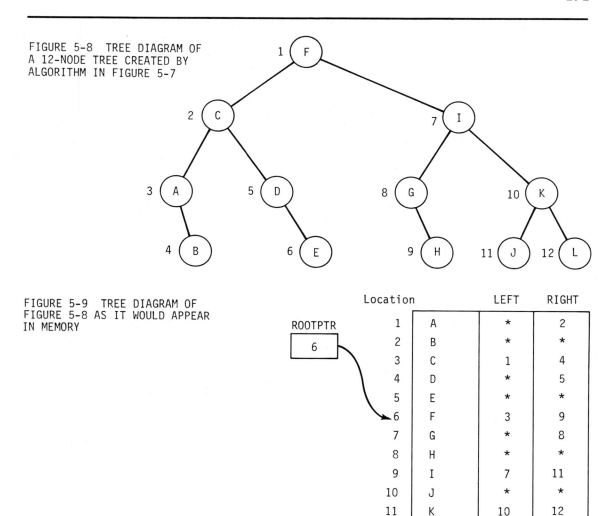

FIGURE 5-8   TREE DIAGRAM OF
A 12-NODE TREE CREATED BY
ALGORITHM IN FIGURE 5-7

FIGURE 5-9   TREE DIAGRAM OF
FIGURE 5-8 AS IT WOULD APPEAR
IN MEMORY

ROOTPTR

Location		LEFT	RIGHT
1	A	*	2
2	B	*	*
3	C	1	4
4	D	*	5
5	E	*	*
6	F	3	9
7	G	*	8
8	H	*	*
9	I	7	11
10	J	*	*
11	K	10	12
12	L	*	*

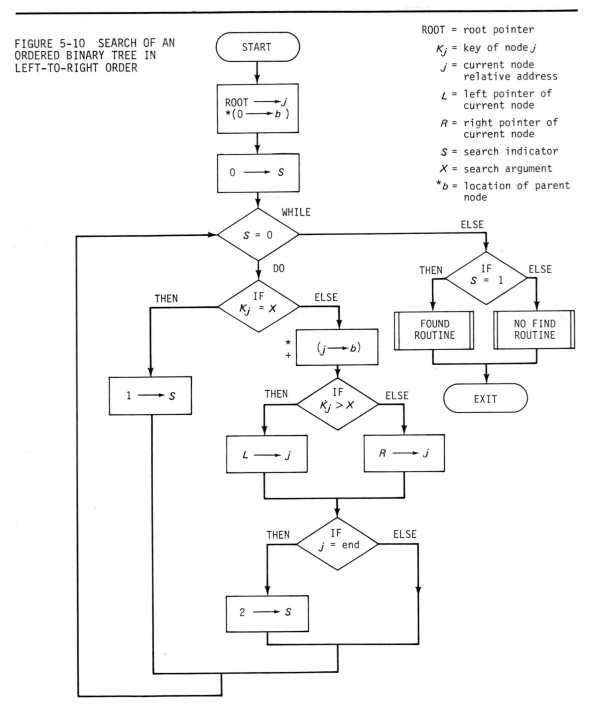

FIGURE 5-10 SEARCH OF AN ORDERED BINARY TREE IN LEFT-TO-RIGHT ORDER

*If routine is to be used for updating, location of parent node must be saved.
+When routine is used with balanced insertion, stacking of nodes is done here.

SEARCH OF AN ORDERED
BINARY TREE IN
LEFT-TO-RIGHT ORDER

```
/*  ROOT = pointer to root of tree */
/*  J,K(J) = location and key of current node */
/*  L,R = left and right pointers of current node */
/*  S = search switch */
/*  X = search argument */
/*  B = location of parent of current node; needed
        for updating */


PROC    BINARY-TREE-SEARCH
    J = ROOT
   *(B = 0)                          /* statements marked *(   )
    S = 0                               are needed for updating */
    WHILE  S = 0  DO
        IF   K(J) = X
            THEN  S = 1                     /* record found */
            ELSE *(B = J)      /* for balancing, node stacking
                 IF   K(J) > X                is done here */
                    THEN  J = L
                    ELSE  J = R
                 ENDIF
                 IF  J  = end
                    THEN   S = 2        /* record missing */
                    ELSE   continue
                 ENDIF
        ENDIF
    ENDDO
    IF  S = 1
        THEN   do found routine
        ELSE   do nofind routine
    ENDIF
END PROC
```

TRAVERSAL OF BINARY TREES

There are times at which it is desirable to examine or process each node in a binary tree structure. A simple example is to print out each node in a binary tree in order. At other times, we want to initiate a procedure that would result in the processing of each node in a tree structure if a given condition is or is not met. An example of this is to search a tree structure for a match on a field that is not the key on which the structure is ordered. In either case, we need an orderly procedure that will terminate after processing each node in a tree structure exactly once; such a procedure is called a *tree traversal*.

Every traversal algorithm for binary trees faces three choices at each node during the process. These are:

1. Process the node.

2. Follow the left branch (that is, process the left subtree).

3. Follow the right branch (that is, process the right subtree).

It should be clear that no matter which of these three choices is taken, the other two must be tended to later. It is the order in which the three choices are treated that classifies the traversal method.

A *preorder* traversal processes the node first and then processes each of the two subtrees. If N, L, and R represent choices 1, 2, and 3, respectively, then algorithms that follow a NLR or NRL order are both preordered.

An *inorder* traversal processes one subtree, then the node, and then the other subtree. Therefore, both LNR and RNL are inordered.

A *postorder* traversal processes both of the subtrees and then the node. Thus LRN and RLN are postordered.

Since binary trees are symmetric in nature, any one of the two examples for each type of traversal can be converted to the other by simply reversing L and R in the algorithm (for example, change LNR to RNL by switching L and R in the algorithm).

Each type of traversal is preferable to the other two under certain conditions. For instance, a preorder traversal is preferable in the case of searching an unordered binary tree or searching on a field other than the key field. In this case, a hit terminates the traversal (search), and we want to process a subtree only if the current node is not the one sought. A flowchart of this procedure is given after the general traversal algorithms.

Given that a binary tree is ordered according to the algorithm described earlier, such that the leftmost leaf and the rightmost leaf mark the endpoints of the order, then an *inorder* traversal processes the nodes exactly in ascending or descending order.

Postorder traversals are indicated anytime we want to process nodes in a bottom-up fashion based on the hierarchy of the tree; in other words, when we want to process the children before processing the parent. The use of postorder traversals in the evaluation of arithmetic expressions represented as binary trees, in which operations form the parent nodes and operands form the leaf nodes, is common in the literature. For example, the expression $G - (1000 * D + R)$ can be represented as shown in Figure 5-11.

Processing the left subtree yields simply G. Processing the right subtree results first in the processing of the left subtree of node 3, which yields the product of 1000 and D, and which we call P, and the processing of the right subtree of 3, which yields R. The addition of P and R completes the processing of the right subtree and, therefore, this result is added to G as node 1 is processed.

In summary, the diagram of a binary tree is given in Figure 5-12, and the order in which the nodes are processed for each of the three traversal methods is:

Preorder (NLR) – MGAJITU

Inorder (LNR) – AGIJMTU

Postorder (LRN) – AIJGUTM

Algorithms to produce the three types of traversals are given in Figures 5-13, 5-14, and 5-15. Figure 5-16 shows a preorder exhaustive search of an unordered binary tree. In each case, as one of the choices L, R, or N is taken at a node, then any remaining choice is placed in a stack for later processing in the following manner. (For a recursive approach to traversals, see Appendix B.)

The preorder algorithm stacks only right branches since each node is processed immediately and any remaining left branch is then taken.

The inorder algorithm stacks only nodes since left branches are taken immediately and right branches will be available when nodes are popped for processing.

The postorder algorithm stacks both nodes and right branches since we do not want a node to be processed until both branches are taken. In this way, each time a node is popped it is processed immediately. If a right branch is popped, it is taken and the process continues. Had we stacked only nodes, then we would need an indicator as to whether or not its right tree had been processed. The stacking of only right pointers is unsatisfactory since our current binary tree format does not contain parent pointers. Since the algorithm in Figure 5-15 stacks nodes and right branches in the same stack, we include in each stack element a type indicator to distinguish between the

FIGURE 5-11 EXPRESSION EVALUATION
USING A POSTORDER TRAVERSAL

FIGURE 5-12

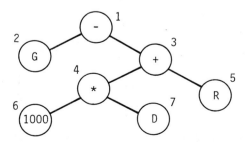

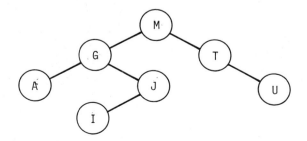

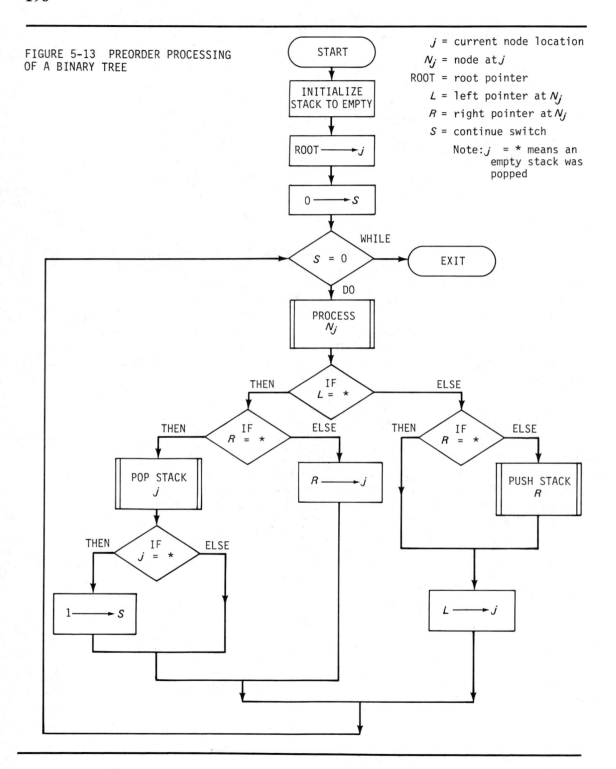

FIGURE 5-13 PREORDER PROCESSING OF A BINARY TREE

```
PREORDER        /*  ROOT = pointer to root of tree */
PROCESSING      /*  J,N(J) = location and identifier of current node */
OF A            /*  L,R = left and right pointers of current node */
BINARY TREE     /*  S = search switch; 0 = continue,
                    1 = processing complete */
                /*  When J = end an empty stack has been popped */


PROC          PREORDER-TRAV
    do, initialize stack to empty
    J = ROOT
    S = 0
    WHILE  S = 0   DO
        do, process node  N(J)
        IF  L = end
            THEN  IF  R = end
                    THEN  POP STACK; return J
                        IF  J = end
                            THEN  S = 1          /* TRAV IS COMPLETE */
                            ELSE  continue
                        ENDIF
                    ELSE  J = R
                ENDIF
            ELSE  IF  R = end
                    THEN  continue
                    ELSE  PUSH STACK; send R
                ENDIF
                J = L
        ENDIF
    ENDDO
END PROC
```

198

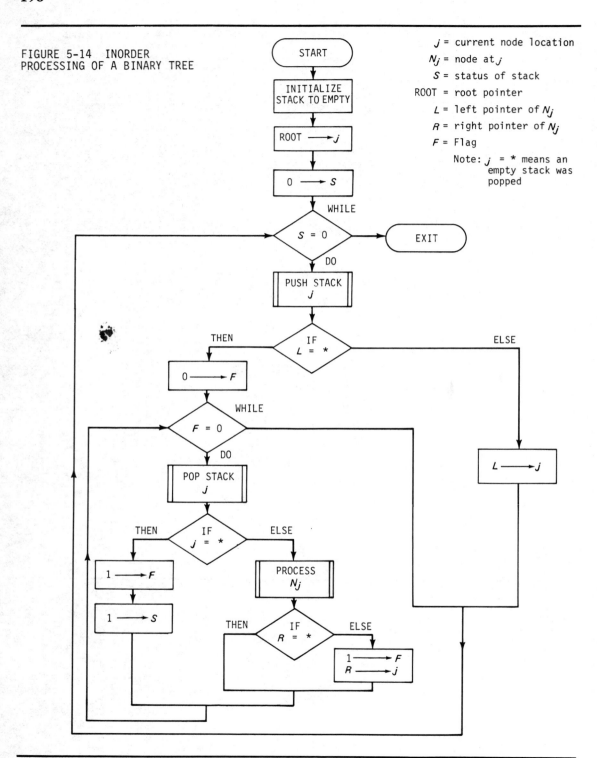

FIGURE 5-14 INORDER
PROCESSING OF A BINARY TREE

j = current node location
N_j = node at j
S = status of stack
ROOT = root pointer
L = left pointer of N_j
R = right pointer of N_j
F = Flag

Note: j = * means an empty stack was popped

START

INITIALIZE STACK TO EMPTY

ROOT ⟶ j

0 ⟶ S

WHILE $S = 0$

EXIT

DO

PUSH STACK j

IF $L = *$

THEN 0 ⟶ F

WHILE $F = 0$

DO POP STACK j

IF $j = *$

THEN 1 ⟶ F

1 ⟶ S

ELSE PROCESS N_j

IF $R = *$

ELSE 1 ⟶ F

R ⟶ j

ELSE L ⟶ j

INORDER PROCESSING
OF A BINARY TREE

```
/*  J,N(J) = location and identifier of current node */
/*  S = status flag for traversal; 0 = continue,
        1 = complete */
/*  ROOT = root pointer */
/*  L,R = left and right pointers of N(J) */
/*  F = internal flag to continue popping stack */
/*  J = end means that an empty stack was popped */


PROC          INORDER-TRAV
    do, initialize stack to empty
    J = ROOT
    S = 0
    WHILE  S = 0  DO
        do, PUSH STACK; send J
        IF  L = end
            THEN  F = 0
                WHILE  F = 0  DO
                    POP STACK; return J
                    IF  J = end
                        THEN  F = 1
                              S = 1
                        ELSE  process N(J)
                            IF  R = end
                                THEN  continue
                                ELSE  F = 1
                                      J = R
                            ENDIF
                    ENDIF
                ENDDO
            ELSE  J = L
        ENDIF
    ENDDO
END PROC
```

FIGURE 5-15 POSTORDER PROCESSING OF A BINARY TREE

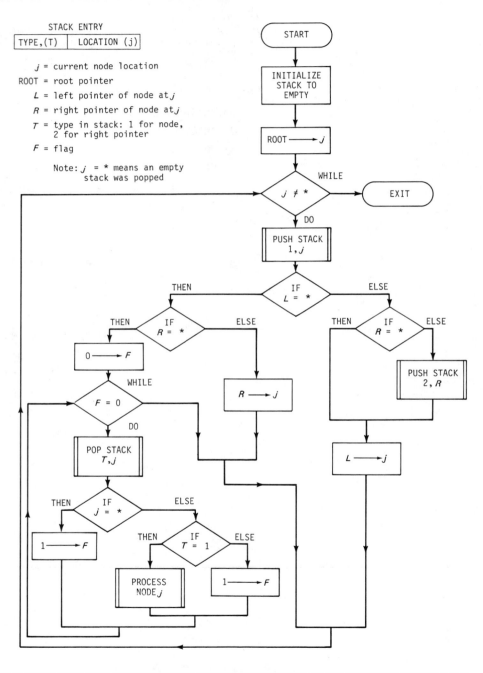

STACK ENTRY

TYPE,(T)	LOCATION (j)

j = current node location
ROOT = root pointer
L = left pointer of node at j
R = right pointer of node at j
T = type in stack: 1 for node, 2 for right pointer
F = flag

Note: j = * means an empty stack was popped

START

INITIALIZE STACK TO EMPTY

ROOT ⟶ j

WHILE
$j \neq *$ → EXIT

DO

PUSH STACK 1, j

IF
L = *

THEN   ELSE

IF
R = *   IF
R = *

THEN   ELSE   THEN   ELSE

0 ⟶ F R ⟶ j PUSH STACK 2, R

WHILE
F = 0

DO

POP STACK T, j L ⟶ j

IF
j = *

THEN   ELSE

1 ⟶ F IF
T = 1

THEN   ELSE

PROCESS NODE j 1 ⟶ F

POSTORDER PROCESSING
OF A BINARY TREE

```
/*  J,N(J) = location and identifier of current node */
/*  ROOT = root pointer */
/*  L,R = left and right pointer of current node */
/*  T = type of entry in stack; 1 = node,
    2 = right pointer */
/*  F = flag to pop stack; 0 = pop stack,
    1 = exit pop loop */
/*  J = end means an empty stack was popped */


PROC     POSTORDER-TRAV
    initialize stack to empty
    J = ROOT
    WHILE  J ≠ end  DO
        PUSH STACK; send 1,J
        IF  L = end
            THEN  IF R = end
                        THEN  F = 0
                            WHILE  F = 0  DO
                                POP STACK; return T,J
                                IF  J = end
                                    THEN  F = 1
                                    ELSE  IF T = 1
                                                THEN process N(J)
                                                ELSE  F = 1
                                            ENDIF
                                ENDIF
                            ENDDO
                        ELSE J = R
                    ENDIF
            ELSE  IF  R = end
                        THEN  continue
                        ELSE  PUSH STACK; send 2, R
                    ENDIF
                    J = L
        ENDIF
    ENDDO
END PROC
```

FIGURE 5-16 EXHAUSTIVE
SEARCH OF AN UNORDERED
BINARY TREE
(PREORDERED)

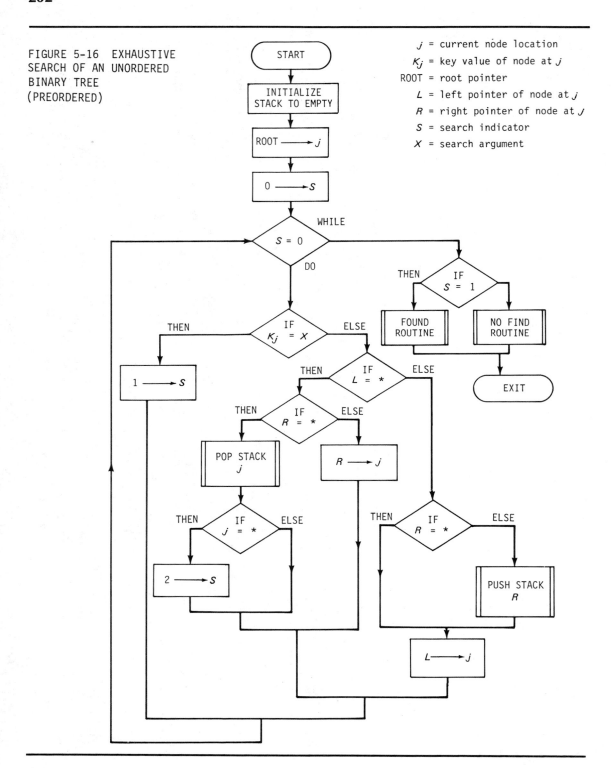

```
EXHAUSTIVE SEARCH OF      /*  J,K(J) = location and key of current node */
AN UNORDERED BINARY       /*  ROOT = root pointer */
TREE (PREORDERED)         /*  L,R = left and right pointers of node at J */
                          /*  S = search indicator; 0 = continue search,
                              1 = found, 2 = missing */


             PROC     SEARCH-BINARY-EXHAUSTIVE
                initialize stack to empty
                J = ROOT
                S = 0
                WHILE  S = 0  DO
                    IF  K(J) = X
                          THEN  S = 1
                          ELSE  IF  L = end
                                THEN  IF  R = end
                                      THEN POP STACK; return J
                                          IF  J = end
                                              THEN S = 2
                                              ELSE continue
                                          ENDIF
                                      ELSE  J = R
                                      ENDIF
                                ELSE  IF  R = end
                                      THEN   continue
                                      ELSE   PUSH STACK; send R
                                      ENDIF
                                      J = L
                          ENDIF
                    ENDIF
                ENDDO
                IF  S = 1
                    THEN  do found routine
                    ELSE  do nofind routine
                ENDIF
             END PROC
```

two; a type value of 1 indicates a node, while a type value of 2 indicates a right branch. Thus, we traverse the tree by first stacking the location of the current node, next stacking the right branch of the current node if it has one, and then following the left branch if it is valid. When we reach a node with a null left branch, we attempt to continue the process by taking the right branch. Should the right branch be null also, we pop the stack until we find a right branch to continue or until the stack is empty, at which time the traversal is complete. During the popping of the stack, each time a node is popped, it is processed immediately.

An alternative to the implementations of the three traversal methods just described involves the use of *threads* in place of stacks. A thread is a pointer carried in a leaf node that points to the successor of the node according to one of the specific traversal methods, such as LNR. Threads usually replace the end-of-list or null pointers found in leaf nodes; therefore, they must be distinguished from the regular left and right subtree pointers. One solution is to carry a thread flag in each node to indicate whether the content of a pointer field is a thread; another method is to carry threads as negative values. For example, a thread that points to a node at location 500 would be carried as −500.

Threads can be created as the tree is created or by making a single traversal according to the methods described earlier and then copying the stack contents into the proper pointer fields as the stack is popped each time.

An example of a preordered, threaded binary tree with right threads (that is, threads replace only right pointers of leaf nodes with successors) is shown in Figure 5-17. Figure 5-18 shows an inorder binary tree with right threads.

Threads provide us with a more efficient means of searching a tree according to a predescribed order than repeated use of the traversal algorithms, but the use of threads increases the overhead to maintain a tree structure. Therefore, we should consider using threads for a given tree structure if we have a frequent requirement to process the tree according to a particular order and the volume of updating is not excessive. Otherwise, the use of the traversal algorithms, or their functional equivalents, is likely to be preferable.

FIGURE 5-17 DIAGRAM OF NLR (PREORDERED) RIGHT-THREADED TREE. THE RIGHT POINTER OF THE LAST NODE CARRIES A NULL OR END MARKER

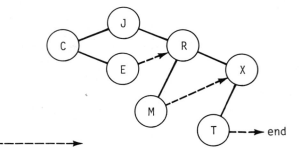

Denotes thread ⎯ ⎯ ⎯ ⎯ ⎯ ⟶

UPDATING WITHOUT BALANCING

The problem of updating an ordered binary tree is treated in two ways. First we examine how the tree can be updated *without considering balance*. We readdress the problem while maintaining balance in the next section.

When we eliminate the restriction for maintaining balance, adding nodes is simpler than deleting them because, if we always choose to add nodes as leaf nodes, then we are not required to rearrange our existing tree structure. On the other hand, in the case of deletions, we cannot assume that only leaf nodes will be deleted. Therefore, we must provide for the restructuring of the tree when nodes other than leaf nodes are deleted.

The process of adding nodes is reduced to locating the parent of the node to be added and replacing its empty subtree with the new node.

Consider the diagrams (Figure 5-19) that illustrate a series of three additions to a given ordered tree.

In Figures 5-19 (b) and (c), we added a node (subtree) to a parent that was initially a leaf node whereas, in (d) we added a node to a parent that was not a leaf node initially but had one empty subtree. In each case, however, the process is the same, and this can readily be seen in the algorithm in Figure 5-20.

The problem of deletions involves not one but three cases that must be considered: (1) the deletion of a leaf node; (2) the deletion of nonleaf node with one empty subtree; and (3) the deletion of a nonleaf node with no empty subtrees.

The deletion of a leaf node (Figure 5-21) involves simply replacing the pointer found in the parent node, which points to the node being deleted, with a null or end-of-list indicator.

For the deletion of a nonleaf node with one empty subtree (Figure 5-22), we replace the pointer in the parent to the node being deleted with the nonempty subtree pointer from the node being deleted. Fortunately, if we simply check to see if the node being deleted has one empty pointer field and then always move the remaining pointer to the parent, case 1 and case 2 are reduced to the same process, which can be seen in the algorithm on page 210.

FIGURE 5-18 DIAGRAM OF LNR (INORDER)
RIGHT-THREADED TREE

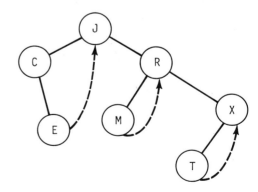

FIGURE 5-19 (a) The initial tree; (b) after adding A; (c) after adding B;
(d) after adding X.

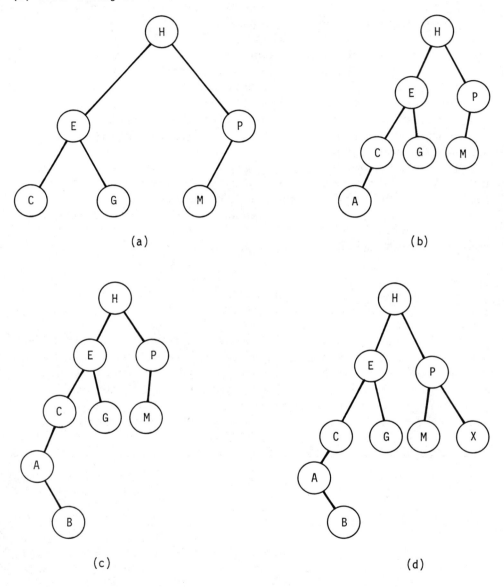

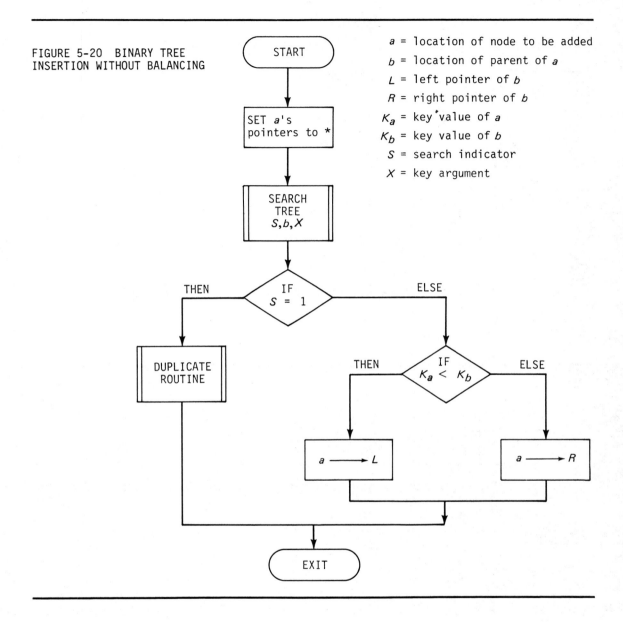

FIGURE 5-20 BINARY TREE
INSERTION WITHOUT BALANCING

a = location of node to be added
b = location of parent of a
L = left pointer of b
R = right pointer of b
K_a = key value of a
K_b = key value of b
S = search indicator
X = key argument

```
BINARY TREE        /* A = location of node to be added */
INSERTION          /* B = location of parent of node at A */
WITHOUT BALANCING  /* L,R = left and right pointers of node at B */
                   /* K(A),K(B) = keys of nodes at A and B */
                   /* S = search indicator from search routine;
                      1 = found, 2 = missing */
                   /* X = key search argument */


           PROC    BINARY-INSERTION
                   set pointers of node at A to end
                   do  BINARY-TREE-SEARCH; send X return S,B
                   IF  S = 1
                       THEN  do duplicate routine
                       ELSE  IF  K(A) < K(B)
                                 THEN  L = A
                                 ELSE  R = A
                             ENDIF
                   ENDIF
           END PROC
```

For the deletion of a nonleaf node with no empty subtrees (Figure 5-23), the rightmost node of the left subtree of the node being deleted will replace the deleted node. This involves finding the rightmost node and placing the pointer to it in the appropriate pointer field of the parent of the deleted node. Choosing the leftmost node of the right subtree achieves the same results. However, to present an algorithm a choice must be made. Therefore, a choice was made (based purely on the whim of the author without any thought of what psychological or philosophical implications might be involved), and the algorithm is given in Figure 5-24.

We see that the updating of an ordered binary tree is a relatively simple process if we ignore balancing; so questions arise as to when we should be concerned about balancing. If we can assume that our initial tree was created so that it was optimally balanced to begin with, and if the volume of adds and deletes is relatively small compared to the number of nodes in the tree, then balancing is not a major concern. Also, if we can be assured that update activity is spread somewhat evenly throughout the tree structure then, once again, balancing should not be a major concern, but this condition is not likely to be predictable. Therefore, in the practical sense, we should consider balancing anytime the condition of a low volume of adds and deletes is not met.

Consider the example in Figure 5-25(a) in which an optimally balanced binary tree, containing only three nodes with keys A, B, and C, is created. When insertions are made in ascending order we have what is shown in Figure 5-25(b).

FIGURE 5-21 THE DELETION OF A LEAF NODE: (a) before; (b) after deleting F

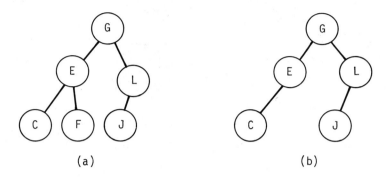

(a)   (b)

FIGURE 5-22 THE DELETION OF A NONLEAF NODE WITH ONE EMPTY SUBTREE: (a) before;
(b) after deleting L

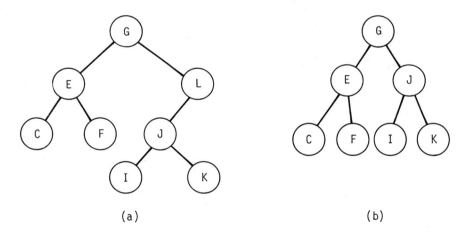

(a)   (b)

FIGURE 5-23 THE DELETION OF A NONLEAF NODE WITH NO EMPTY SUBTREES: (a) before;
(b) after deleting I

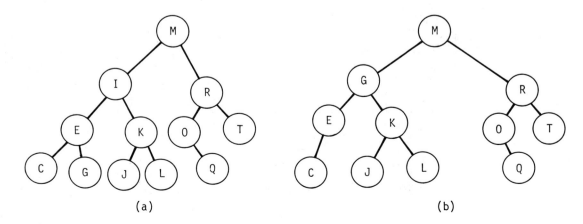

(a)   (b)

210

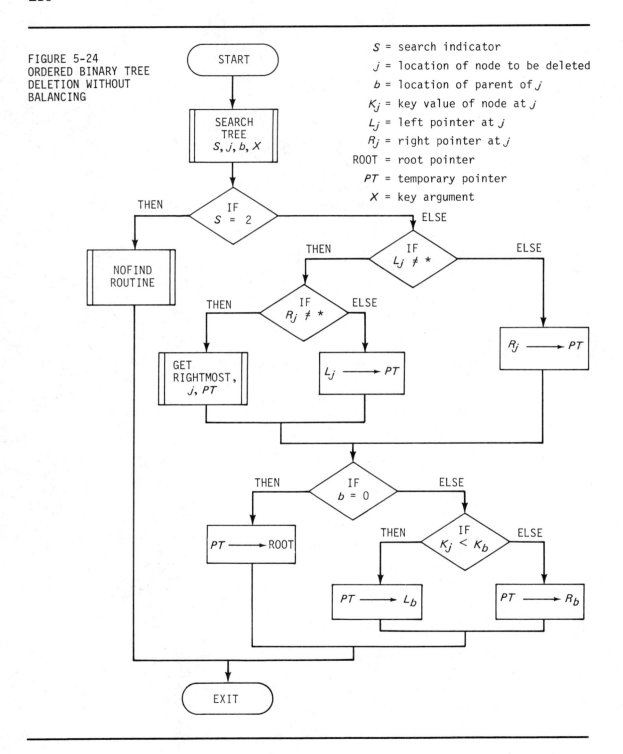

FIGURE 5-24
ORDERED BINARY TREE
DELETION WITHOUT
BALANCING

S = search indicator
j = location of node to be deleted
b = location of parent of j
K_j = key value of node at j
L_j = left pointer at j
R_j = right pointer at j
ROOT = root pointer
PT = temporary pointer
X = key argument

START

SEARCH
TREE
S, j, b, X

THEN

IF
S = 2

ELSE

NOFIND
ROUTINE

THEN

IF
$L_j \neq *$

ELSE

THEN

IF
$R_j \neq *$

ELSE

$R_j \longrightarrow PT$

GET
RIGHTMOST,
j, PT

$L_j \longrightarrow PT$

THEN

IF
b = 0

ELSE

$PT \longrightarrow$ ROOT

THEN

IF
$K_j < K_b$

ELSE

$PT \longrightarrow L_b$

$PT \longrightarrow R_b$

EXIT

FIGURE 5-24 (continued)

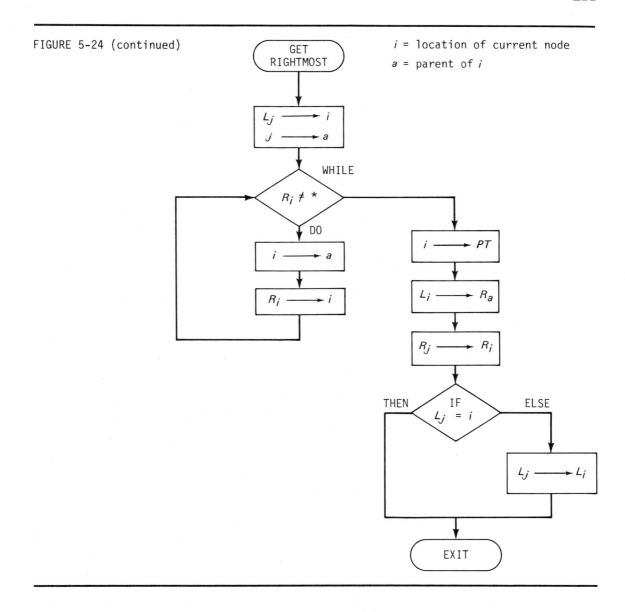

i = location of current node

a = parent of i

This tree structure has now degenerated to the point that the right subtree of the root is six times longer than its left subtree, and should we, by chance, delete node A, then our tree has degenerated into a single linked list! Obviously, if we are working with only a few nodes, then this is still not a major problem, but when this situation occurs in a tree with many nodes, the problem becomes acute, and we must employ some scheme to achieve a better distribution of nodes.

ORDERED BINARY TREE
DELETION WITHOUT
BALANCING

```
/*  S = search indicator; 1 = found, 2 = no find */
/*  J = location of node to be deleted */
/*  K(J),L(J),R(J) = key, left pointer, right pointer
    of node at J */
/*  B = location of parent of node at J */
/*  ROOT = root pointer */
/*  X = key search argument */
/*  PT = temporary pointer save area */


PROC    BINARY-TREE-DELETION
    do  BINARY-TREE-SEARCH; send X return J,B,S
    IF  S = 2
        THEN  nofind routine          /* record to be deleted
                                         is missing */
        ELSE  IF  L(J) ≠ end
                  THEN  IF  R(J) ≠ end
                            THEN-GET-RIGHTMOST; send J return PT
                            ELSE  PT = L(J)
                        ENDIF
                  ELSE  PT = R(J)
              ENDIF
              IF  B = 0
                  THEN  ROOT = PT
                  ELSE  IF  K(J) < K(B)
                            THEN  L(B) = PT
                            ELSE  R(B) = PT
                        ENDIF
              ENDIF
        ENDIF
END PROC
```

The reason that maintaining a balanced tree over an optimally balanced tree is attractive is that, in 1962, two Russian scientists—Adel'son-Vel'skii and Landis—proved a theorem that shows, in effect, that the height of a balanced tree will never be more than 1.4 times the height of an optimally balanced tree. Techniques for maintaining balance require less processing than those required for maintaining optimal balance, therefore we present them in the following section.

GET RIGHTMOST
(SUBROUTINE)

```
/*  GET-RIGHTMOST is subroutine for BINARY-TREE-DELETION */
/*  I = location of current node */
/*  A = location of parent of I */
/*  all other variables are the same as main routine */
/*  routine finds the rightmost node of a left subtree */


PROC      GET-RIGHTMOST
    I = L(J)
    A = J
    WHILE  R(I) ≠ end  DO
        A = I
        I = R(I)
    ENDDO
    PT = I
    R(A) = L(I)
    R(I) = R(J)
    IF  L(J) = I
        THEN  continue
        ELSE  L(I) = L(J)
    ENDIF
END PROC
```

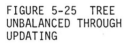

FIGURE 5-25 TREE
UNBALANCED THROUGH
UPDATING

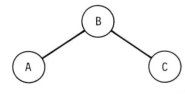

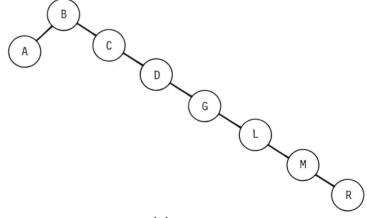

(a)   (b)

BALANCING

Once a balanced tree has been created, it is often desirable for the tree to remain balanced to maintain high efficiency in processing the tree structure. Maintaining balance becomes more important as update activity increases because, without balancing, the only insurance against poor performance is to recreate the tree structure frequently by a procedure such as the one described earlier.

Since a balanced tree can only become unbalanced through the addition or deletion of nodes, we now consider how balance can be maintained during these two processes. We have already established procedures to add and delete nodes to a binary tree; so our problem is reduced to rebalancing after a node has been added or deleted. We need to define a new field to be carried in every node called a *balance factor*. The balance factor (b.f.) will have a value of +1, 0, or −1, which is the height of the left subtree minus the height of the right subtree (Knuth, *Sorting and Searching*) (see Figure 5-26).

Consider the following additions to Figure 5-26.

1. Adding node L would change the b.f. of node K to 0 and not affect anything else.

2. Adding node A would change the b.f. of nodes M, H, E, and C to +1.

3. Adding node Q would change the b.f. of node S to 0 and node P to −1.

None of these additions affect the structure of the tree. They affect only the balance factors since, after each addition, both subtrees of each node are still balanced.

4. Adding node Z causes an imbalance at V since its right subtree would have a height of 2 more than its left subtree. But if we transform Figure 5-27(a) to Figure 5-27(b), the imbalance is corrected. This is called a *left rotation* of the tree rooted at V. After the rotation, V, Y, and Z would each have a b.f. of 0.

5. Adding node I would cause a *right rotation* of the tree rooted at K. This single rotation is all that is needed when the b.f. of the parent node of the added node is equal in direction to the b.f. of the next highest ancestor node with an imbalance.

6. Adding node X is slightly more complex since the b.f. of Y would be +1 and the imbalance at V would be negative or to the right. This can be corrected by a double rotation, first of the parent of X in the direction of the imbalance at V and then at V to correct the imbalance (Figure 5-28).

The algorithm for insertion with balance then must:

1. Add the new node.

2. Adjust the balance factors.

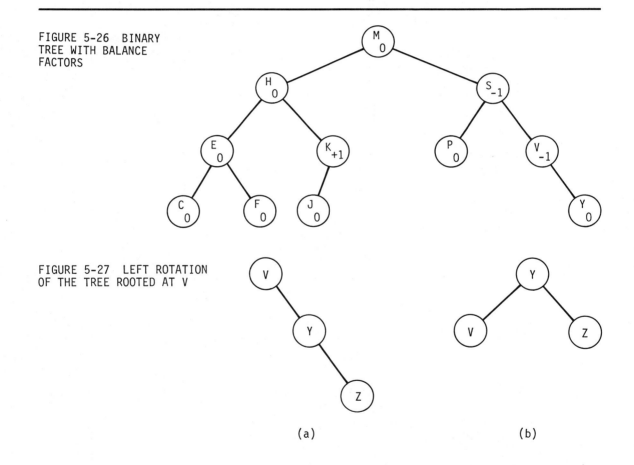

FIGURE 5-26 BINARY
TREE WITH BALANCE
FACTORS

FIGURE 5-27 LEFT ROTATION
OF THE TREE ROOTED AT V

(a)   (b)

3. Perform a single or double rotation as needed to correct the imbalance if an imbalance exists.

It should be noted that a rotation does not always take place between a leaf node and its two immediate ancestors, or between nodes whose subtrees that are not part of the ancestoral chain from our added node are empty.

Consider the situation in Figure 5-29(a) in which node B has just been inserted. In this case, the imbalance occurs at the root node M. Therefore, our insertion algorithm must account for a possible delayed imbalance as well as providing for all nonempty subtrees that may be involved in the rotation. The resulting imbalance from inserting B can be corrected by the rearrangement in Figure 5-29(b). This is just a single right rotation of MHE with the right subtree of H becoming the left subtree of M.

Similarly, the adjustment required for Figure 5-30(a) to be balanced is given by Figure 5-30(b), which is a double right rotation of MHE with the right subtree of H transferring to the left subtree of M.

FIGURE 5-28 DOUBLE ROTATION

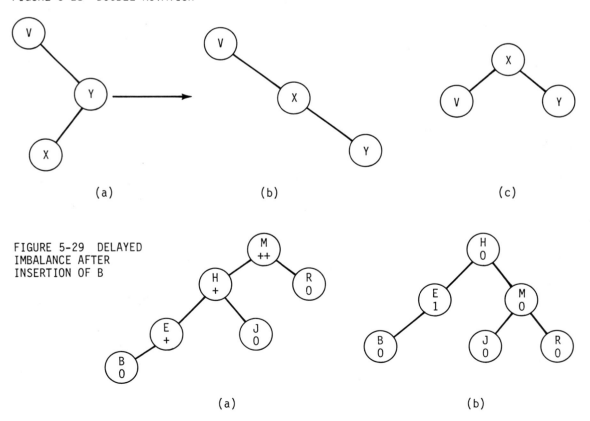

FIGURE 5-29 DELAYED
IMBALANCE AFTER
INSERTION OF B

In general, given a node J, its parent P, the next ancestor A (parent of P), and the pointer to A, AP, a single right rotation involves the following steps:

1. AP $\rightarrow$ SAVE
2. L_A $\rightarrow$ AP
3. R_P $\rightarrow$ L_A
4. SAVE $\rightarrow$ R_P

This is represented graphically in Figure 5-31. Likewise, in general, a double right rotation requires:

1. AP $\rightarrow$ SAVE
2. R_P $\rightarrow$ AP
3. L_J $\rightarrow$ R_P
4. L_A $\rightarrow$ L_J
5. R_J $\rightarrow$ L_A
6. SAVE $\rightarrow$ R_J

This is represented graphically in Figure 5-32.

Thus a single rotation requires the manipulation of three pointers, and a double rotation requires the manipulation of five pointers, together with the proper adjustment of the balance factors.

FIGURE 5-30
DELAYED IMBALANCE
AFTER INSERTION
OF J

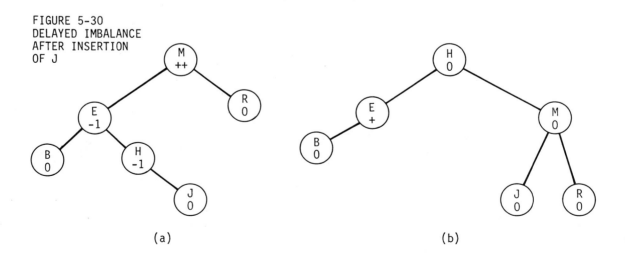

(a) (b)

The algorithm in Figure 5-33 satisfies the requirements for insertions with balancing. It shows only the subroutine for right rotations since left rotations involve a symmetric process. Indeed, it would probably be more effective to implement procedures for single and double rotations and then supply the necessary pointers as parameters. However, this particular implementation was chosen so that readers can readily trace the movement of pointers during this rather complex process. Once again, all insertions initially form leaf nodes, but a double rotation can change this relationship.

FIGURE 5-31 (a) Before; (b) after single rotation

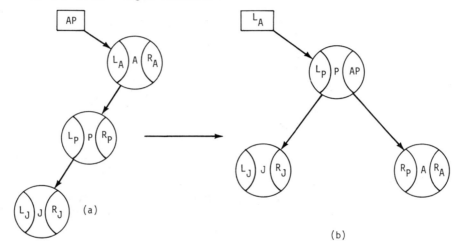

FIGURE 5-32 (a) Before; (b) after double rotation

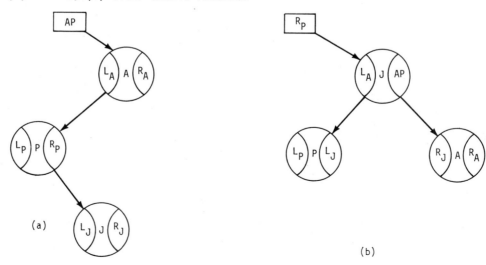

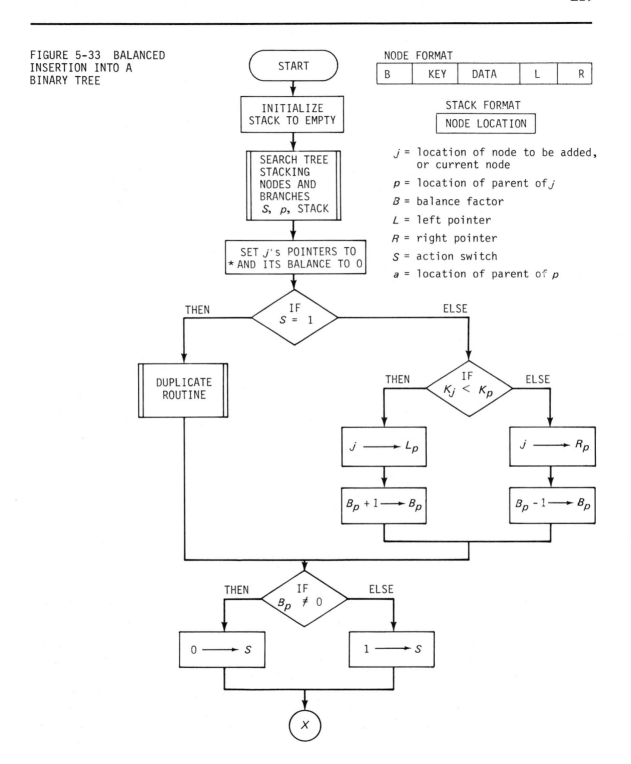

FIGURE 5-33 BALANCED INSERTION INTO A BINARY TREE

NODE FORMAT

| B | KEY | DATA | L | R |

STACK FORMAT

| NODE LOCATION |

j = location of node to be added, or current node

p = location of parent of j

B = balance factor

L = left pointer

R = right pointer

S = action switch

a = location of parent of p

START

INITIALIZE STACK TO EMPTY

SEARCH TREE STACKING NODES AND BRANCHES S, p, STACK

SET j's POINTERS TO * AND ITS BALANCE TO 0

IF $S = 1$

THEN — DUPLICATE ROUTINE

ELSE — IF $K_j < K_p$

THEN — $j \longrightarrow L_p$ — $B_p + 1 \longrightarrow B_p$

ELSE — $j \longrightarrow R_p$ — $B_p - 1 \longrightarrow B_p$

IF $B_p \neq 0$

THEN — $0 \longrightarrow S$

ELSE — $1 \longrightarrow S$

X

FIGURE 5-33 (continued)

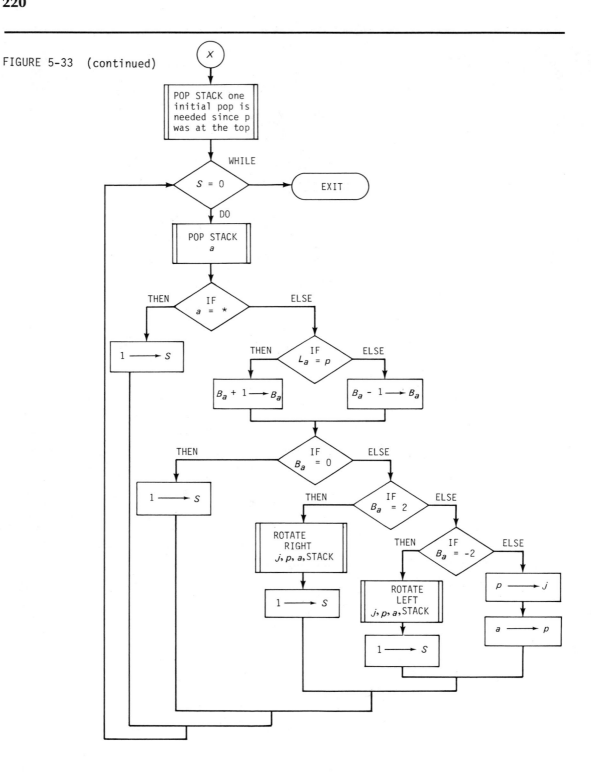

FIGURE 5-33 (continued)

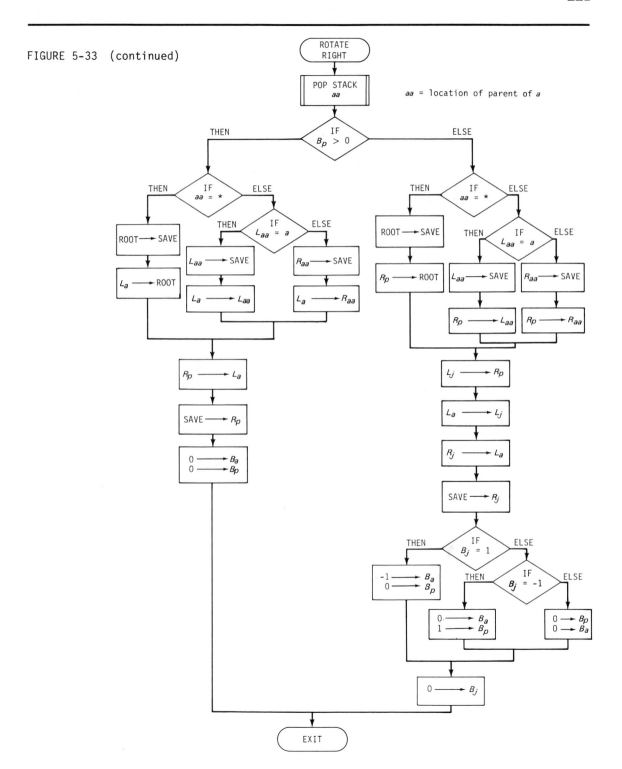

MULTIWAY TREES

Multiway trees are trees in which a node may have more than two children, as shown in Figure 5-34(a). The representation of such a structure in memory depends on its use. If the tree is used simply to show a hierarchical relationship of nodes without ordering, then each node needs pointer fields to accommodate the maximum number of children that can occur. For instance, Figure 5-34(a) might appear in memory like Figure 5-34(b).

It is obvious that the great majority of the pointer fields are empty, a situation that can result in a considerable waste of storage. This problem is intensified if an ordered tree is represented in this fashion, for in this case each node must carry a key associated with each subtree of a node in addition to the pointers to provide for an ordered search. A possible implementation of an ordered multiway tree is shown in Figure 5-35. In this case, each node may have as many as four children. Therefore, each node must contain space for four pointer fields as well as the four corresponding high keys in the respective subtrees.

One partial solution to wasted pointer and key fields is to represent each node of the multiway tree with exactly two pointer fields, a *first child pointer* and a *sibling pointer*. The tree in Figure 5-34(a) now becomes the one in Figure 5-36(a). In memory, we have what is shown in Figure 5-36(b).

This figure shows, in effect, a conversion from a multiway tree to a binary tree, and it is essentially the format of the level directories described earlier. The subdirectories and sublists are children of a directory entry at the level above, and entries within a particular sublist or subdirectory are siblings.

The processes for creating, searching, and updating multiway trees are not treated explicitly, and they are addressed only briefly as follows:

1. Creation of a multiway tree in first child-sibling form can be accomplished much as the level directories were earlier. However, creation in the general form is more difficult and is not attempted since the B tree, to be discussed later, usually suffices.

2. Searching a multiway tree is very similar to searching for a binary tree. For example, a preordered exhaustive search requires the stacking of possibly more than one alternate pointer, but other than that, the procedure is identical to a preordered search of a binary tree.

FIGURE 5-34 (a) Example of multiway trees; (b) example of how (a) might appear
in memory

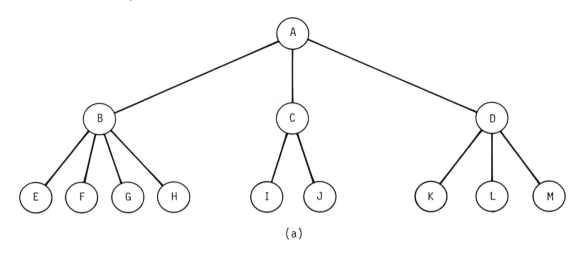

(a)

Location		PTR1	PTR2	PTR3	PTR4
1	A	2	3	4	*
2	B	5	6	7	8
3	C	9	10	*	*
4	D	11	12	13	*
5	E	*	*	*	*
6	F	*	*	*	*
7	G	*	*	*	*
8	H	*	*	*	*
9	I	*	*	*	*
10	J	*	*	*	*
11	K	*	*	*	*
12	L	*	*	*	*
13	M	*	*	*	*

ROOT
1

(b)

FIGURE 5-35 (a) A possible implementation of an ordered multiway tree; (b) example of how (a) might appear in memory

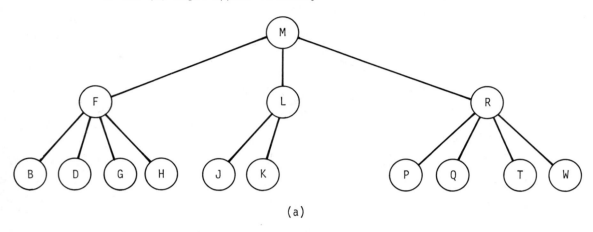

(a)

Location		HIGH KEY SUBTREE 1	PTR1	HIGH KEY SUBTREE 2	PTR2	HIGH KEY SUBTREE 3	PTR3	H.K. 4	PTR4
1	B	*	*	*	*	*	*	*	*
2	D	*	*	*	*	*	*	*	*
3	F	B	1	D	2	G	4	H	5
4	G	*	*	*	*	*	*	*	*
5	H	*	*	*	*	*	*	*	*
6	J	*	*	*	*	*	*	*	*
7	K	*	*	*	*	*	*	*	*
8	L	J	6	K	7	*	*	*	*
9	M	H	3	L	8	W	12	*	*
10	P	*	*	*	*	*	*	*	*
11	Q	*	*	*	*	*	*	*	*
12	R	P	10	Q	11	T	13	W	14
13	T	*	*	*	*	*	*	*	*
14	W	*	*	*	*	*	*	*	*

ROOT
9

(b)

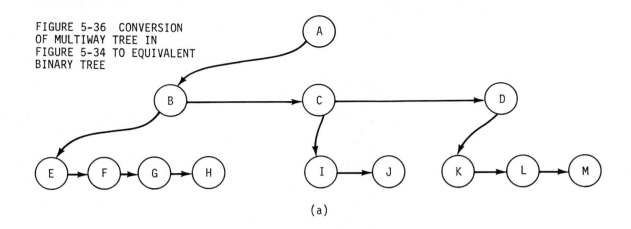

FIGURE 5-36 CONVERSION OF MULTIWAY TREE IN FIGURE 5-34 TO EQUIVALENT BINARY TREE

(a)

		First Child Pointer	Sibling Pointer
1	A	2	*
2	B	5	3
3	C	9	4
4	D	11	*
5	E	*	6
6	F	*	7
7	G	*	8
8	H	*	*
9	I	*	10
10	J	*	*
11	K	*	12
12	L	*	13
13	M	*	*

(b)

3. Updating is also similar to updating for a binary tree. Additions are made at the leaf level, and deletions require a procedure similar to replacing a node with an appropriate descendant node. These algorithms are left for the reader to develop.

DECISION TREES

We have discussed the use of trees as directories or indices and as files structured as search trees. Another use of trees is as decision trees. A *decision tree* is a model that represents all of the sequences of steps that lead to a possible solution of a given problem. In the tree, the root is a fixed starting position or step; every other node represents a particular step choice or decision from its parent, and each branch of the tree represents a sequence of steps that lead to a possible solution to the problem. In other words, a decision tree gives us a model whereby we can consider every possible solution to a given problem.

Consider the classic traveling salesman problem in which a salesman needs to visit a given list of cities and then return home so that the total distance covered (or the total cost of travel) is at a minimum.

For illustrative purposes, let us assume that the salesman must visit three cities. If we represent the salesman's home city by *A* and the other three cities with *B, C,* and *D,* then each branch of the tree diagram in Figure 5-37 represents a possible sequence in which he can visit the cities.

Using the model in this figure, a preordered traversal produces all of the branches such that each time a leaf node is reached, a new branch is started. If

FIGURE 5-37   TRAVELING SALESMAN PROBLEM

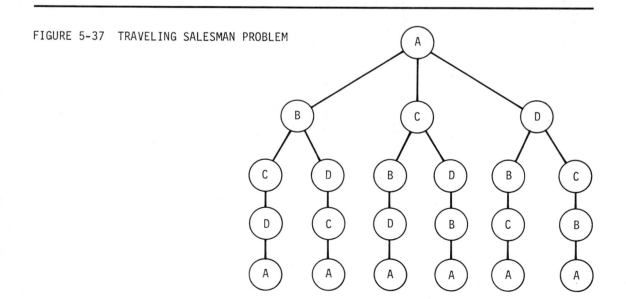

we devise an algorithm that will keep track of the current branch being traversed as well as the shortest branch encountered so far, then we will obtain the shortest route at the end of the complete traversal.

For this problem, the number of branches will be equal to the number of permutations that can be obtained from the number of cities to be visited, not counting the home city. Therefore, if there are n cities to be visited, then there will be $n!$ branches. In this case, we have three cities to be visited. Thus we have $3! = 6$ branches. Readers should be cautioned that this solution to the traveling salesman problem is appropriate for only a relatively small value of n, such that n does not exceed 10 or 12 cities, depending on the speed of the computer used and the efficiency of the algorithm employed.

For example, suppose that for a given algorithm and computer, the average time to reach the end of a branch is 200 microseconds. Then, for 10 cities to be visited, we have:

$$n! = 10! = 3,628,800 \text{ branches}$$

and $\qquad 3,628,800 \times 0.0002 = 725.76 \text{ seconds}$

or approximately 12 minutes to search. But 12! would increase this time by a factor of 132 yielding 132 (12) = 1584 minutes or 26.4 hours, which would cause considerable consternation at most computer centers!

Fortunately, no matter what n is used, a physical representation of decision tree *does not* need to exist anywhere. The algorithm simply considers choices in a sequence that would be represented by a tree structure. At each step where more than one choice exists, choices not taken are stacked in the identical fashion of a traversal of a tree. This fact will become evident in the next example, which is also a classic in the literature of interesting problems for solution with a computer.

This problem is called the Knight's Tour and seeks to find a sequence of moves such that from some given position on a chessboard, a knight must visit each square on the board exactly once.

The following approach to the Knight's Tour problem was suggested by S. E. Goodman and S. T. Hedetniemi in their text, *Introduction to the Design and Analysis of Algorithms* (1977), although their solution is not the exhaustive type presented here.

The chessboard is presented as an N by N array of squares to which the knight must move, surrounded by a guard perimeter two squares deep to prevent the knight from "jumping" off the board. Initially, all of the squares on the game part of the board are set to 0, while the squares in the guard perimeter are set to some nonzero value such as 99 or -1 (see Figure 5-38).

Readers have no doubt noticed that the chessboard in this figure contains only 25 positions instead of the normal 64. The reason for this is that an exhaustive approach to a solution from any given position on a regulation 8 by 8 board can be prohibitive with respect to execution time unless the programmer is lucky enough to encounter a solution branch very early in the traversal. Should an initial position from which there is no tour that covers the whole board be chosen, then the entire decision tree must be traversed. Such a traversal is quite long for the 5 by 5 board and astronomical for the 8 by 8 board.

Moves are generated by using a table consisting of the eight pairs of increments that can be added to the knight's present coordinates on the board to generate a possible legal move. A legal move is one that resides on the board, has not been visited before, and lies $\pm 2 \times \pm 1$ squares or $\pm 1 \times \pm 2$ squares from the present position. See Figure 5-40.

A tour begins by replacing the 0 in a given square on the board with a 1. As each new move is made, the move is recorded on the board by replacing the new position's zero value with the move number so that, at the end of the tour, the sequence of moves can be shown by simply printing out the board.

At each position on the board, all eight possible next moves are tested; any of these that will produce a legal move is stacked. Then the stack of legal moves is popped to produce the next move, and the process continues. If the number of moves made reaches the maximum (25 for the 5 by 5 board), a successful tour has been generated. Otherwise, if the stack of legal moves is emptied before the maximum is reached, then no tour exists from the given position.

The algorithm in Figure 5-39 makes use of two stacks, one to record the sequence of moves for the tour being created (TOUR STACK) and the other for the choice of moves that remain to be taken during the traversal (CHOICE STACK). The TOUR STACK is necessary to provide backtracking capability, since backtracking to a choice not previously taken requires resetting to zero any squares prior to this in the new sequence.

The algorithm in Figure 5-39 was implemented in COBOL on an IBM 370/125 computer, and it produced tours from positions (1,1) and (3,3) in less than 5 minutes on a 5 by 5 board. In all, tours were found from 13 positions on the 5 by 5 board. However, no tour was found from position (1,2) or any of its seven other equivalent positions.

The algorithm in Figure 5-40 produces the tour starting from position (1,1) on the board (Figure 5-41).

FIGURE 5-38 INITIAL BOARD
ARRANGEMENT FOR KNIGHT'S
TOUR PROBLEM

99	99	99	99	99	99	99	99	99
99	99	99	99	99	99	99	99	99
99	99	0	0	0	0	0	99	99
99	99	0	0	0	0	0	99	99
99	99	0	0	0	0	0	99	99
99	99	0	0	0	0	0	99	99
99	99	0	0	0	0	0	99	99
99	99	99	99	99	99	99	99	99
99	99	99	99	99	99	99	99	99

FIGURE 5-39 EXHAUSTIVE
SOLUTION TO KNIGHT'S
TOUR PROBLEM

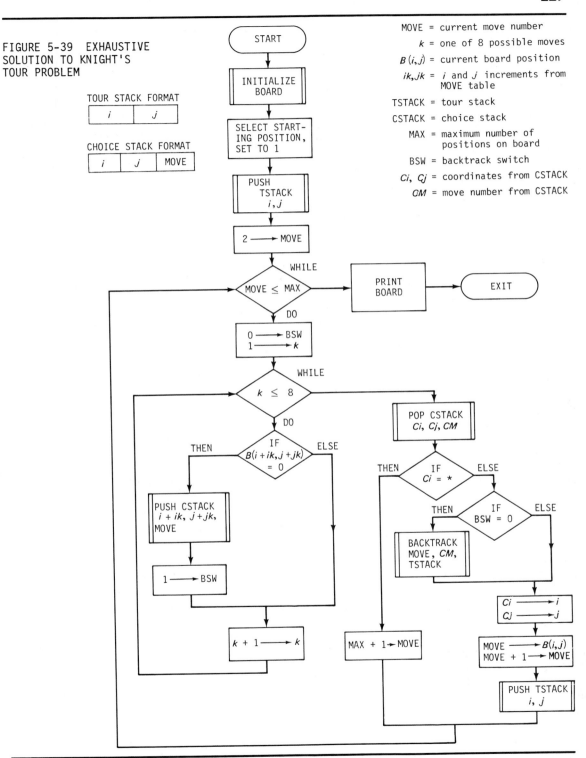

FIGURE 5-39 (continued)

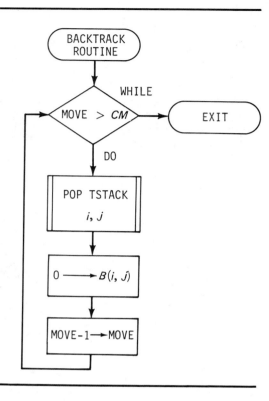

FIGURE 5-40 MOVE TABLE

k	ik	jk
1	-2	+1
2	-1	+2
3	+1	+2
4	+2	+1
5	+2	-1
6	+1	-2
7	-1	-2
8	-2	-1

i,j = board position
ik = i increment
jk = j increment
MOVE = move number

FIGURE 5-41 SOLUTION TO KNIGHT'S TOUR
USING ALGORITHM IN FIGURE 5-39

1	10	15	20	23
16	5	22	9	14
11	2	19	24	21
6	17	4	13	8
3	12	7	18	25

EXHAUSTIVE
SOLUTION TO
KNIGHT'S TOUR
PROBLEM

```
/*  MOVE = current move number */
/*  K = one of the 8 possible moves from a given
    position */
/*  B(I,J) = current board position */
/*  IK,JK = increments to I and J, from move table */
/*  TSTACK,CSTACK = tour stack and choice stack */
/*  MAX = maximum number of positions on board */
/*  BSW = backtrack switch */
/*  CI,CJ,CM = board coordinates and move number
    from move stack */


PROC        KNIGHTS-TOUR
    initialize board
    input I,J
    B(I,J) = 1
    PUSH TSTACK; send I,J
    MOVE = 2
    WHILE  MOVE ≤ MAX  DO
        BSW = 0
        K = 1
        WHILE  K ≤ 8  DO
            IF  B(I+IK,J+JK) = 0
                THEN  PUSH CSTACK; send I+IK,J+JK,MOVE
                    BSW = 1
                ELSE  continue
            ENDIF
            K = K + 1
        ENDDO
        POP CSTACK; return CI,CJ,CM
        IF  CI = end
            THEN  MOVE = MAX + 1
            ELSE  IF  BSW = 0
                    THEN BACKTRACK; send MOVE,CM,TSTACK, return MOVE
                    ELSE  continue
                  ENDIF
                  I = CI
                  J = CJ
                  B(I,J) = MOVE
                  MOVE = MOVE + 1
                  PUSH TSTACK; send I,J
        ENDIF
    ENDDO
    print board
END PROC
```

BACKTRACK
(SUBROUTINE OF
KNIGHT'S TOUR)

```
/*  all variables same as main routine */

PROC    BACKTRACK
    WHILE   MOVE > CM    DO
        POP STACK; return I,J
        B(I,J) = 0                /* clear out old moves */
        MOVE = MOVE -1
    ENDDO
END PROC
```

B TREES

B trees are ordered, optimally balanced, multiway trees with additional restrictions described here. A *B tree of order n* has the following properties:

1. Each node has at most n children.

2. Each node, except the root and leaf nodes, has at least $n/2$ children.

3. The root has at least 2 children, unless it is a leaf node.

4. All leaf nodes are on the same level and contain no information. (These are represented simply by null pointers in their parent nodes and therefore require no additional storage.)

5. A nonleaf node with K children contains $K - 1$ keys.

B trees are extremely useful because they are easy to search, relatively easy to maintain when compared to multiway trees in general, and provide fast retrieval times when used as indices to external files. Data base management systems, such as System 2000 as well as IBM VSAM access methods, use B-tree indices.

B trees maintain their balance by splitting and contracting nodes. When the addition of a new key or record would cause a node to have $n + 1$ children, the node is split into two nodes and the middle key from what would have been an oversized node is moved up to the parent node. This move can possibly cause a splitting again, and the process can be propagated all the way to and including the root. When the root splits, a new level is added to the tree so that the tree adds levels from the root upward instead of downward from the leaves. Deletions cause nodes to contract, and when a deletion would cause a node to have less than $n/2$ descendants, this node is combined with a neighbor that can also propagate contractions upward through the structure. Figure 5-42 shows a B tree of order 5. The general node format for a B tree of order n is

$$P_1, K_1, P_2, K_2, \ldots, P_{n-1}, K_{n-1}, P_n$$

We would rarely want to construct a B tree that contains only a system of keys. Normally there is a record, or at least some additional information, associated with each key. Therefore, we can either carry the additional information with the corresponding key or include a pointer to this information. If we use a pointer to each record, our B-tree node is modified as follows:

$$P_1, (K_1, R_1), P_2, (K_2, R_2), \ldots, P_{n-1}, (K_{n-1}, R_{n-1}), P_n$$

where P_i and K_i are as before, and R_i is a pointer to the record that corresponds to K_i.

Since nodes may contain a variable number of keys, processing of the node can be facilitated by including a count of the number of keys in the node as the first entry of the node. This option is used in the following illustration of a B tree residing in memory and also in each of the B-tree algorithms that follow.

Using the preceding format, our B tree of order 5 would appear in memory as shown in Figure 5-43.

The deletion of any of the level-three keys in the previous example, except for 819 or 872, would not cause combining of nodes or affect the content of the nodes at levels one or two. However, the deletion of 872 invokes a more involved process.

First, after the deletion of 872,

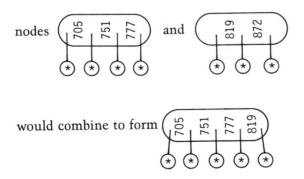

This would cause the key 806 at the next highest level to be replaced by 902, which will now result in a reinsertion of 806, which in turn causes a split. The final result is shown in Figure 5-44.

234

FIGURE 5-42 B TREE OF ORDER 5

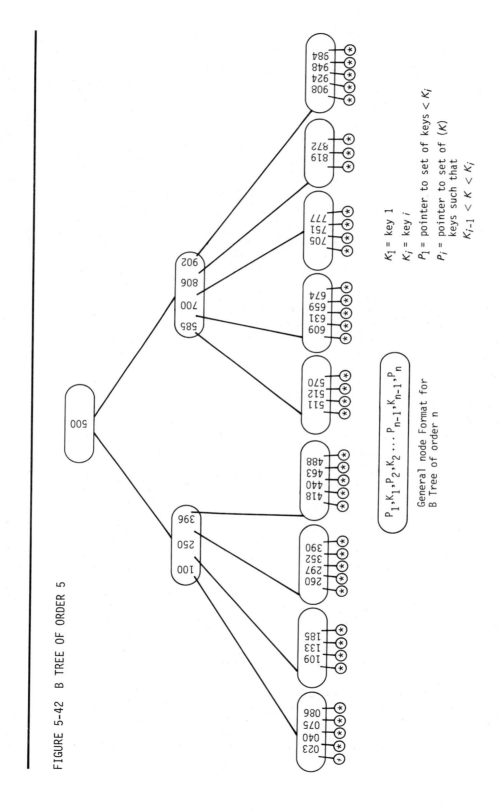

K_1 = key 1

K_i = key i

P_1 = pointer to set of keys < K_i

P_i = pointer to set of (K)
      keys such that

      $K_{i-1} < K < K_i$

$P_1, K_1, P_2, K_2 \ldots P_{n-1}, K_{n-1}, P_n$

General node Format for
B Tree of order n

FIGURE 5-43 B TREE OF ORDER 5 AS IT WOULD APPEAR IN MEMORY: (a) we assume that
the records are physically in ascending order starting at relative
location 1; (b) records associated with the B-tree index

Node	Key Count	P_1	K_1	R_1	P_2	K_2	R_2	P_3	K_3	R_3	P_4	K_4	R_4	P_5
1	1	2	500	19	3									
2	3	4	100	5	5	250	9	6	396	14	7			
3	4	8	585	23	9	700	28	10	806	32	11	902	35	12
4	4	*	023	1	*	040	2	*	075	3	*	086	4	*
5	3	*	109	6	*	133	7	*	185	8	*			
6	3	*	260	10	*	297	11	*	352	12	*	390	13	*
7	4	*	418	15	*	440	16	*	463	17	*	488	18	*
8	3	*	511	20	*	512	21	*	570	22	*			
9	4	*	609	24	*	631	25	*	659	26	*	674	27	*
10	3	*	705	29	*	751	30	*	777	31	*			
11	2	*	819	33	*	872	34	*						
12	4	*	908	36	*	924	37	*	948	38	*	984	39	*

(a)

	Key	Data
1	023	
2	040	
3	075	
4	086	
5	100	
6	109	
7	133	
8	185	
9	250	
10	260	
11	297	
12	352	
13	390	
14	396	
15	418	
16	440	
17	463	
18	488	
19	500	
20	511	
21	512	
22	570	
23	585	
24	609	
25	631	
26	659	
27	674	
28	700	
29	705	
30	751	
31	777	
32	806	
33	819	
34	872	
35	902	
36	908	
37	924	
38	948	
39	984	
40		

(b)

Continuing with our original example of the B tree of order 5, consider the addition of key 450.

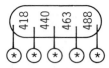

must now split yielding the result shown in Figure 5-45.

SEARCHING B TREES

Since we plan to present the creation of a B tree as an insertion process, and since insertion requires searching, we discuss searching first.

Searching a B tree is similar to searching a binary tree except that, for a B tree of order N, we must consider up to $N-1$ keys with N pointers for each node instead of the fixed single key with two pointers for each node in a binary tree. This means that not only must we search from node to node, as before, but now we must also search each node internally as well to determine which key will indicate our next branch.

The algorithm in Figure 5-46 makes use of a key-count field in the first field of every node to specify the number of valid keys that reside in the node. Each key has associated with it (1) a low pointer for the node at the next lower

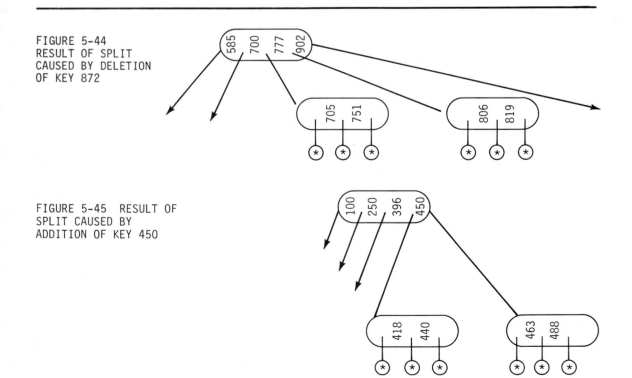

FIGURE 5-44
RESULT OF SPLIT
CAUSED BY DELETION
OF KEY 872

FIGURE 5-45   RESULT OF
SPLIT CAUSED BY
ADDITION OF KEY 450

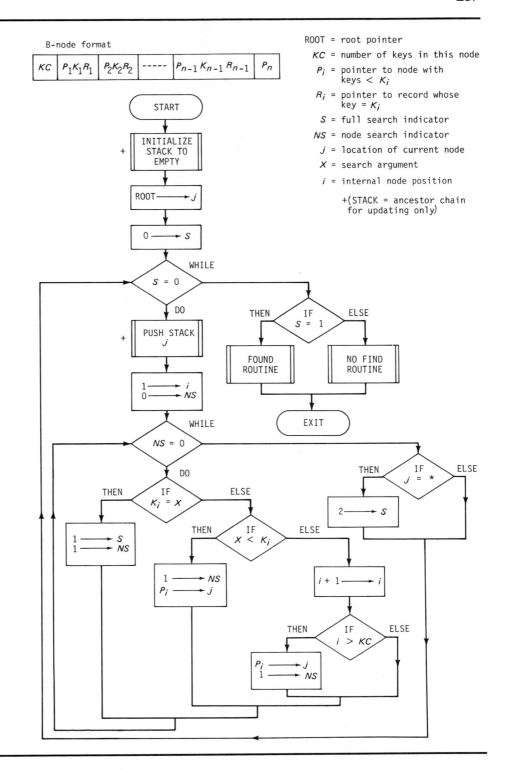

FIGURE 5-46
SEARCH OF A
B TREE

B-node format

| KC | $P_1K_1R_1$ | $P_2K_2R_2$ | ----- | $P_{n-1}K_{n-1}R_{n-1}$ | P_n |

ROOT = root pointer
KC = number of keys in this node
P_i = pointer to node with keys < K_i
R_i = pointer to record whose key = K_i
S = full search indicator
NS = node search indicator
j = location of current node
X = search argument
i = internal node position

+(STACK = ancestor chain for updating only)

```
SEARCH OF A B TREE          /*  ROOT = root pointer */
                            /*  P(I) = pointer to node with keys < K(I) */
                            /*  R(I) = pointer to record whose key = K(I) */
                            /*  KC(J) = key count of node at J */
                            /*  J = location of current node */
                            /*  I = internal position within current node */
                            /*  X = search argument */
                            /*  S = full search indicator */
                            /*  NS = node search indicator */
                            /*  STACK = ancestor chain (for updating only) */

                    PROC B-TREE-SEARCH
                        *(do initialize STACK to empty)    /* for updating only */
                        J = ROOT
                        S = 0
                        WHILE S = 0 DO
                            *(PUSH STACK; send J)     /* for updating only */
                            I = 1
                            NS = 0
                            WHILE NS = 0 DO
                                IF K(I) = X
                                    THEN S = 1
                                         NS = 1
                                    ELSE IF X < K(I)
                                            THEN NS = 1
                                                 J = P(I)
                                            ELSE I = I + 1
                                                IF I > KC
                                                    THEN J = P(I)
                                                         NS = 1
                                                    ELSE Continue
                                                ENDIF
                                         ENDIF
                                ENDIF
                            ENDDO
                            IF J = end
                                THEN S = 2
                                ELSE Continue
                            ENDIF
                        ENDDO
                        IF S = 1
                            THEN do found routine
                            ELSE do nofind routine
                        ENDIF
                    END PROC
```

level with all key values less than it, (2) a record pointer to the record with a key value equal to it, and (3) a high pointer to the node at the next lower level that contains key values greater than it. Therefore, the key-count field is useful in processing the entire node.

The algorithm will return: (j), the location of the node that contains the target key or the node in which the new key must be inserted; (S), the search indicator of whether the target key was found or not; (i), the position within the node at j at which the target key is located, or the location of the key position at which the target key must be inserted; and finally (ASTK), which is a stack of all nodes processed during the search, including j. The stacking of the search path is needed only if this routine is to be used for updating.

CREATION AND UPDATING OF B TREES

Creation of a B tree can be accomplished by creating an initial tree with a single node and then inserting all other keys one at a time. Since the B tree must, by definition, remain balanced, we perform balanced insertions. Thus the resulting structure is also balanced. Creation, then, is basically reduced to developing an insertion algorithm for B trees.

There are essentially two types of insertion. The first case involves insertion of a key into a node that is not full. This process is a relatively simple one that requires little more than shifting the current node contents to accommodate a new entry, much in the fashion of the basic insertion sort.

The second case is the insertion of a key into a node that is already full. This case requires splitting the node and the insertion of an entry into the parent of the node that was split. This, in turn, may cause another split, which may cause another, and so on, until even the root splits.

The algorithm in Figure 5-47 reduces all inserts to the case of insertion into a nonfull node. When splitting is required, the full node is split into two nonfull nodes, and then the insertion of the new key is made to one of these, while the central key from the original full node is passed up for insertion in the parent node. If the order of the B tree is an even number (that is, it contains an odd number of keys), then the selection of the central key is simply the key found at internal position m, where $m = \lceil KC_j/2 \rceil$. However, when we have an even number of keys, the central key must be chosen such that, after the split, both of the new nodes satisfy the requirements for the minimum number of children. Our algorithm for the split solves this problem by selecting a central key that is found at either $m = \lceil KC_j/2 \rceil$ or $m = \lceil (KC_j + 1)/2 \rceil$ from the original node, or by choosing the central key as the new key to be inserted, in the special case when the new key would in fact be the center of an oversized node if we allowed insertion without splitting. The problem of the propagation of the splitting is handled by following the ancestor chain of the first node, and treating each node along the chain in the same fashion as the first by inserting the key produced by the split. When a nonfull node is encountered along the chain, a final insertion is made and the process stops. In the special case when the root node splits, a new root is created with a single key.

FIGURE 5-47
(a) Insertion into a B tree

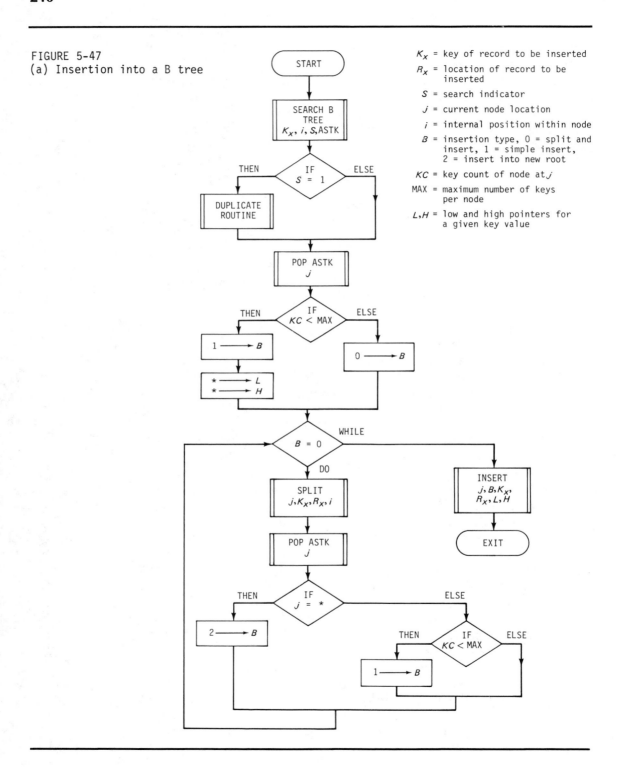

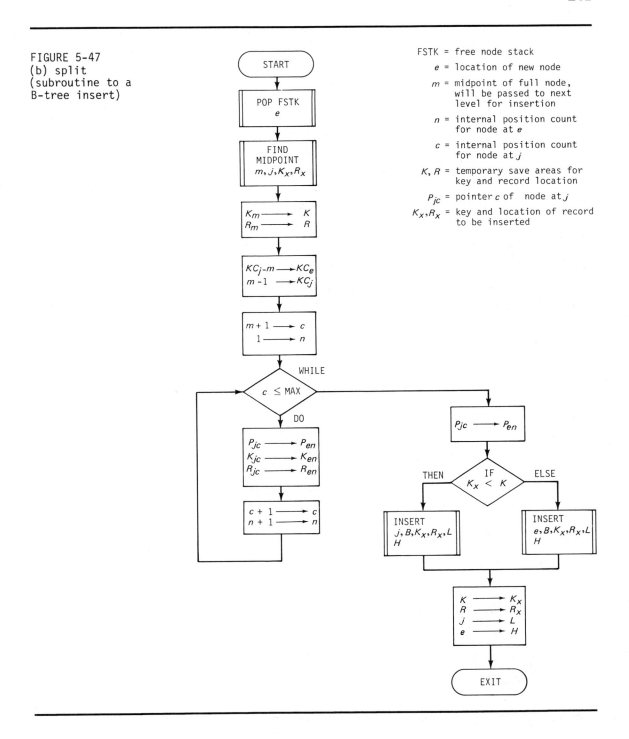

FIGURE 5-47
(b) split
(subroutine to a
B-tree insert)

FSTK = free node stack

e = location of new node

m = midpoint of full node, will be passed to next level for insertion

n = internal position count for node at e

c = internal position count for node at j

K, R = temporary save areas for key and record location

P_{jc} = pointer c of node at j

K_x, R_x = key and location of record to be inserted

242

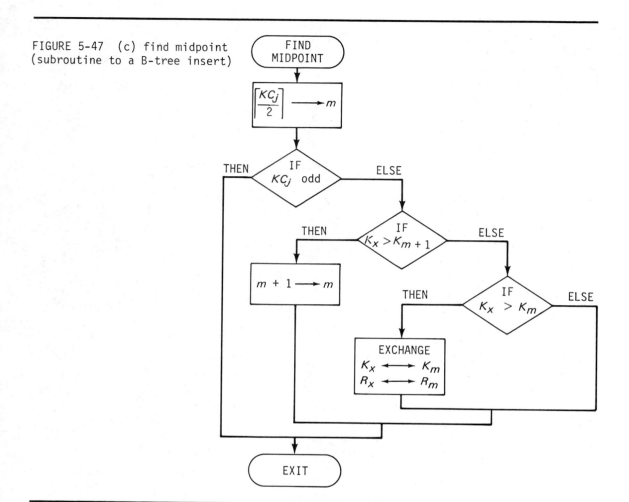

FIGURE 5-47 (c) find midpoint
(subroutine to a B-tree insert)

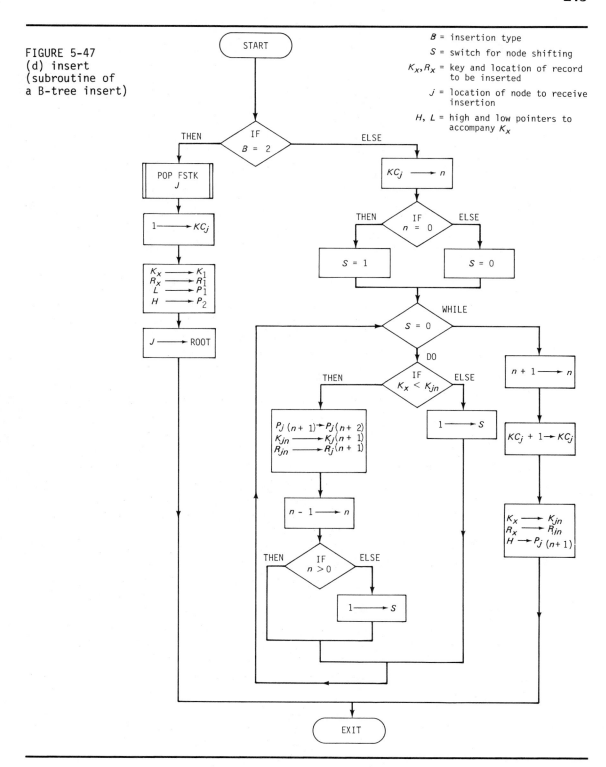

FIGURE 5-47
(d) insert
(subroutine of
a B-tree insert)

INSERTION INTO A B TREE

```
/*  It is assumed that the B tree is nonempty and
    of order ≥3 */
/*  KX,RX = key and location of record to be inserted */
/*  S = search indicator; 1 = found, 2 = no find */
/*  J = current node location */
/*  I = internal key position for node at J */
/*  B = insertion type; 0 = split and insert,
    1 = simple insert, 2 = insert into new root */
/*  KC = key count of node at J */
/*  MAX = maximum number of keys per node */
/*  L,H = low and high pointers for a given key value */
/*  ASTK = ancestor stack from search routine */


PROC      B-TREE-INSERT
    SEARCH B-TREE; send KX return I,S,ASTK
    IF  S=1
        THEN  do duplicate routine
        ELSE  continue
    ENDIF
    POP ASTK; return J
    IF  KC < MAX
        THEN  B = 1
                L = end
                H = end
        ELSE  B = 0
    ENDIF
    WHILE  B = 0   DO
        SPLIT; send J,I,KX,RX
        POP ASTK; return J
        IF  J = end
            THEN B = 2
            ELSE  IF  KC < MAX
                      THEN  B = 1
                      ELSE  continue
                  ENDIF
        ENDIF
    ENDDO
    INSERT; send J,B,KX,RX,L,H
END PROC
```

SPLIT (SUBROUTINE
TO B-TREE-INSERT)

```
/*  FSTK = free node stack; used to create
    new nodes */
/*  E = location of new node */
/*  M = midpoint of full node, will be passed
    to next level */
/*  N = internal position for node at E */
/*  C = internal position for node at J */
/*  K,R = temporary save areas for key and
    record location */
/*  P(J,C) = pointer C of node at J */
/*  other variables same as main routine */

PROC    SPLIT
    POP  FSTK; return E
    FIND MIDPOINT send M,J,KX,RX return M,J,KX,RX
    K = K(J,M)
    R = R(J,M)
    /* midpoint record from full node is extracted
       to pass up to next level */
    KC(J) = M - 1
    KC(E) = KC(J) - M
    C = M + 1
    N = 1
    /* shift half of node J contents to node E */
    WHILE  C ≤ MAX      DO
        P(E,N) = P(J,C)
        K(E,N) = K(J,C)
        R(E,N) = R(J,C)
        C = C + 1
        N = N + 1
    ENDDO
    P(E,N) = P(J,C)    /* shift high pointer from J to E */
    IF  KX < K
        THEN INSERT; send J,B,KX,RX,L,H
        ELSE INSERT; send E,B,KX,RX,L,H
    ENDIF
    KX = K
    RX = R
    L = J
    H = E
END PROC
```

FIND MIDPOINT
(SUBROUTINE TO
B-TREE-INSERT)

```
                              /*  all variables same as split subroutine */

              PROC    FIND-MIDPOINT
                  M =  KC(J) / 2
                  IF  KC(J) is odd
                      THEN continue
                      ELSE IF KX  > K(M + 1)
                              THEN  M = M + 1
                              ELSE IF KX > K(M)
                                      THEN exchange KX,K(M)
                                           exchange RX,R(M)
                                      ELSE continue
                                      ENDIF
                              ENDIF
                      ENDIF
              END PROC
```

Readers may have already surmised from the earlier examples of inserting and deleting keys that the deletion process is a bit more involved than insertion. Deletion of keys can cause both contraction and splitting of nodes to maintain a B-tree structure.

Contraction will occur anytime the result of a deletion leaves a node, other than the root, with less than $N/2$ children for a B tree of order N. Contraction is accomplished by combining the deficient node with an adjacent node at the same level. However, anytime nodes are combined, we may have more than N children and thus a split must occur. A split can also occur when the combining of two nodes with the same parent produces a full node for, at this point, the parent node will have an extra pointer. Therefore, one of its keys must be inserted in the new node, thus causing a split.

A deletion algorithm is not presented here since it is long and contains a combination of techniques that we have studied before. A detailed procedure for a deletion algorithm is presented in *Algorithms + Data = Programs* by Niklaus Wirth (1975).

```
INSERT (SUBROUTINE     /*  all variables same as in other routines */
OF B-TREE-INSERT)

                PROC    INSERT
                   IF  B = 2
                       THEN  POP FSTK; return J          /* check for no room here */
                             KC(J) = 1
                             K(J,1) = KX
                             R(J,1) = RX
                             P(J,1) = L
                             P(J,2) = H
                       ELSE  N = KC(J)
                          IF  N = 0              /* For B tree of order 3, N may
                              THEN   S = 1                equal 0 */
                              ELSE   S = 0
                          WHILE S = 0  DO
                             IF   KX < K(J,N)                    /* shift contents */
                                  THEN   P(J,N+2) = P(J,N+1)
                                         K(J,N+1) = K(J,N)
                                         R(J,N+1) = R(J,N)
                                         N = N - 1
                                         IF  N > 0
                                             THEN   continue
                                             ELSE   S = 1
                                         ENDIF
                                  ELSE   S = 1
                             ENDIF
                          ENDDO
                          N = N + 1
                          KC(J) = KC(J) + 1                       /* count new entry */
                          K(J,N) = KX
                          R(J,N) = RX
                          P(J,N+1) = H
                          ROOT = J
                   ENDIF
                END PROC
```

REVIEW EXERCISES

1. Define a tree.

2. Describe one example of an application in which a tree structure is used.

3. Show how the binary tree structure shown here would appear in memory by completing the table.

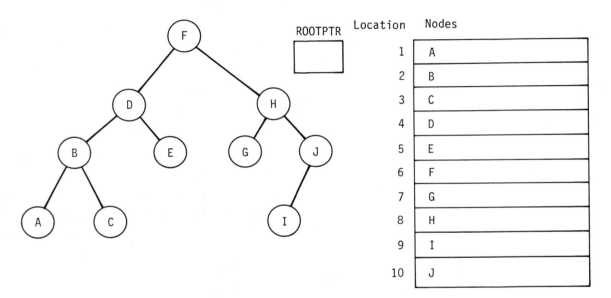

4. Draw a flowchart of a routine that is to search a left-to-right-ordered binary tree. (The example in problem 3 is ordered in this fashion.)

5. Indicate whether or not the following binary trees are balanced.

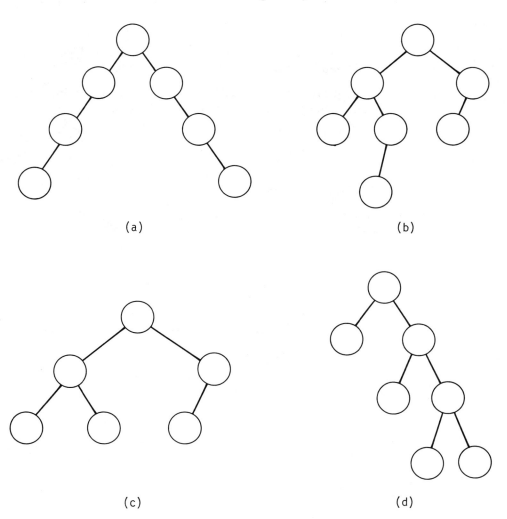

(a)   (b)

(c)   (d)

6. (a) Draw a B-tree structure of order 4 for the following keys with a root
   node that contains exactly one key. The keys are 10, 20, 30, 50, 55,
   60, 66, 72, 80, 88, 90, 96, 100.

   (b) Show what happens when keys 2, 4, and 8 are added to the structure.
   (You need show only the affected nodes.)

PROGRAMMING ASSIGNMENTS

Building on the previous programming assignments (see problems 1 and 2 on page 181), modify problem 2 on page 181 such that:

(a) The inverted file is now created as a binary tree in ascending order (left to right) that will now allow for a logical binary search.

(b) Print out the physical inverted file area to show that the tree has been created properly.

(c) Next print out the tree in inorder, which should yield the ascending logical order of the records.

(d) Process the inquiries to the file as before to show that the program still works.

REFERENCES

Augestein, Moshe J., and Aaron M. Tenenbaum. *Data Structures and PL/I Programming.* Englewood Cliffs, N.J.: Prentice-Hall, 1979.

Birkhoff, Garrett, and Saunders MacLane. *A Survey of Modern Algebra.* Rev. ed. New York: Macmillan, 1962.

Brillinger, Peter C., and Doron J. Cohen. *Introduction to Data Structures and Non-Numeric Computation.* Englewood Cliffs, N.J.: Prentice-Hall, 1972.

Bureau of the Budget. *Automatic Data Processing Glossary.* U.S. Government Executive Office of the President. Washington, D.C.: U.S. Government Printing Office, 1963.

Coleman, Derek. *A Structured Programming Approach to Data.* New York: Springer-Verlag, 1979.

Comer, Douglas. "The Ubiquitous B-Tree." *ACM Computing Surveys*, vol. 11, no. 2 (June 1979).

Digital Equipment Corp. *Peripherals Handbook.* Maynard, Mass.: Digital Equipment Corp., 1980.

Donovan, John J. *Systems Programming.* New York: McGraw-Hill, 1972.

Elson, Mark. *Data Structures.* Palo Alto, Calif.: Science Research Associates, 1975.

Flores, Ivan. *Assemblers and BAL.* Englewood Cliffs, N.J.: Prentice-Hall, 1971.

Flores, Ivan. *Data Structure and Management.* Englewood Cliffs, N.J.: Prentice-Hall, 1970.

Flores, Ivan. *Data Structure and Management.* 2d ed. Englewood Cliffs, N.J.: Prentice-Hall, 1977.

Gear, William C. *BASIC Language Manual.* Palo Alto, Calif.: Science Research Associates, 1978.

Goodman, S. E., and S. T. Hedetniemi. *Introduction to the Design and Analysis of Algorithms.* New York: McGraw-Hill, 1977.

Gotlieb, C. C., and L. R. Gotlieb. *Data Types and Structures.* Englewood Cliffs, N.J.: Prentice-Hall, 1978.

Graham, J. W., and J. W. Welch. *Waterloo BASIC: A Structured Approach.* Waterloo, Ontario, Canada: WATFAC Publications, 1979.

Gruenberger, Fred. *Computing a Second Course.* New York: Canfield Press, 1971.

Hibbard, T. N. "An Empirical Study Of Minimal-Storage Sorting." *Communications of the ACM*, vol. 6, no. 5 (May 1963).

Horowitz, Ellis, and Sartaj Sahni. *Fundamentals of Data Structures.* Potomac, Md.: Computer Science Press, 1976.

IBM. *Introduction to IBM Direct-Access Storage Devices and Organization Methods.* GC20-1649-9.

IBM. *IBM DOS Full American National Standard COBOL.* GC28-6394-6.

IBM. *Series 1 Digest.* G360-0061-3.

IBM. *IBM System/370 Principles of Operation.* GA22-7000-6.

IBM. *IBM System/370 Model 125 Functional Characteristics.* GA33-1506-3.

IBM. *IBM System/370 Model 145 Functional Characteristics.* GA24-3557-4.

IBM. *OS Sort/Merge Program.* GC28-6543-7.

James, Robert C., and Glenn James. *Mathematics Dictionary.* 3d ed. Princeton, N.J.: Van Nostrand, 1968.

Knuth, Donald E. *The Art of Computer Programming.* Vol. 1. Reading, Mass.: Addison-Wesley, 1969.

Knuth, Donald E. *The Art of Computer Programming.* Vol. 3. Reading, Mass.: Addison-Wesley, 1973.

Kroenke, David M. *Business Computer Systems: An Introduction.* Santa Cruz, Calif.: Mitchell Publishing, Inc., 1981.

Lewis, T. G., and M. S. Smith. *Applying Data Structures.* Atlanta: Houghton Mifflin, 1976.

Lorin, Harold. *Sorting and Sort Systems.* Reading, Mass.: Addison-Wesley, 1975.

Lum, V. Y., et al. "Key-to-Address Transform Techniques: A Fundamental Performance Study on Large Existing Formatted Files." *Communications of the ACM,* vol. 14, no. 4 (April 1971).

Martin, James. *Computer Data-Base Organization.* 2d ed. Englewood Cliffs, N.J.: Prentice-Hall, 1977.

Murach, Mike. *Business Data Processing.* 3d ed. Palo Alto, Calif.: Science Research Associates, 1980.

Pratt, Terrence W. *Programming Languages: Design and Implementation.* Englewood Cliffs, N.J.: Prentice-Hall, 1975.

Shelly, Gary B., and Thomas J. Cashman. *Advanced ANSI COBOL Disk/Tape Programming Efficiencies.* Fullerton, Calif.: Anaheim, 1974.

Sperry Univac. *Sperry Univac 1100 Series Operating System.* UP-8225 Rev. 2.

Standish, Thomas A. *Data Structure Techniques.* Reading, Mass.: Addison-Wesley, 1980.

Struble, George W. *Assembler Language Programming: The IBM System/360 and 370.* 2d ed. Reading, Mass.: Addison-Wesley, 1975.

Tremblay, Jean-Paul, and Richard B. Bunt. *An Introduction to Computer Science.* New York: McGraw-Hill, 1979.

Tremblay, J. P., and R. G. Sorenson. *An Introduction to Data Structures with Applications.* New York: McGraw-Hill, 1976.

Wirth, Niklaus. *Algorithms + Data Structures = Programs.* Englewood Cliffs, N.J.: Prentice-Hall, 1975.

Wohl, Gerald. *Structured COBOL.* Palo Alto, Calif.: Science Research Associates, 1979.

Yourdon, Edward. *Techniques of Program Structure and Design.* Englewood Cliffs, N.J.: Prentice-Hall, 1975.

APPENDIX A:
CALLING SUBPROGRAMS IN COBOL

In COBOL, a module that is implemented as a formal subroutine must exhibit the same basic structure as any COBOL program. Specifically, it must have all four divisions (IDENTIFICATION, ENVIRONMENT, DATA, and PROCEDURE) consisting of all sections that are required of any COBOL program and any others that are pertinent to the module. The significant differences are summarized as follows:

1. A USING clause with its corresponding parameter list is appended to the PROCEDURE DIVISION statement. Example: PROCEDURE DIVISION USING LIST-AREA, REC-COUNT.

2. A LINKAGE SECTION is inserted in the DATA DIVISION immediately after the WORKING-STORAGE SECTION, which contains data definitions for the parameters in the parameter list. These definitions must agree in size, type, and alignment with their counterparts in the calling module.

3. If the subroutine contains no I/O statements, then its ENVIRONMENT DIVISION will be null, and its DATA DIVISION will not contain a FILE SECTION (see the example that follows).

The calling module simply issues a CALL statement together with a USING clause that specifies the appropriate parameter list. The parameter list consists of data names defined in the calling module.

The following example shows the relationship of a calling module and a call subroutine.

```
                              .
                              .
                              .
                    DATA DIVISION
                              .
                              .
                              .
Calling Program    77   REC-COUNT  PIC  S9(5)  USAGE COMP.
                   01   LIST-AREA.
                        02   REC OCCURS 50 TIMES.
                             03   REL-KEY  PIC  X(20).
                             03   FILLER   PIC  X(30).
                              .
                              .
                              .
                    PROCEDURE DIVISION.
                              .
                              .
                        CALL 'SHELLSRT' USING LIST-AREA, REC-COUNT.
                              .
                              .
                              .
Subprogram          IDENTIFICATION DIVISION.
                    PROGRAM-ID.  SHELLSRT.
                              .
                              .
                              .
                    ENVIRONMENT DIVISION.
                    DATA DIVISION.
                    WORKING-STORAGE SECTION.
                              .
                              .
                              .
                    LINKAGE SECTION.
                    77   NUM-RECS  PIC  S9(5)  USAGE COMP.
                    01   LIST-AREA.
                         02   ELEMENT OCCURS 50 TIMES.
                              03   E-KEY  PIC  X(20).
                              03   FILLER PIC  X(30).
                              .
                              .
                              .
                    PROCEDURE DIVISION USING LIST-AREA, NUM-RECS.
                              .
                              .
                              .
                        GOBACK.
                              .
```

APPENDIX B:
RECURSION

Recursion has been relegated to an appendix primarily because of the overall philosophy of this book. We stated in the preface that one of the goals of the book was to present all algorithms without the use of recursive techniques since the majority of applications programmer/analysts must program in languages that do not support recursion. Therefore, the body of the text can be studied without considering or using recursion. It is highly desirable, however, for a professional programmer to understand the concept and use of recursion since much of the literature on algorithms employs recursion as a common technique, and the increasing popularity of Pascal and Ada indicates that what is desirable now will be mandatory in the future.

A *recursive routine* is one that can call itself in the proper implementation of a procedure. The two types of recursion are direct and indirect. In *direct recursion*, a given routine calls itself. In *indirect recursion*, a given routine A calls a routine B that results in a call back to A before returning control to A.

As we will see, algorithms for providing solutions to certain kinds of problems can be expressed more simply (and sometimes more naturally) with recursion than with nonrecursive techniques. Unfortunately, recursion is not supported in programming languages such as COBOL, FORTRAN, and BASIC, and it is not supported at instruction level in any of the common machine-level languages. On the other hand, recursion is supported in languages such as Pascal, PL/I, and ALGOL.

At first glance it may appear that the study of recursion is of value only to those who program in languages that support recursion. By understanding how recursion is used, however, we can develop algorithms to solve problems that would be very difficult to express by other means. Then, by understanding the underlying process of how recursive routines are implemented internally, we can often convert these recursive algorithms to equivalent nonrecursive routines by simulating the internal processes.

The classic example found in the literature for demonstrating the use of recursion is the calculation of $N!$ as:

$$N! = 1 \quad \text{when } 0 \leq N \leq 1$$

$$N! = N * (N - 1)! \quad \text{when } N > 1$$

On the other hand, the classic comment accompanying this example is that even though it illustrates beautifully the concept of recursion, it is also a good example of the kind of routine that should *not* be implemented using recursion. We will cover in greater depth the question of when to use recursion later, but first we will return to our factorial example.

Since every recursive routine has the potential of creating a sequence of calls to itself, it must also contain a provision for always terminating this call sequence after a reasonable number of calls. Otherwise we face the logical possibility of an infinite loop or of exhausting all resources available to the routine for its execution. Typically, this termination provision is reached by ensuring that each successive recursive call progresses to a simpler version of the original problem until the problem is reduced to a trivial case and the process stops. This is exactly what happens in the factorial problem. On each successive call we ask for a factorial of an integer that is one less than the previous call until we call for the factorial of 1 (which is defined as 1) and the process ends.

We now formalize our recursive factorial routine using Figure B-1.

FIGURE B-1 RECURSIVE
ROUTINE TO CALCULATE N!

```
Line Number
  1  /*  N = the integer to find the factorial of */
  2  /*  FACT = the value of N! */
  3  /*  NTEMP = intermediate variable used in
            place of N during recursive calls */
  4  PROC  FACTORIAL (N,FACT)
  5     IF N ≤ 1
  6        THEN FACT = 1
  7        ELSE NTEMP = N - 1
  8             CALL FACTORIAL send NTEMP return FACT
  9             FACT = N * FACT
 10     ENDIF
 11  END PROC
```

The execution of the FACTORIAL routine to calculate 4! results in Figure B-2.

To answer the question of how a routine may call itself, we return to our discussion of nonrecursive calls presented in Chapters 1 and 3 when we covered stacks. In any routine, recursive or not, when a call is made in routine A to some other routine B, we assume that control will return to the point that immediately follows the call in routine A when the called routine B has completed execution. Of course, a called routine may in turn call another routine and so on, but the return path from all of these calls is exactly the reverse order in which they were made; therefore, we resort to the use of a stack in which each of these return addresses is stored. When a routine completes execution, we simply pop the stack to obtain the return address of the routine that has called it. This process continues until we return to our original routine and its execution is completed.

We still need this return path when we use recursive routines, but when we have a recursive call we must save not only the return address but also the current values of all parameters and local variables, since parameters are call-dependent and local variables are execution-dependent for each execution of the routine. As we return from a recursive call, we must restore all nonvariable parameters and local variables to the values they had when the call was issued, and we must provide for variable parameters to be passed back from one execution of the routine to the execution that preceded it. We can satisfy these requirements by creating a separate *return record* each time the routine is called (see Figure B-3). Each return record is composed of the return address from this call and a complete data area containing values for all parameters and local variables.

As return records are created, they are placed into stack. Each time the end of the routine is reached, the return address is taken and the stack is popped to restore previous values. In this way the top of the stack always contains the current values of the parameters and local variables. This process

---

FIGURE B-2

Values of Variables

STEP		N	FACT	NTEMP
0	initial entry to routine	4	?	?
1	NTEMP = N - 1	4	?	3
2	Call1 FACTORIAL	4	?	3
3	NTEMP = N - 1	3	?	2
4	Call2 FACTORIAL	3	?	2
5	NTEMP = N - 1	2	?	1
6	Call3 FACTORIAL	2	?	1
7	FACT = 1	1	1	?
8	return from Call3	2	1	1
9	FACT = N * FACT	2	2	1
10	return from Call2	3	2	2
11	FACT = N * FACT	3	6	2
12	return from Call1	4	6	3
13	FACT = N * FACT	4	24	3
14	exit routine	4	24	?

continues until the end of the routine is reached with only one entry in the stack. At this point, the return address to the original calling routine is taken. Since variable parameters must somehow be passed back to the data area of the previous call (and if we assume parameters are passed by address as in COBOL and FORTRAN), one technique that we can use to accomplish this is to simply allow the current execution of the routine to post the final value of the variable parameters directly in the stack entry that precedes the top entry. If we are willing to accept overhead for simplicity, we can simply post all parameters in the preceding stack entry since nonvariable parameters will still have the same value.

Figure B-4 shows how the stack of return records for routine FACTORIAL given in Figure B-1 would appear after the execution of the statement FACT = 1.

A nonrecursive simulation of routine FACTORIAL is given in Figure B-5. This simulation is basically a mechanical implementation of the internal processes described earlier. The return addresses are eliminated from the equivalent recursive stack since they have no use or meaning here, but no other attempt has been made to improve the efficiency of the routine. This simulation, however, is reasonably close to the process that would be generated by an equivalent recursive routine in a programming language that supports recursion. When the routine in Figure B-5 is compared with the iterative calculation of $N!$ shown in Figure B-6, we are led to the conclusion that recursion will not, in general, lead to more computer-efficient routines to solve problems. Therefore, recursive solutions should be avoided when other direct methods are readily available. The main advantage in using recursion is in problem solving and savings in programming time.

For another example that is more appropriate for the use of recursion, we will readdress the problem of defining an algorithm that produces a preorder traversal of a binary tree. Basically, we want to produce an algorithm that, given a nonempty binary tree, will: process the root of the tree, process the left subtree of the root preorder, and then process the right subtree of the root

FIGURE B-3 FORMAT OF RETURN RECORD FOR FACTORIAL

Return address	Current value N	Current value FACT	Current value NTEMP

FIGURE B-4 DIAGRAM OF STACK OF RETURN RECORDS FOR ROUTINE FACTORIAL

STK-PTR

4

K	Return address	N	FACT	NTEMP
1	Exit address	4	?	3
2	Addr. line 9	3	?	2
3	Addr. line 9	2	?	1
4	Addr. line 9	1	1	?

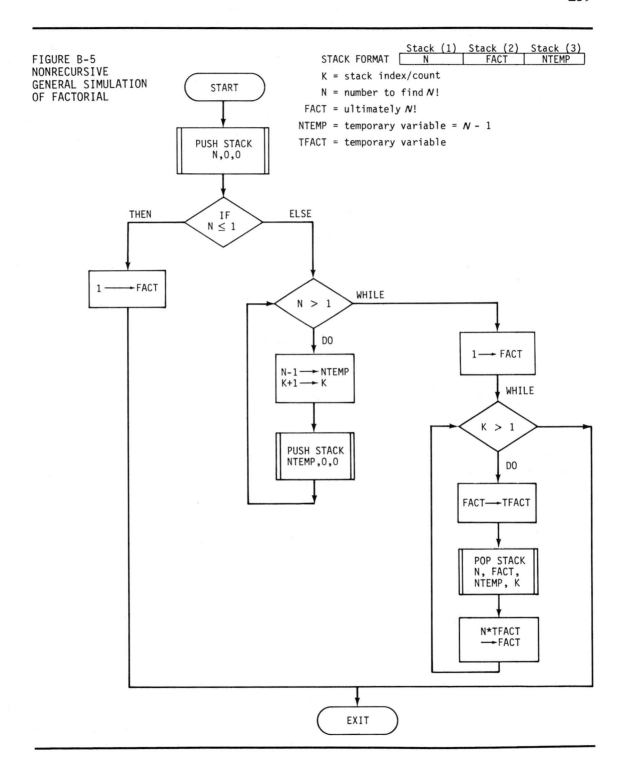

FIGURE B-5
NONRECURSIVE
GENERAL SIMULATION
OF FACTORIAL

STACK FORMAT

	Stack (1)	Stack (2)	Stack (3)
	N	FACT	NTEMP

K = stack index/count
N = number to find $N!$
FACT = ultimately $N!$
NTEMP = temporary variable = $N - 1$
TFACT = temporary variable

START

PUSH STACK
N,0,0

IF
N ≤ 1

THEN

ELSE

1 ⟶ FACT

N > 1

WHILE

DO

N−1 ⟶ NTEMP
K+1 ⟶ K

PUSH STACK
NTEMP,0,0

1 ⟶ FACT

WHILE

K > 1

DO

FACT ⟶ TFACT

POP STACK
N, FACT,
NTEMP, K

N*TFACT
⟶ FACT

EXIT

FIGURE B-6 ITERATIVE
SOLUTION TO CALCULATION
OF N!

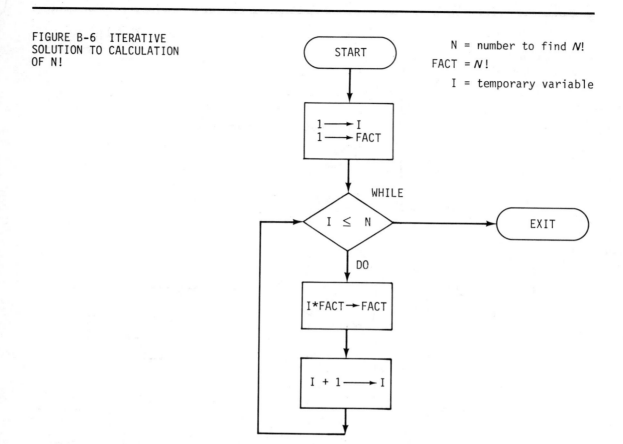

N = number to find *N*!

FACT = *N*!

I = temporary variable

preorder. But since any nonempty subtree of a binary tree is also a binary tree, we can express a preorder traversal of the subtree in the same manner as the primary tree. Thus we have the following recursive algorithm given in pseudocode for a preorder traversal:

```
/*  J = location of current node */
/*  L(J),R(J) = left and right pointers of node at J */
/*  N(J) = node at location J */

PROC PREORDRR (J)  /* J is passed as parameter */

  IF J ≠ end
    THEN process N(J)
           CALL PREORDRR send L(J)
           CALL PREORDRR send R(J)
    ELSE continue
  ENDIF
END PROC
```

Recursive algorithms for inorder and postorder traversals could be expressed as:

```
PROC INORDRR (J)
  IF J ≠ end
    THEN CALL INORDRR send L(J)
           process N(J)
           CALL INORDRR send R(J)
    ELSE continue
  ENDIF
END PROC


PROC POSTORDRR (J)
  IF J ≠ end
    THEN CALL POSTORDRR send L(J)
           CALL POSTORDRR send R(J)
           process N(J)
    ELSE continue
  ENDIF
END PROC
```

These algorithms for tree traversals are much simpler than their non-recursive counterparts found in Chapter 5, and they are more natural with respect to expressing the concept of tree traversals. For a closer look at the internal processes involved in these algorithms, we will first trace the execution of PREORDRR on a given tree and then simulate the algorithm nonrecursively.

Consider the tree shown in Figure B-7, in which key values are shown within the nodes and relative node locations are given next to the corresponding nodes.

The execution sequence of PREORDRR is shown in Figure B-8, with current data values beside corresponding execution steps.

In order to implement the simulation (shown in Figure B-10), we need to identify the entry and return points in the original routine and the corresponding actions that take place at each of these points. Figure B-9 identifies these entry points.

Entry point 1 is never a return point, but it is the entry each time we wish to process a node. If we have a valid node at point 1, we process the node and take the left pointer; otherwise we must pop the stack to obtain a new node. At point 2 we simply take a right pointer and continue. At point 3 we always pop the stack to obtain a new node.

Using these guidelines we now develop the algorithm given in Figure B-10. If we compare the algorithm in Figure B-10 with the algorithm in Chapter 5, which is a direct approach to a preorder traversal, we do not find the wide discrepancy with respect to complexity that we did in the two corresponding algorithms for calculating $N!$. The direct method is still slightly more efficient, which should be the case since the internal mechanisms for recursion will generally build in some overhead. Given the simplicity, however, of the original recursive algorithm for preorder traversals written in a few lines of code, we may well wish to choose it if we have the use of a programming language that supports recursion.

Even without the use of a programming language that supports recursion, we have now provided a technique for first stating an algorithm recursively and then simulating the internal processes to produce an equivalent non-recursive algorithm.

FIGURE B-7

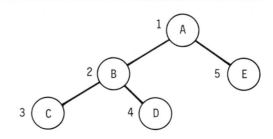

FIGURE B-8

Values of Variables

	STEP	J	L(J)	R(J)
0	initial entry to routine	1	(2)+	(5)
1	process A	1	2	5
2	Call1 PREORDRR (L(J))	1	2	5
3	process B	2	3	4
4	Call2 PREORDRR (L(J))	2	3	4
5	process C	3	*	*
6	Call3 PREORDRR (L(J))	3	*	*
7	J = end	*	?	?
8	return from Call3	3	*	*
9	Call4 PREORDRR (R(J))	3	*	*
10	J = end	*	?	?
11	return from Call4	3	*	*
12	return from Call2	2	3	4
13	Call5 PREORDRR (R(J))	2	3	4
14	process D	4	*	*
15	Call6 PREORDRR (L(J))	4	*	*
16	J = end	*	?	?
17	return from Call6	4	*	*
18	Call7 PREORDRR (R(J))	4	*	*
19	J = end	*	?	?
20	return from Call7	4	*	*
21	return from Call5	2	3	4
22	return from Call1	1	2	5
23	Call8 PREORDRR (R(J))	1	2	5
24	process E	5	*	*
25	Call9 PREORDRR (L(J))	5	*	*
26	J = end	*	?	?
27	return from Call9	5	*	*
28	Call10 PREORDER (R(J))	5	*	*
29	J = end	*	?	?
30	return from Call10	5	*	*
31	return from Call8	1	2	5
32	exit routine	1	(2)	(5)

+ Initial and exit values of L(J) and R(J) are dependent on J and
  may or may not be considered as defined on entry to PREORDRR.

Tree traversals and other problems that employ backtracking processes such as the Knight's Tour problem and B-tree insertion are likely candidates for recursive solutions. For a fuller discussion of other appropriate applications, refer to the books by Augestein and Tenenbaum, Tremblay and Sorenson, and Wirth, cited in the references of this book. It has been our intent here to present the fundamental properties of recursion and the internal processes that are involved, and then to briefly describe techniques whereby recursive algorithms can be simulated in nonrecursive programming languages.

FIGURE B-9 ENTRY AND
EXIT POINTS FOR RECURSIVE
ROUTINE PREORDRR

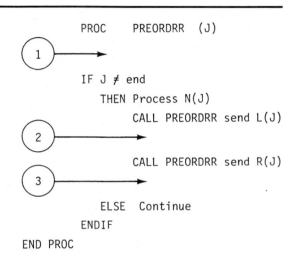

```
PROC     PREORDRR  (J)

  ①────▶

  IF J ≠ end
      THEN Process N(J)
            CALL PREORDRR send L(J)
  ②──────────▶

            CALL PREORDRR send R(J)
  ③────────▶

      ELSE  Continue
  ENDIF
END PROC
```

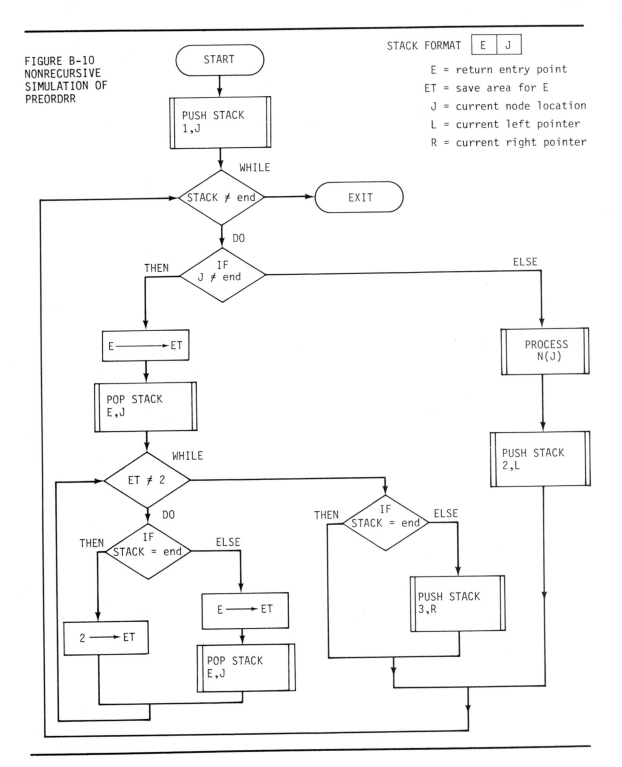

FIGURE B-10
NONRECURSIVE
SIMULATION OF
PREORDRR

INDEX